The Synoptic Gospels:
A Journey Into the Kingdom

by Edward L. Bleynat, Jr.

Volume I:
From Bethlehem to the River Jordan

R. BRENT AND COMPANY
Asheville, North Carolina

THE SYNOPTIC GOSPELS: A JOURNEY INTO THE KINGDOM: VOLUME I: FROM BETHLEHEM TO THE RIVER JORDAN. Copyright © 2004 by Edward L. Bleynat, Jr. and The Synoptic Project, Ltd. All rights reserved. No part of this book may be used or reproduced in any manner whatsoever without written permission, except in the case of brief quotations embodied in critical articles and reviews. For information, contact Edward L. Bleynat Jr., 21 Broad Street, Asheville, NC 28801

The Scripture quotations contained herein are from the New Revised Standard Version Bible, copyright © 1989 by the Division of Christian Education of the National Council of the Churches of Christ in the U.S.A., and are used by permission. All rights reserved.

Published in Asheville, North Carolina
by R.Brent and Company
50 Deerwood Drive
Asheville, NC 28805

Editor and publisher: *Robbin Brent Whittington*
Cover illustration: *Chappell Studio, New Orleans*
Cover design: *johndietzdesigns.com, Asheville*
Interior design: *Robbin Brent Whittington and Rick Soldin*
Compositor: *Electronic Publishing Services, Inc.;*
          Jonesborough, Tennessee

Library of Congress Cataloging-in-Publication Data

Bleynat, Edward L. Jr.
The Synoptic Gospels: A Journey Into The Kingdom: Volume I: From Bethlehem to the River Jordan—1st ed.
        p.   cm.
    ISBN 0-9678061-2-7
    1. Bible Commentaries 2. Religion 3. Adult Christian Education
    I. Title

                                    200315020   LCCN

First Edition

2 4 6 8 10 9 7 5 3 1

Printed in the United States of America

Dedication

This series is dedicated to the ancient Waldenses, who risked (and frequently lost) all for the right to read and interpret the Scriptures for themselves; to WEB, Elizabeth, and Luke Bleynat, three of their more recent descendants, who happen to live with me and whose frequent interruptions were not unwelcome; and to their mother, Anne, whose many contributions of time and energy made this work possible. Though she is not herself a Waldensian, she is more than principled, compassionate, and stubborn enough to pass for one.

✝✝✝

†††

Contents

Foreword ix

Preface xi

Biblical and Church Timeline xx

Introduction: The Ancient and Timeless Journey of Faith 1

The Composition of The Bible 2

Gospels 5

The Canonical Gospels 5

From an Ancient to a Modern Application 7

The Responsible Interpretation of Scripture 8

    Tools for Interpreting Scripture 10

Our Silence Will Not Save Us 12

1 **Beginning Our Journey** 13

The Synoptic Problem 15

And if we do not tell it the stones will speak … 19

2 **The Synoptic Journeys** 21

The Rebel's Journey 21

The Galilean Journey of the Q Community 26

The Rabbi's Journey 27

The Chronicler's Journey 34

3 **Out of Ur in the Chaldees and into Occupied Israel** 39

Tamar 54

Rahab 55

Ruth 55

Bathsheba 56

Mary 56

Contents

4 From the Jerusalem Temple to the Judean Hill Country 59

The Time 63
The Occasion 64
The Players 64
The News 65
The Reaction 65
What of Elizabeth? 66
The Time 69
The Occasion 69
The Players 69
The News 70
The Reaction 70
What of Joseph? 71
John and Jesus: Shared Patterns and Paths 71
  Of Men and Angels 74

5 From Denial to Acceptance: Two Journeys to Fatherhood 81

The Circumcision and Naming 83
Zechariah Speaks 84
The Friends and Relations Respond 85
Zechariah Sings 85
The Benedictus 87
Preliminary Matters 91
Joseph's Dilemma and his "Righteous" Response 92
A Change of Direction: An Angelic Message 96
The Virgin Birth 96

6 From Nazareth to Bethlehem 105

An Occasion for a Trip to Bethlehem 107
  An Old Story 112
The God of the Lowly 113
  A New Story 114
Out of Bethlehem 118
An Ethereal Visit 121
The Religious Traditions of the Wise Men 122
The Sign 124
The Gifts 124

The Title   125
The Future   125
The Traditions   125

7 From Bethlehem to Nazareth: A Transitional Journey   129

The Rites of Circumcision and Purification   130
Blessings and Honors Bestowed   135
A Proclamation   136
   Poetry and Evangelism   138
In the World of a Tyrant   141
Connections to the Past, According to Matthew   143
A Theological Problem with Matthew's Story   145
On the Place of Dreams in Scripture   147

8 From Nazareth to the Jerusalem Temple: A Journey to Adulthood   151

A Pilgrimage with a Twist   153
A Different Tradition   158
   Gnosticism   159
   The Infancy Gospel of Thomas   160
A Broader Orthodoxy   162
Jesus and Moses; Jesus and Augustus   165

**9 Out of the Old Order and into the New: 171
John Proclaims the Ultimate Return from Exile**

John the Baptist Appears   172
John the Baptist Speaks   183

**10 From Nazareth to the River Jordan: 193
"You Are My Son, the Beloved; with You I Am Well Pleased"**

Looking Ahead   213

Acknowledgments   215

Reading List   219

Synoptic Gospels Scripture Excerpts   223

Index   225

Maps

Mark's World   24
Mark written in Rome, Syria or Galilee (64–75 C.E.?)

Matthew's World   28
Matthew written in Antioch of Syria (75–90 C.E.?)

Luke's World   35
Luke written in Southern Greece, Northern Egypt, or Asia Minor (85–95 C.E.?)

Abraham's World   40
Ur in the Chaldees to Canaan (2000–1900 B.C.E.)

The Divided Kingdoms of Judea and Israel   42
(922–722 B.C.E.)

Babylonian Exile   53
The Rivers of Babylon and the Land of Zion (587–539 B.C.E.)

The Jerusalem Temple   63
(circa 4 B.C.E. – 33 C.E.)

The Division of Herod's Kingdom after his Death   107
(4 B.C.E.)

The Kingdom of Herod the Great   107
(37–4 B.C.E.)

David's Kingdom   119
(1000–961 B.C.E.?)

The Holy Family's Flight into Egypt   141
(circa 4 B.C.E.)

The Ultimate Return from Exile   178
(circa 30 C.E.)

Nazareth and the Jordan   204
(30 C.E.?)

Foreword

We Christians are never called to keep our faith to ourselves, but to respect the faith of others as we share our faith with them.

How do we do that? Using the different gifts we are given, we must first reach into our own hearts and share what we've found there with others in our homes, in our workplaces, in our church, and in our communities. We do this while also allowing ourselves to be fully present to others who want to share what is in their hearts. This helps to build a diverse, vibrant and love-filled faith community.

With this book, Ed Bleynat, from Trinity Church, Asheville, a parish in the Episcopal Diocese of Western North Carolina, invites others to do just that. He has shared his knowledge of, interest in, and passion about the message contained in the synoptic Gospels with other adults in his church community. And now, with this book, he shares it with a larger community. The book offers powerful tools that give us a better understanding and an immediate application of our Christian calling, and will enrich our own "journey into the kingdom."

This is a book that can be read and studied for one's own personal benefit. It's also a most helpful Christian education resource. In this instance, I speak specifically of the study guide and commentary about the synoptic Gospels that promote and support biblical study and spiritual growth in a way that compels group discussion and personal discovery of the meaning and value that the synoptic Gospels, and the story of Jesus, continue to have in our lives today.

There are resources here that class members can take home and incorporate into their daily lives. Ed invites the reader to share with others what they believe, hear what others believe, and trust deeply that in this sharing, the Holy Spirit will help the reader to grow daily in faith.

This is an invaluable approach to Scripture that promotes inclusion, diversity, historical understanding, discussion and learning through inquisitiveness. It deeply touches me that our church has committed and knowledgeable lay people who are willing to take on projects like this book, as an outward and visible sign of their commitment to their faith journey.

Regardless of one's denominational perspective, this book will be useful, not only in understanding the personal dimension of the gospel message, but also in building community by constructively relating to people of different faiths in this ever increasing religiously diverse country of ours.

—Rt. Rev. Robert H. Johnson, Bishop
Episcopal Diocese of Western North Carolina

Preface

What would lead someone, particularly a layman, to write a book about any part of the Bible generally, or a commentary about the synoptic Gospels particularly? And why should anyone read it?

To answer these questions for myself—a practicing attorney with no formal theological training, and much of his time properly devoted to his family, career, and own church—I have looked to a framework that the medieval theologian St. Thomas Aquinas has provided. Thomas was a prodigious author; *Summa Theologiae* is one of the classics of Christian theology. Now, I do not possess this little tidbit of information from having read the work as a whole, Latin being outside my knowledge and the opus itself being rather large, particularly when considered with its companion volumes. So, I must confess, I have only read small excerpts of it in translation.[1]

Thomas Aquinas started with the theories of the classical Greek philosopher Aristotle, and then developed them further. He articulated the idea that every event has its cause, and that if you connect any such event to its cause, and that one to its cause, and so forth *ad infinitum,* you will eventually reach the Uncaused Cause, a concept identified with the Deity. This approach is called the "cosmological argument" for proving the existence of God. So, the book you hold in your hands is a result of a chain of events that can theoretically be traced back to the Uncaused Cause, as can other things in the world, notwithstanding critiques of Thomas' system.

However, in explaining my own story, I will not go all the way back to the Uncaused Cause, but will stop along that path and tell why I wrote this book. I hope this will help to show where I have been, and how I have come to the place where I now stand. It may also show how the story of Jesus—particularly as told in the synoptic Gospels—has become, for me, what twentieth-century theologian Paul Tillich calls a matter "of ultimate concern."[2] The story

---

[1]A similar approach holds true for other materials used in writing this book. I relied on numerous sources for my research, some of which were studied closely, others more superficially, and then synthesized what I considered to be key aspects for purposes of contributing to what Thomas Jefferson called "the marketplace of ideas," a foundational theme of this book.

[2]*The Essential Tillich: An Anthology of the Writings of Paul Tillich,* edited by F. Forrester Church.

of Jesus demands "infinite attention, unconditional devotion, ultimate passion."[3] It has become central to me, and has led me to compose a book that I hope has lasting value, not only for me, but also for you.

It is also my desire, in the telling of my journey, to offer you a more complete understanding about the perspective from which *The Synoptic Gospels: A Journey into the Kingdom* is written. And perhaps you may find, within these pages, some paths that are similar to the ones you have trod, and so find a place from which to view more clearly the road ahead. And, just as I connect my own story, and my people's story, to the way that this "ultimate concern" can be experienced today, I hope that you, too, can make similar connections about your own story.

The Ancient History of a People

The Synoptic Gospels: A Journey into the Kingdom is dedicated to, among others, the ancient Waldenses, a people from whom I am descended on my father's side. While they might be considered the first Protestants, their origin is not entirely clear. Some theorize that they date back to the Apostolic era, with the earliest participants in the movement being St. Paul's converts on his route to Iberia. Others date the Waldensian movement as beginning closer to the twelfth century. As the Bible starts in the beginning, and each of us have our own beginnings, I want to highlight the Waldensian story as a beginning point for me.

Regardless of where in the murky past the beginnings of the Waldenses lie, their subsequent history is drawn in clearer lines. The Waldenses held church services for their own edification and evangelized others in Europe during the Middle Ages. They were committed to the principle that all persons should be able to read and interpret the Scriptures for themselves. And they were persecuted for doing so by the power structure of the Medieval Roman Catholic Church and the people who supported it and enforced its will. The Waldensian sense of independence and insistence on freedom from the rule that only clergy could properly read and interpret the Scriptures was considered heresy. Left unchecked, it was a sufficiently serious threat to Rome's power that the Waldenses could not be tolerated.

The Waldenses' history was marked by thousands of their number, over a span of centuries, suffering from treachery and oppression at the hands of the ecclesiastical and political

---

[3]*Id.* at 33.

powers.[4] The brutal torture and slaughter of the innocent was rampant in more than one season, with methods too terrible to describe. Throughout this time, the Waldenses displayed a remarkable resiliency and carried on with their faith inspired by the dictates of their consciences.

The Cottian Alps, in what is currently Northwest Italy, became the largest Waldensian enclave. Waldenses also lived in French portions of that rugged area. After Good King Henry IV of France issued the Edict of Nantes in 1598, the French Waldenses enjoyed religious liberties for the first time in generations. Those on the Italian side, in Savoy, also benefitted from the general spirit of tolerance from the edict.

But Henry IV was assassinated and the edict was eventually revoked. Persecutions were recommenced by those who could not tolerate Protestants enjoying freedom of religion. By now, the Waldenses were identified with the Reformation and had formed alliances with the Calvinists in Geneva. The old ways resumed, and death and destruction befell the Waldensian Valleys. Refugees sought solace in Geneva and wherever else they might find a little bit of relief and freedom. While the Duke of Savoy was titular sovereign over most of the Waldensian Valleys, men bearing that title could not disregard the strong influence exerted by the neighboring great power, France, and by the Roman Church.

The Waldensian history waxed and waned, from persecution to ghetto existence to a modicum of liberty, coming full circle time and again. Finally, in 1848, Charles Albert, Duke of Savoy and King of Sardinia, issued the Emancipation Proclamation, which guaranteed greater civil liberties and effectively bestowed religious freedom upon the Waldenses. These rights did not go the way of the enlightened but ill-fated Edict of Nantes, but survived, and the local Waldensian populace entered into a time of relative peace. But long-term prosperity did not follow; the Alpine habitat became overburdened with the quickly expanding population in the post-persecution era. Emigration to the New World occurred, and the largest North American settlement was founded as my hometown of Valdese, North Carolina, in 1893. There, with the support of the mother church, the Waldenses were absorbed into what is now the Presbyterian Church in the United States of America.

America was an ideal place for Waldensian immigrants, not only because of the opportunity to prosper economically in a way that had become impossible in their homeland, but also because religious freedom embodied in the principle of separation of church and state provided a just framework for those whose ancestors had suffered miserably under a different system.

---

[4]Some of the Waldenses themselves contributed to the reprisals. My sister's genealogical research disclosed at least one early member from a branch of our family tree who collaborated with the Roman Church, even directing its ire toward members of his own family.

A Stroke of American Genius

This separation of church and state, a core value upon which the United States was founded, is a principle currently under assault by people who are able to disregard that neither God, nor the Church, nor Jesus of Nazareth, nor the Holy Bible are mentioned in the United States Constitution. And so, they argue that this is a "Christian" nation in some way that favors one particular faith system. Those who would dismantle the Jeffersonian wall between church and state learned little from the framers of the Constitution, most of whom identified themselves as Christian (though some of the most influential were Deists), and still established an intentionally secular government. As if the absolute silence on religion in the original text of the Constitution were not enough to protect religious liberty, the hold-out states on the issue of ratification (including my own North Carolina) insisted on a Bill of Rights. The very first clause of the First Amendment therein provides that "Congress shall make no law respecting an establishment of religion, or prohibiting the free exercise thereof. . . . "

The wisdom of separation of church and state was hard learned. The European norm had been national religion. We Americans steadfastly refused to follow it, insisting instead on government that does not meddle in matters of faith, and on religious institutions that do not impose any belief system or religious affiliation on the citizenry. These lessons, learned from the experience of the Waldenses and so many others, should not be disregarded. Rather, they should be affirmed. And part of that affirmation—the flip side of the coin of religious liberty—is the responsibility to educate and improve ourselves in our chosen faith traditions.

A Formative Experience

Growing up and residing in North Carolina, I am in the Bible Belt, where many people believe in God, practice their faith, and are vocal about it. I am glad of that, as there should, and must, be a great deal of room for religious discourse in the Jeffersonian marketplace of ideas. What I am not glad of is that the loud voices from the far right tend to set the vocabulary and prompt most major discourse in the media. In doing so, they seek to impose their theology on others, much as the medieval Roman Church did to my Waldensian ancestors for centuries.

My most critical formative experience in grappling seriously with the language and practices of the religious right, and the implications of their theology for the rest of us, was during college in the mid-1980s. This was around the time that Charles Stanley ran against

Wilfred Moore in an election to head the Southern Baptist Convention, a body which has more members than any other religious affiliation in the South. Both men took well-known Bible stories, such as Jonah and the Great Fish, literally. The difference was that Stanley thought others had to do so as well, while Moore held the traditional Baptist position that all Christians were entitled to read and interpret the Scriptures for themselves. Stanley won the election, the fundamentalists took over the Convention, and eventually took over the Southern Baptist seminaries. They terminated academics who had honest questions that would not let them pledge to abide by the idea that the Bible is inerrant in all respects. Non-literalists were not sufficiently Christian, it seemed, to satisfy the new guard.[5]

The modern far-right doctrinaire approach to theology was at odds with what I already believed in my early twenties to be the truth. It was also at odds with the spirit of tolerance I learned with particular clarity from my mother. She was raised Irish Catholic, but joined the Presbyterian Church after marrying a Waldensian descendant. She never seemed to think that any one group was more or less Godly than another. Further, the extreme right-wing theology, contrary to my upbringing, was also totally at odds with my experience in the mainline church. And, it was at odds with my core belief that God would not consign to Hell for all eternity multitudes of people who, for some reason, just couldn't or didn't "get with the program" and believe certain things told in, and about, the Bible to be absolutely true.

However, at that age, I did not possess the necessary tools to carve out some alternative approach to Scripture. An approach that stood against religious authoritarianism and enforced biblical literalism, that stood for inclusion. Without those tools, I also had to worry whether the literalists were right about what it meant to be Christian. If they were, I had to wonder, was I wrong in my earlier conception of God? Was he really a tyrant ready to drop us all into the pit, "sinners in the hands of an angry God," as the Puritan clergyman Jonathan Edwards would have it? That was a highly unpalatable way, but was it **the** Christian way? And if it was, would I feel compelled to remove myself from it and drift into some sort of Deism, or Agnosticism, or perhaps the civilized, humane, and cultivated, but seemingly less spiritual world of Unitarianism? As rigid

---

[5]Among the critical differences between medieval European Roman Catholic authoritarianism and modern versions of authoritarianism are the forms of power that the institutions wield. The medieval church, with the cooperation of the political authorities, could go so far as to kill a dissident, dissenter, or heretic. Separation of church and state eliminates that unholy marriage of religion and politics in modern America. Hopefully, an increased respect for the rights of others contributes as well. But, the fact remains that those who have power are all too often willing to use it to stamp out what they perceive to be sins of doctrinal impurity. The tools now might include cutting off someone's livelihood (in the case of the seminary inerrancy pledges) or engaging in theological bullying by questioning another's faith (in the case of seeking to impose religious views on public school students by the more subtle coercion of official prayer).

literalism was not compatible with either my honest intellectual inquiry, or my ideas about a just and merciful God, I would either have to abandon the field of Christian practice and debate and retreat into some other philosophy or religion, or rebuild my Christian viewpoints in a manner that specifically relied on a different set of principles than biblical literalism.

My family, a few friends, and the clergy of the Waldensian Presbyterian Church in Valdese, where I was a member, helped by listening and talking and nudging me along out of this distressed state and in a better direction. My father shared that he had been in a similar struggle theologically at about the same age, as no doubt have many young people. My pastor and associate pastor, Paul Felker and the late Jack Parse, introduced me to William Barclay's commentaries on the New Testament. Here, I found a rational, historical, and contextual approach to Scripture that was nonetheless devout, not to mention delightful reading.

I also spent time in a weekly summer Bible study with some friends and acquaintances at a moderate Baptist congregation, where a young man named Jeff Hyde led a study group centered largely around the synoptic Gospels. We approached the Scriptures with an historical and inquisitive bent. Buddy Corbin, then the pastor at that church, heard my interpretive thoughts and questions and suggested I write my own commentary on the Bible. I think that statement was meant more as a challenge to explore deeply my personal faith life than as a literal suggestion that I write a book for publication. But, it appears I am now taking his suggestion quite literally.

Beginning with the good advice of these people, given almost twenty years ago, I have followed a course of reading thousands upon thousands of pages of biblical text, commentary, theology, and the like, talking frequently with people, and letting the Spirit move me along. I find my core theology much the same as it was before I started this process, but with the ensuing years of study and fund of knowledge expanded, I now know the place from which I speak much better. In this journey I have time and again been reminded of T.S. Eliot's *Four Quartets*. In *Little Gidding*, a poem from that volume, Eliot speaks of coming at the end of the journey to the place where he began, and knowing it for the first time.

Moving Forward

My journey has been a continuous one. I have come to believe that Christian faith to be precisely that—a journey that lasts a lifetime. The synoptic Gospels themselves involve near constant movement. They follow Jesus and his band from place to place, physically and theologically, venturing more deeply into the way God has set before them. Because of that, I have chosen a title for this series that reflects a journey.

I have also been blessed in my companions along the way. In having Anne Elizabeth Freels Bleynat as my wife since 1990, I share life with someone who explores the same questions I explore, even though we are rather different people and so have different ways. She has an intuitive mysticism that is uncommonly well-grounded in reality. I suspect that she could step on a cloud and know there is something solid underneath. I, however, am more analytical and skeptical, more grounded in logic than intuition. Sometimes, I think there is something I lack in my thought-oriented world. And occasionally, I catch a glimpse of another place, and even participate in it, stepping briefly through the unseen doorways that Anne and other mystically inclined people have opened.

Anne, a graduate of the University of the South (an Episcopal institution), also got me out of my content Presbyterian world and into the Episcopal Church, where I have surprised myself by being quite at home (at least once I got more accustomed to the *Book of Common Prayer*, though I still at times mumble through it). I even submitted myself to a confirmation process that involved kneeling in front of an Episcopal bishop. My Waldensian precursors had died for the right not to do so before a Roman one. The principal difference, of course, is the voluntariness of the act. When I pointed out the irony of the situation to the Suffragan bishop who confirmed me at Holy Trinity Church, Greensboro, North Carolina, he told me that I didn't have to kneel; standing would have been fine except for the fact that I, being 6' 10", was about a foot taller than he.

The journey has brought my family to Asheville, North Carolina, where we are parishioners at its large downtown church, Trinity Asheville. When Trinity was in the process of beefing up its Christian Education programs for both children and adults, it occurred to me that Jeff Hyde's summer study course on the synoptic Gospels had been enough of an eye-opening experience on my road to greater biblical literacy that I wanted to offer something like it to others. I recruited parishioners Terri Roberts to teach Mark, and Katie Chappel to teach Luke. I accepted responsibility for course planning and administration, also teaching Matthew. We were fortunate to begin this class around the time that a strong rector, Bill Whisenhunt, was installed. We gladly took advantage of his ability to fill up the pews during worship by encouraging more folks to get there an hour early for Sunday School.

One parishioner suggested that short summaries be prepared to help people catch up if they missed a class. I began writing those, but they turned out not to be particularly "short." Another person suggested that with those summaries, I had the beginnings of a book. Finally, Robbin Brent Whittington, fellow parishioner and class member, agreed to bring her skills as a publisher and editor to bear in arranging, producing, and publishing this material. An installment of the product is what you have before you. It includes biblical text, questions we bring to the study of Scripture, commentary on the synoptic Gospels, questions raised by the texts, insights, discussion points, and other matters that emerged from our shared lives as Christian students of the Word. It can be used individually or in Christian education, the domain where lay people in particular have met and taught and learned and discussed for years.

I owe much of this work to the people in my class, a group that has included those in diverse places in life's journey, from college or graduate school at one end, through parenthood, careers, and other stages, right up and into retirement. Of the last group, I mention by name Jim and Nancylee Petty, a retired Episcopal priest and his wise better half, whose presence constantly reassure me that the process of exploration does not end when we leave the workaday world.

Preparing this book, and the work already done on other volumes in this series, has been a labor of love. It reflects something of the journey I have taken and the people along the way. Now, it is my fondest hope that it assists you on your journey into the kingdom of God.

—**Edward L. Bleynat, Jr.**

†††

Biblical and Church Timeline

2000 B.C. to 1900 B.C. (?)	Abram called out of Ur in the Chaldees (modern south Iraq)
1700 B.C. to 1300 B.C. (?)	Descendants of Abraham and Sarah sojourn in Egypt
1350 B.C. (?)	Oppression of the Hebrews begins
1290/1270 B.C. to 1250/1230 B.C. (?)	Exodus from Egypt begins; Moses then leads people in the desert for "forty years"
1250/1230 B.C. to 1100 B.C. (?)	Conquest of Holy Land by Israelites and era of governance by the judges
1020 B.C. to 1000 B.C.	Saul's reign; the United Monarchy of The Jews begins
1000 B.C. to 961 B.C.	David's reign
961 B.C. to 922 B.C.	Solomon's reign; United Monarchy ends at close of Solomon's reign
950 B.C.	Solomon's temple constructed
922 B.C. to 722 B.C.	Divided Monarchy; Judea (capital city is Jerusalem) and Israel (capital city is Samaria)
722 B.C.	The Assyrian Empire (centered in north of modern Iraq, encompassed parts of Turkey, and reached Mediterranean) conquers The northern kingdom of Israel
612 B.C.	The Assyrian Empire Collapses
587 B.C.	Fall of southern kingdom of Judea to Babylonian Empire, destruction of Jerusalem and its temple
587 B.C. to 539 B.C.	Babylonia exile; Jewish leadership deported to Babylon
539 B.C.	Cyrus of Media, king of the Medes and the Persians (modern Iran) captures Babylon without a fight; the Holy Land is under Persian control
538 B.C.	Cyrus allows the deported Israelites to return home,
515 B.C.	Second temple construction completed in Jerusalem
334 B.C. to 323 B.C.	Alexander The Great of Macedonia (modern Greece) conquers the known world
333 B.C.	Alexander the Great defeats Persia
325 B.C.	Greeks conquer Palestine
323 B.C.	Alexander the Great dies and is succeeded by Ptolemy and his heirs; the Ptolemaic reign over Judea was a period of tolerance and generally favorable treatment of the Jews.
Third Century B.C.	Hebrew Bible translated into Greek, called "The Septuagint"
198 B.C.	The dynasty of Selucids (modern Syria) succeeds the Ptolemaic dynasty and attempts to force Hellenism on the Jews of Palestine
175 B.C. to 164 B.C.	Antiochus, IV Epiphanes, Greco/Syrian Ruler Occupies Judea. During his reign, he erects an altar to Zeus in the Jerusalem Temple and loots the temple; one of his subordinates sacrifices swine on the temple altar
166 B.C.	Maccabean Revolt begins
164 B.C.	Judas Maccabeus successfully prosecutes revolt against the Selucid dynasty; Antiochus IV dies; Jerusalem Temple rededicated
63 B.C.	Pompey conquers Palestine and makes Syria a Roman province; Israel was part of Syrian administrative region

37 B.C. to 4 B.C.	Herod the Great's reign in Israel; collaborator client-king installed by Rome, descendants were also client rulers; further reconstruction and improvements of Jerusalem Temple
27 B.C. to 14 A.D.	Reign of Roman Emperor Augustus
6 B.C. to 6 A.D.	Jesus is born (most likely date is 4 B.C.)
6 B.C. to 2 B.C.	Matthew's Holy Family flees to Egypt, relocates to Nazareth
4 B.C. to 6 A.D.	Archelaus is Jewish Ethnarch of Judea; Rome then resumes direct rule of Judea
4 B.C. to 34 A.D.	Phillip is Jewish Tetrarch of Iturea, Trachonitis, etc.
4 B.C. to 39 A.D.	Herod Antipas is Jewish Tetrarch of Galilee and Perea
6 A.D.	Quirinius begins term as Roman governor of Syria
8 A.D.	Luke's Jesus visits Jerusalem Temple as a child
14 A.D. to 37 A.D.	Reign of Roman Emperor Tiberius
26 A.D. to 29 A.D.	Jesus baptized by John the Baptist
26 A.D. to 36 A.D.	Pontius Pilate, Roman procurator of Judea
30 A.D.	Approximate year of Jesus' crucifixion
34 A.D. to 35 A.D.	Saul the Pharisee's conversion; becomes Paul the Apostle
37 A.D.	Paul's first visit to Jerusalem after conversion
37 A.D. to 41 A.D.	Reign of Roman Emperor Caligula
37 A.D. to 44 A.D.	Herod Agrippa I, Jewish client-king over Judea, Galilee, and Perea
41 A.D. to 54 A.D.	Reign of Roman Emperor Claudius
49 A.D.	Jerusalem conference determined Gentile converts to Christianity did not have to become Jewish proselytes
50 A.D.(?)	The Q source compiled
53 A.D. to 100 A.D.	Herod Agrippa, II, Jewish client-king
54 A.D. to 68 A.D.	Reign of Roman Emperor Nero
64 A.D.	Nero's persecution of Christians in Rome; Peter and Paul martyred?
64 A.D. to 75 A. D.	The Gospel According to St. Mark written
66 A.D. to 73 A.D.	Jewish Rebellion against Rome
68 A.D. to 69 A.D.	Reign of Three Roman Emperors
69 A.D. to 79 A.D.	Reign of Roman Emperor Vespasian
70 A.D.	Destruction of Jerusalem and the Temple
73 A.D.	Masada, the last Jewish stronghold, falls to Rome; rebellion ends
75 A.D. to 90 A.D.	The Gospel According to St. Matthew written
79 A.D. to 81 A.D.	Reign of Roman Emperor Titus
81 to 96 A.D.	Reign of Roman Emperor Domitian; persecuted Christians
85 A.D. to 95 A.D.	The Gospel According to St. Luke written
132 A.D. to 134 A.D.	Second Jewish rebellion
325 A.D.	Roman emperor, Constantine the Great, convenes Council of Nicaea
367 A.D.	Easter Letter of St. Athanasius published; settles Orthodox Canon
525 A.D.	The traditional Christian calendar was devised by a Roman abbot who miscalculated the probable date of Jesus' birth

Introduction

The Ancient and Timeless Journey of Faith

The Holy Bible is the best of books. It starts "in the beginning," with God bringing order out of chaos, light out of darkness, forming matter and infusing energy, adding layers of complexity to simple beginnings. Time and again God beholds the creation, and declares it to be good. The narrative continues with the entry of living beings, including those created in God's image, onto the stage of the nascent world. It tells of their rejection—our rejection—of a state of blessedness, as we opt to follow the inducements of our own will rather than God's good way set before us. It tells the story of our alienation from our Maker, and from each other.

The Bible also tells of the redemptive process. God calls a man named Abram out of Ur in the Chaldees, and into a new place where he and his progeny are to provide a means to restore humanity to a state of blessedness, a state of reconciliation with the Creator, and with each other. It tells the story of the generations that follow, as they transcend the pagan world around them, and develop a certain imperfect understanding of, and faith in, a monotheistic God. They come to believe him to be sovereign of the whole created order, not just some petty deity in a pantheon populated by petty deities striving against each other for power. The Bible tells of the repeated failure and redemption of this people; it tells of their building and losing and rebuilding a kingdom and a temple where the holy rites of the one God, Yahweh, are observed.

The Bible describes God as the one who creates, redeems and sustains us. It tells tales of the people of God rebelling and reconciling, loving and hating, giving and abusing. It is the story of peace and war, passion and treachery, the conquerors and the conquered, the battle between good and evil.

And, after the people of God emerge from their murky and contentious beginnings, and live through slavery, escape, conquest, kingdom, exile, and return, the Bible then tells the story of the one who is as God intended all of us to be. Out of Nazareth in Galilee, a man named Jesus comes. He heals the sick, preaches good news to the poor, confronts the powerful, restores the broken, transforms the ordinary, declares the immediate presence of the kingdom of God, and leads those who will follow him on an astounding journey out of darkness and into the light—that same light which was declared to be good "in the beginning."

Yet, many times in his story—our story, God's story—the darkness appears to have the upper hand. The story of Jesus' earthly life ends in the blood and sweat and shame and agony of the particularly brutal form of Roman execution typically reserved for those whom the empire deemed to be political criminals. It was a type of execution intended to send a dire warning signal to others who might dare to threaten the peace and power of Rome with insolent rebellions. Now, with his friends having betrayed or abandoned him, and, as The Gospel According to Saint Mark tells it, with even God's peace having somehow deserted him, Jesus dies an indescribably violent and brutal death. And he dies alone.

But his death is not the end. Reports circulate that he lives again. The once chastened disciples are now emboldened. His message is spread throughout the Roman Empire. Instead of the end, his death is only a beginning.

The Composition of The Bible

The Bible is not just one book; it is many. The Old Testament consists of thirty-nine books written over a thousand-year period. It was first set down in the Hebrew language. A Greek translation of the Old Testament, known as the Septuagint, was widely used at the time of Christ, and was often the source that New Testament authors used when referencing the Old Testament.

The books of the New Testament were written in Greek over a period of about a century, and only later compiled into one corpus. Even though Greek is the original language of authorship, the Gospels and Acts of the Apostles remain translations of sorts. Jesus and his followers' primary tongue was Aramaic. Their words had to be translated into Greek so that a record could be preserved in the most universal language of the time, rather than being bogged down and limited in the more colloquial Aramaic tongue.

The first record we have of any compilation of New Testament-era text was that of Marcion. His canon consisted of revised letters of Paul, and part of Luke's gospel. While he was declared a heretic for his gnostic views,[1] and a theology that deemed the God of the Old Testament and the God of the New Testament to be entirely different beings, he did set a precedent in the Christian age for compiling sacred writings.

The earliest catalogue we have of the twenty-seven books forming our New Testament Canon is found in the Easter Letter of St. Athanasius, dated 367 A.D. This particular canon, still in use in the Western Church, was decided upon in a time that followed protracted and bloody doctrinal disputes that lasted, literally, for decades. Athanasius himself was a principal participant in these controversies, which we will visit from time to time in this series. The canon compilation reflects actual usage of its constituent parts in Christian study and worship, particularly among a coalition of churches around the Mediterranean that are the ancestors of much of the modern Church. Other churches, such as the Coptic and Syrian ones, developed different canons.

Most writers of the New Testament worked independently of each other. They had no way of knowing that their works would be compiled into a single book that would be considered

---

[1]Gnosticism is an ancient Christian movement described in places in this series, and summarized here. It was considered heretical by the Orthodox movement, which prevailed in the struggle for leadership of the emerging Church. The idea underlying Gnosticism was that acquisition of special knowledge, or *gnosis*, was a central part of the salvation process. It often involved initiation rites, secret ceremonies, and arcane genealogies. Some strands of Gnosticism argued for a dichotomy between spirit, which was considered good, and matter, which was considered evil. While not itself a gnostic work, The Gospel According to Saint John has an esoterica and mystical bent to it that led some ancients to question its inclusion in the canon on the grounds that it leaned too much toward Gnosticism.

sacred Scripture by people almost 2,000 years later. On the contrary, many seemed to believe that the second coming of Christ was at hand, and the end of the world as they knew it was imminent. Different approaches to eschatology, or theological understandings about the expected end of history, are found in the New Testament. The varying degrees of urgency these writings express may reflect changing expectations among different Christian communities about the culmination of their world. As time passed, and the passion, crucifixion, and resurrection of Jesus became more historically remote, the Church extended its predictions about the time period in which all would come to fulfillment. In this series on the synoptic Gospels, we will eventually see how the anticipated end of time is expressed differently by each writer.

Paul's letters are among the oldest books of the New Testament, written in the 50s and 60s A.D. The Gospels were probably written between 65 A.D. and, perhaps, 100 A.D. They would have been written on scrolls of papyrus, each scroll being about the length of a chapter in our New Testament. However, the books of the New Testament were not actually divided into chapters until 1248 A.D., nor into verses until 1551 A.D.

There are thousands of variations found in the ancient texts that have been passed down to us.[2] Indeed, we only possess texts written several hundred years after the originals. In translating and publishing versions of the Bible, scholars have attempted to get as close as possible to the original contents by relying on various techniques, such as by putting emphasis on older texts rather than on newer ones, and on those that were used widely rather than only locally. One result of these methodological efforts is found in the New Revised Standard Version, or "NRSV," which is our primary translation in this series and the most widely used one today. It is as close as a particular interdenominational group of scholars has gotten to the original writings, given the records before them. Particularly notable variations among their source texts are identified in NRSV footnotes, and sometimes reflected here.

The books of the New Testament are believed originally to have been letters written to be read aloud, and in full, to Christian congregations. An obvious example of this genre is found in letters of Paul, where he sends personal greetings to members of the Christian communities that he is addressing. There is evidence that the letters were intended to meet certain critical needs at that time, a trait most visible in his Letter to the Galatians, where Paul argues against a doctrine that would have required Gentile converts to the Christian movement to adopt Jewish law and customs in order to become Christians. Paul obviously won this battle, rendering the Letter to the Galatians as a key testament to Christian liberty and

---

[2]Most variations involve minor spelling or syntax; others are substantive.

an essentially constitutional basis to justify the expansion of the early Jesus movement into the primarily gentile world. Paul's success eliminated serious barriers to entry, such as adult circumcision and dietary restrictions. Gentile membership in the Church became freely available to those who came and professed faith in Jesus as the Christ.

Gospels

Among the books of the New Testament are four that we call "Gospels." This particular series is about three of those books—Matthew, Mark, and Luke—that we call "synoptic."[3] But before we move into a reading of each of their texts, some background information would be helpful.

There is much more information available for consideration in understanding the story of Jesus than just the synoptic Gospels standing alone. Archaeologists have uncovered more than twenty different pieces of Christian literature meeting the definition of "gospel." Some are fragmentary. Others are more complete copies of longer works. Obviously, not all of them made their way into the New Testament. Nor are they all about the mission and ministry of Jesus as an adult. At least one of the so-called "infancy gospels" describes the child Jesus engaging in anti-social behavior, arbitrarily exercising his immense power in order to cause another child to shrivel up and die because he had failed to understand properly certain theological or metaphysical principles. One suspects such depictions of the abuse of power and the lack of grace led tales of that ilk to lack credibility, and to be used sparingly in the early Church before the canon was settled, and to their ultimate exclusion from the final canon.

The Canonical Gospels

The four Gospels that became part of the New Testament—Matthew, Mark, Luke and John—achieved their canonical status more by usage than by mandate (though a mandate appeared in due course, as the Orthodox leaders opposed the study of other gospels, and eventually required that they be destroyed). Their common use was a grass roots acknowledgment that

---

[3]Definitions of these terms are found at the beginning of chapter 1.

these stories of Jesus offered a sense of authenticity to the particular coalition of Greek-speaking churches around the Mediterranean; they gained a heightened status and were eventually considered to be inspired literature. This particular group of churches came to be described as "Catholic," in this sense meaning "universal" or "pervasive," rather than describing an affiliation with a particular denomination. The universal Church was later carved into parts. The Schism between the Eastern Orthodox and Roman Catholics occurred in 1052. It was followed half a millennium later in the West by the Reformation and the separation of Protestant denominations from Rome.

Both the Schism and the Reformation arose, at least in part, out of our human tendency to define ourselves more by our differences than by our similarities. One can see the emergence of this tendency within Christianity, even in the earliest years of the Church. The biblically reported dispute between Paul—who did not want to impose Judaic ritual law on Gentile converts—and the Jerusalem Church leadership—who did want to impose these requirements—is one example.

Yet even in divisiveness we can see inclusion and compromise and, in some cases, consensus. These virtues were concretely displayed by the incorporation of four Gospels into the canon. This incorporation encompassed the broad array of theologies that were acceptable within Orthodoxy, a diversity reflected in the differences found in the gospel stories themselves. Had inclusion not been a key value in settling the canon, one gospel would have been sufficient.

But diverse views often gave way to enforced Orthodoxy, as power was concentrated in the few, particularly in the Medieval Church. The Reformation, and the traditions that have arisen from it, turned the tide away from unbridled ecclesiastical authority and toward the priesthood of all believers with its emphasis on individual conscience and responsibility and the right to read and interpret the Scriptures for oneself. In some ways, this historical movement ushered in a return to the Church's roots at the time the canon was being developed.

Through the present day, the Protestant movement has done much to restore theological pluralism. Rather than being totally wedded to the received canon simply because it had been around for over a millennium, Martin Luther would have gone so far as to eject the letters of James and Jude, along with Revelation, from the New Testament for the reason that Luther did not believe them to be sufficiently Christ-centered for inclusion. The tolerance and inclusiveness of the Roman Church has also expanded in later days, as the Second Vatican Council of the 1960s revisited age-old practices and moved toward services in the vernacular, rather than in Latin, as well as becoming more ecumenically oriented and broad-minded about Bible study by the laity.

From an Ancient to a Modern Application

As we have seen, the Bible is an ancient book, written against the unfolding story of an ancient people. It began as a compilation of works about Jewish faith and history. Layers were added to it as times changed and new events occurred, or old events needed to be (re)interpreted. In the case of the Christian Bible, the sacred history is brought forward in and through the story of Jesus of Nazareth.

The ancient words of the Bible have a timeless power that continue to speak profoundly to our own age. These words tell us stories of brokenness and of its transformation into wholeness. But the Bible can also be misused to advance a desire for power, instead of to enhance a call to service. And so, in light of the tremendous possibilities it presents, we must take seriously the whole enterprise of reading and interpreting the Bible. We must faithfully and intelligently seek a fitting application of its ancient and timeless words to a changing age and so discover something about God's meaning for our lives.

To appreciate just how serious a business it is to read and study Scripture, we need not look much further than the nightly news for a current perspective. Nor do we need look much further than a basic text book on Western Civilization for an historical one. The divisions of the world, now and through the ages, have often been marked with lines drawn by the swords of religious fervor. Zealots separate "them" from "us" based on one's adherence to a particular religious faith, or even adherence to particular traditions within the same faith. One group will often treat another as infidels or heretics because its members do not subscribe to the proper creed or dogma.

We live in an era when extremist elements of "the people of the Book" create crisis conditions that affect us all. Radical Islam seeks to expel others from the land of Mohammed, and attacks civilian targets as a means to this end. Radical Judaism jeopardizes possibilities for peace in the Middle East by resisting compromise with Palestinians who still suffer from their people having been involuntarily divested of their lands when the State of Israel was formed. Radical Christianity still encompasses the shedding of blood in Northern Ireland, and argues in the Holy Land for restoration of Israel to biblical borders as God's definitive will, even if the inhabitants reap the whirlwind in the process.

These people follow in the footsteps of predecessors who instituted Islamic Jihads, Christian Crusades, and Israelite Conquests that occurred centuries, even millennia, earlier. Whether demagogues are laying claim to the Koran, the Hebrew Bible, or a particular version of the Christian one, the Scriptures, which various peoples call sacred, have been invoked with self-righteous fanfare and their proof texts cited with utter confidence to justify atrocious acts. As my father has often said, more people have been killed in the name of religion than any other cause.[4]

Yet, criticism of authoritarian religious systems, or of an enforced sort of literalism itself, is of limited usefulness if there is not a positive alternative one can offer. Gladly, there are plenty of positive ways to interpret the Bible generally, and the synoptic Gospels in particular. In furtherance of that end, this book is intended to expand the marketplace of ideas in some beneficial way by offering a synthesis of biblical scholarship.

I have compiled and synthesized a number of viewpoints, packaging them with questions to ponder and suggested ways of looking at the biblical texts. I hope this is useful to you and others as a tool to better understand the story of Jesus and also to live it out. It is written from the perspective of laity, expressing not only my own views, but also what has come out of the views of many thoughtful participants during several years of teaching adult Christian education.

†††

The Responsible Interpretation of Scripture

This much is clear: when the Bible is read and studied thoroughly and with intellectual honesty, one cannot insist on an inerrancy standard where others are required to accept the Bible as the literal, historical truth in all respects. Where there is any contradiction in how the same story is told in two different places, both cannot be completely factually accurate. To insist on inerrancy and verbal inspiration as the norm in light of such a simple point is to cast an all-knowing God as a little confused or forgetful about what actually happened. Similarly, when there are two conflicting biblical themes, neither can express an absolute truth. The Bible contains both human perspective and holy paradox.

---

[4]The wars, murders, and purges of Nazis, Stalinists, and Maoists may be exceptions to this rule. But if one looks at how invasive were their ideologies, and how public deviation from them was met with swift reprisal, it becomes difficult to see where their politics and philosophy end and a fundamentalistic quasi-religious fervor begins.

So, how are we to proceed responsibly into the Scripture and glean what God would impart to us through it? In order to bring the boundless resources of the Bible to bear in advancing the welfare of all God's children—and not just those whom we happen to like—we do well to begin by grappling with methods to use when interpreting Scripture.

The phrase "interpreting Scripture" implies that one accepts certain limits or guidelines. Indeed, limitations and guidelines are always characteristic of any form of ordered liberty. Freedom in interpreting the Scriptures should not go beyond its logical conclusion: the priesthood of all believers grounded in sound—if divergent—theology, to an illogical extreme: any interpretation of Scripture is valid just because someone likes it and has memorized proof texts to support it. Scripture should be read responsibly.

The fear that this principle would not be followed, or that religious liberty would be misused, concerned even so great a man as Martin Luther. He worried that Protestant liberty had led every "milk maid" to believe she could be a sound interpreter of Scripture without reference to commentary or other learned resources. Forgiving his sexist choice of a straw (wo)man to make his point, Luther does identify a potential problem. Like any other intellectually challenging discipline, the interpretation of Scripture is best done from an informed position, taking into account history, nuance, language, context, the writers' possible agendas or priorities, and the spirit of the times. Responsible interpretation of Scripture does not involve reading an isolated passage, removed from the rest of the text or the circumstances of its writing, and leaping to conclusions about how the will of God can be divined from it. Responsible interpretation is about learning what can be learned in each situation, including the circumstances around the composition of biblical text, so that its themes and implications are given due regard. When we do so, we won't lose the forest for the trees.

Responsible interpretation is also about trusting that the Holy Spirit is at work in others as well as within oneself. We must respect our own experience and the experiences of our fellow Christians, and honor tradition and reason and a sense of justice and mercy when studying the Bible. Interpreting Scripture involves using tools available to us, not the least of which is critical thought, and bringing them to bear when trying to understand and apply ancient texts. If we also add into the mix the notion that this great privilege and responsibility is something we undertake better together than alone—a concept implied in the Episcopal catechism declaring that the Holy Spirit guides "the Church in the true interpretation of the Scriptures"—then we are well on our way to becoming someone other than Luther's metaphorical milkmaid. Let's highlight some tools or points to consider in interpreting Scripture responsibly:

Tools for Interpreting Scripture

✝   Historical context

✝   Alternative translations, or even the original languages of composition

✝   Commentaries and other resources (preferably from diverse groups with different vantage points)

✝   Opinions of others, including those who, by virtue of education, wisdom, or temperament, can provide sound input or guidance

✝   The use of reason to ensure sound interpretations

✝   Consistency of interpretation with overriding biblical themes, such as justice, mercy, faith, hope and love

✝   Prayerful consideration

✝   Sharing our own viewpoints and inviting responses

✝   Group study

✝   Practical experience

✝   Daily commitment to our faith journey

These timeless tools have been used throughout the history of the Church. While they are not new, we sometimes forget to use them.

Striving for a responsible interpretation of Scripture is not simply an intriguing intellectual exercise; it is also part of our search for truth. It involves an effort to see what was communicated to the original audiences by the original authors in order to understand better what lay at the heart of Jesus' work and words. To paraphrase Texas Christian University School of Divinity Professor M. Eugene Boring's introduction to his commentary on The Gospel According to Saint Matthew in *The New Interpreter's Bible* series:

The responsible interpretation of each gospel must correspond to the nature of the gospel itself. Gospels are *literary* works interpreting the *theological meaning* of concrete *historical events* to *a community of people* in a particular situation. These approaches to understanding the Gospels are not mutually exclusive, but rather correspond to the natures of the key texts. We must address what each gospel meant to its readers—the intended, immediate audience—to discover better what it means to us now.

It is important to maintain each concept, italicized above, in a certain balance. An overemphasis on the *literary* aspects of a gospel can result in our losing sight of the historical Jesus. An underemphasis can lead to a literalism which obscures the true meaning or intent.

An overemphasis on the *theological* meaning of the works can deprive us of the personal reality experienced by Christ's disciples. An underemphasis can result in the gospel being reduced to a collection of stories without unifying themes.

An overemphasis on the *historicity* of the events can lead to different risks, which are actually opposite sides of the same coin. On one side, a hyper-skeptical approach to the stories of Jesus limits their spiritual significance and potentially discounts crucial data because the methodology being used requires "multiple attestation" of the same story before it is deemed authentic. This quickly becomes a question of corroboration or confirmation. On the other side of that coin, an excessive focus on the historical aspects of the Gospels, treating them principally as strictly factual accounts, misapprehends the spiritual and symbolic meaning the authors intended.

Finally, an overemphasis of the *communities* to which the Gospels were written limits our ability to explore their meaning for our lives today. An underemphasis makes us lose the cultural context, and thus the original intent of the works.

Rather than deviating too far into one interpretive direction or another, a reasoned balance of the literary, theological, historical and communal aspects of the gospel stories is necessary to aid us in our interpretive efforts. By following this path, we will not stray out of the bounds of proper understanding. We will stay well within the realm of sound reasoning.

†††

Our Silence Will Not Save Us

Today, more than ever, it is vital that mainline voices speak up and be part of the chorus having something to say about what it means to be Christian, and how that role is grounded in a biblically oriented faith. Otherwise, those who are speaking the loudest will be the ones leading by default. And we may not want to go in the direction they are taking us.

Our silence will not save us. If we remain silent, and a rigid and judgmental orthodoxy becomes the norm, we will bear responsibility for the lack of tolerance and diversity in our midst. To preserve an inclusive Christianity, mainline churches must reclaim the language of faith for the voices of moderation and the progressive Christian tradition.

It is important for us to reclaim the name "Jesus" and the title "Christian" to help us sustain the cardinal virtues of faith, hope, and love, and the practices of doing justice, loving mercy, and walking humbly with God. This *is* the core of the Christian way. We must speak out on behalf of the One who called the peacemakers "blessed" and who still calls us to love our enemies. We must help others recognize him in the good and kind. We must retell the story—the whole story—and let people judge for themselves what is right, as Jesus instructed his first disciples to do almost 2,000 years ago.

1

Beginning
Our
Journey

T he word "synoptic" means "to see together."
The word "gospel" means "good news of God's
saving action." So, the synoptic Gospels of
Matthew, Mark and Luke proclaim good news of
God's saving action in a way that allows them to
be seen or read together. In fact, the three works
can best be studied together when set out in
columns and read side-by-side, such as done in
Gospel Parallels.[1] Their ample shared material, seen
together, allows them to be better understood as
they converge and diverge, meet and depart.

We will get to know these stories best as we
take the synoptic Gospels and read them against
the backdrop of history, and within the socio-
political-cultural context of Jesus' time and place.

---

[1]*Gospel Parallels* is a book using The New Revised Standard
Version of the Synoptics, and is designed to facilitate their
comparative study.

The vistas these gospels offer greatly expand when we approach them thoroughly, inquisitively, honestly, and even passionately.

John Dominic Crossan of the University of Chicago, a contemporary scholar of the historical Jesus, offers a way of looking at the gospel texts. If we were to read each of the synoptic Gospels, one after the other, we would no doubt be struck by how much they have in common. They contain a similar chronology, a frequent duplication of stories, and many of the same characters. While each of the Synoptics begins in a different place and way, they converge around the baptism of Jesus and continue along comparable (though not identical) paths through his journeys of healing and preaching, and on to his crucifixion and resurrection.

But if we read these three Gospels side-by-side, we observe other things. We might begin to notice the similarities in the stories less, and their differences more. Then, we might ask questions and seek answers about why the differences exist and what meanings they hold.

With that in mind, chapters in this book (and some subparts of each chapter) have introductory sections that describe some of what is to follow. Questions for consideration are often presented just after setting out a section of gospel text in order to encourage immediately reflecting on it in a particular way or with a particular idea. Following many sections are summaries, commentary, further questions to ponder, suggestions to aid in interpretation, or other thoughts that may help illuminate the interpretive path. I have also included topics that do not strictly arise from the synoptic Gospels, but are complementary to the material and may help cast light not only on the story of Jesus, but also on how the people of our very different era might respond to it.

This series describes our three stories of Jesus as a diverging and converging journey. Throughout the synoptic Gospels, Jesus and his disciples are depicted as being on the road, where they encounter a host of people. Some are potential friends. Others are powerful enemies. One of the illuminating traits for understanding Jesus was that he did not stay in one place for long. Instead, he moved constantly about the countryside to teach, preach, heal, and proclaim the good news of the kingdom of God. The books in this series, and the chapters within them, are often arranged around the image of a journey. While it is the journey of Jesus and his followers, it is also the journey of the people of God. It is our journey.

✝✝✝

The Synoptic Problem

The three synoptic Gospels contain an abundant amount of shared material. Many episodes occur in approximately the same place in Mark's story, for example, as they do in Matthew's or Luke's. The presence of such common content and sequence suggests that these Gospels have common origins. Questions about how each gospel relates to the other, and how they came to occupy their current forms, are collectively called "the synoptic problem." Efforts at untangling the synoptic problem have spanned over 150 years and have centered around identifying which versions of the shared material appear to be the earlier, and thus likely the sources, and which ones appear to be the later, and thus likely the uses, of the developing tradition.

A large preponderance of New Testament scholars believe the shortest gospel, Mark, was the first one written. Their reasons are many and varied. For example, over ninety percent of the contents of Mark are found in Matthew, or Luke, or both. Mark also appears to provide the core structure for the other two synoptic Gospels, as they frequently depart from its narrative and then return when telling their stories. While different segments of Mark are sometimes found in different places in Matthew and Luke, the two longer books rarely agree with each other in such a fashion as to cause both to conflict with Mark. So, scholars believe that Matthew and Luke used different editing techniques when retelling what they found in their shared Markan source.

There are other clues to Markan priority. In a number of places, Matthew and Luke seem to shorten Mark's account, and even to sanitize or revise its more scandalous aspects, such as those passages describing just how extreme was the extent of the disciples' failure to understand Jesus' call to them. To decide that these characteristics support the theory of Markan priority requires us to make certain assumptions about the role human nature played in development of early Christian communities and writings. More specifically, Markan priority, to some extent, assumes that Matthew's and Luke's agendas included painting a favorable picture of the disciples. Under this theory, Mark's harsh description of the disciples would be considered the earliest rendering, and Luke's and Matthew's kinder, gentler portrayals would be adaptations of Mark.[2]

---

[2]This idea also presumes that there is some motivation to improve, rather than to impair, how the leadership is portrayed. A more favorable portrayal would have been the norm where loyalty to the movement required loyalty to its early leadership. It is also conceivable that a writer would craft a later version of a story to display the group's leadership in a more negative light than the original work did—particularly if the author were part of a movement that had become disaffected with that leadership.

Assuming Markan priority, with Matthew and Luke relying on it, we gain some clues about how this particular source was used. It appears that The Gospel According to Saint Mark was held in considerable enough regard by later authors for them to incorporate almost all of it into their works. Yet, it was not considered to be beyond improvement or editing, both for style and for content. Further, if Markan priority is assumed to be the case, it is a safe bet that Mark was read in the churches where the authors of Matthew and Luke were active, and that these authors and communities adapted Mark to the needs of their communities in the composition of their longer gospels. Mark's peculiar combination of earthy simplicity in some segments, and extensive details giving an eye-witness flavor in others (including the occasional use of the Aramaic tongue to report words of Jesus), also suggests it was the first canonical gospel written. It appears the authors of the other two synoptic Gospels added their own construction and finishes over the foundation of the house that Mark built.[3]

Though the writers of Matthew and Luke relied upon Mark, they did not feel totally bound by its contents or structure. They rearranged the sequence of some events. They revised language and added or omitted certain details. They addressed different themes. They also used other sources to round out their stories of Jesus.

The latter two gospels contain a considerable amount of material shared between them, but which is not found in Mark. It is the opinion of most scholars that the authors of Matthew and Luke each had access to a common set of sayings by Jesus, which has been dubbed "Q," the first letter in the German word "quelle," which means "source." Matthew and Luke also reflect traditions (which were possibly communicated orally) independent of not only Mark and Q, but also of each other, which scholars call the "M" and "L" sources, respectively, after the first letter of the names of these gospels.

The prelude to The Gospel According to St. Luke—a passage we will study in detail very early in this book—acknowledges that particular author's indebtedness to other people, and implies that he followed something of the process we are reviewing right now. The evangelist describes his reliance upon the traditions "handed on to us by . . . eyewitnesses and servants of the word" and declares that he had undertaken "to write an orderly account" of them for his audience (Luke 1:1-4).

---

[3]A minority, around ten percent, of New Testament scholars believe Matthew came first and the other two relied on it. While they articulate some reasonable grounds for their opinions, the theory of Markan priority holds around a ninety percent adherence and offers arguments at least as compelling as the ones for Matthean priority, if not significantly more so. Rather than taking a point-counterpoint approach to set out each side of the case, this series simply assumes Markan priority, and summarizes some of the reasons underlying that theory.

But how, precisely, did Luke (or any of our other evangelists,[4] for that matter) compile his source material and use it when relating a particular account of the greatest story ever told? The scholarly methodologies and theories described above, and Luke's own suggestion about what he has done, allow us to construct the following chart to trace a likely course from what the historical Jesus said and did, to the events that are incorporated in the synoptic Gospels.

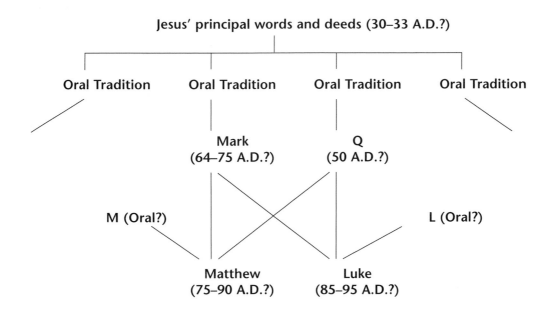

Some of the oral traditions above, whose arrows do not lead to our synoptic Gospels, have been embodied in other works, such as the traditions that led to The Gospel According to Saint John, perhaps, or the sayings Gospel of Thomas, referenced below. It is highly likely that some oral traditions were not preserved in any written record, or that such records were destroyed, with all the strands of information and fabrics of faith of the early Christian communities where they developed being forever lost.

The multiple versions of the story of Jesus, and the potential problems they present for a thoroughly consistent understanding of who he was and what he sought to accomplish, beg the question: Why did the early Church include all these stories, containing not only common

[4]"Evangelist" in this sense means someone who tells good news.

material, but also contradictory or conflicting material, in the compilation now known as the New Testament? Would such an untidy inclusion of different viewpoints not undermine the consistency and the credibility of the message? Was it not important to "get the story straight," and avoid challenges that would arise naturally out of inconsistencies found among the multiple stories?

Could it be that the members of the early Church, whose reading choices greatly influenced what became the New Testament, were aware of, and even embraced, the differences among the gospel accounts of the life of Christ? And, could it be that they were not only smart enough to know of these differences, but also wise enough not to pretend to the role of censor by seeking to impose on widely used and received texts an artificial consistency that the texts themselves do not claim to possess?

The early Church purposefully embraced a diversity of story and belief found within the sources available to it. This understanding of the early Church finds historical support in what happened to one man's effort at penning a comprehensive and entirely consistent gospel. During the middle of the second century, an early church figure named Tatian attempted to write a single gospel harmonizing all four of the canonical gospel stories. Naturally, in writing his gospel story, Tatian would have had to pick and choose from among different segments in the various evangelists' accounts of the life of Christ in order to compose a "unified" whole. The early Church rejected his literary efforts by not including them in the canon, instead preferring the ambiguity often presented in the four canonical Gospels over a forced effort at a single-story account.

Sadly, this early emphasis on diversity within the texts has faded into the background. The focus of some of the most vocal Christians seems to have shifted one hundred eighty degrees away from how the texts differed and moved toward what they have in common. Some groups today insist on claiming literal, historical accuracy and inerrancy for all aspects of the Bible instead of heeding the wise, yet quieter, voices of ambiguity and paradox. If we study the Scriptures with a serious, calmer, less doctrinaire eye, we can still see their diversity and learn a lesson that is somehow closer to the heart of the Gospel than what we previously thought we knew. How do we get to this place of greater understanding?

††††

And if we do not tell it the stones will speak ...

On Palm Sunday, the disciples shouted "Hosanna!" and covered Jesus' path with fronds and cloaks. Hearing this, and fearful of Roman reprisal in the fever pitch of Passover, the Pharisees pleaded for Jesus to control his disciples. "If they are silent," Jesus replied, "the stones will shout aloud!"

How are we, whether stones or disciples, to tell the story of the Christian faith journey in the twenty-first century after Jesus' birth? In examining the body of information from the vantage points of the various gospel writers, we see a little more than we did before, and gain a new appreciation for how truly remarkable the story is. While the world possesses substantial information about the times and life of Jesus, it is neither comprehensive nor entirely consistent. In the next chapter, we will focus on how three of these written records and revisions, or themes and variations, came into being and why.

†††

CHAPTER TWO

The Synoptic Journeys

The central story of Christianity is the story of Jesus. We see that story told in four different ways within the canon—from the vantage points of Matthew, Mark, Luke and John. Each evangelist's verison has a noticeably different tone than the others'. Each tells his own account of the journey in a way that represents not only the author's perspective, but also how the story of Jesus had been told, retold and internalized within their own Christian communities.

We begin with Mark's story.

The Rebel's Journey

New communities of faith developed in the Roman Empire around the preaching, teaching, healing, and oral tradition that the apostles whom Jesus appointed, and the people that followed them, proclaimed. One particular community ended up with a book incorporating certain strands of that oral tradition, which we now know as the Gospel According to St. Mark. For the reasons previously described, Mark is, by most accounts, considered the oldest gospel. It is the shortest, swiftest, most direct story of the critical events late in the life of Jesus. It is written in a relatively unsophisticated style of Greek,[1] suggesting (superficially, at least), a simple author writing to a simple audience. But we will also see a level of complexity in Mark's composition that does not immediately meet the eye. Tradition attributes its authorship to John Mark, a companion of Peter in Rome. John Mark had previously served with Paul, but the two experienced a less-than-amicable parting of ways.[2] Tradition holds that this John Mark found himself in Rome at a time when the mission of the early Church had reached the seat of the empire, and brought his sometimes hidden and underappreciated skill as a writer to bear in furtherance of the ministry Peter was pursuing there.

The composition of Mark's story is sometimes dated around 65 A.D., though a number of scholars place it after the destruction of the Jewish Temple in Jerusalem in 70 A.D. It is described as a "Rebel's Story" in the book *The Four Witnesses: The Rebel, the Rabbi, the Chronicler, and the Mystic*, by Robin Griffith-Jones.[3] Mark chronicles the dark and tragic circumstances surrounding Jesus, including his disciples' almost complete failure to respond, with either faith or understanding, to the way he has set before them. It is written in a fast-paced tempo, frequently using present tense, and often shifting between present and past tenses for no apparent grammatical reason. This method of communication is more in keeping with the storyteller's art of an oral culture than with the careful scholarship of a reflective sage. The breathless style can also lead one to believe that Mark was written in a hurry, maybe even as a desperate effort to preserve a particular record of Jesus when the walls of persecution were quickly closing in.

If the author is John Mark, and the place was Rome, then he was in the most intense of Christian crucibles. According to tradition, Peter and Paul were both martyred in Rome sometime in the 60s A.D., during a persecution by the Emperor Nero. Nero scapegoated the Christians as having been responsible for the great fire in Rome, and Christian casualties mounted. The Gospel According to St. Mark may have arisen out of that setting.

As with all the books of the New Testament, Mark was intended to be read aloud to a church community. While we do not know with any certainty that John Mark, or even someone named "Mark," is the author of the book, we will use that designation to refer both to the book

---

[1]In this series, when descriptions are given of the languages of antiquity, they are based entirely on what scholars say about a given topic. I know neither Greek, nor Hebrew, nor any of the other languages of era. I confess that Southern Highland is more my dialect.

[2]There is also a suggestion of a later reconciliation, though that is uncertain, given that different people described in the New Testament may have had the same or similar names.

[3]Rev. Griffith-Jones wrote his book in John Wesley's study—no doubt a place infused with the Holy.

and to its author, unless context indicates otherwise. We should not fret too much over this lack of certainty about Mark's authorship, though, as we cannot positively identify any of the authors of any of the Gospels. The texts themselves do not name their authors. The traditional nomenclature of "Matthew, Mark, Luke and John," has been used since early generations of the Church to associate these particular works with apostolic authority figures. Mark's gospel was traditionally associated with the preaching of Peter, for reasons outlined earlier. Later, it was circulated among Christian communities along with other gospel writings in leather bindings in a style called "codex" form. The introductory page to the whole compilation was emblazoned with the words "The Gospel." Subsequent cover pages contained the phrase "according to," followed by each putative author's name, and then the gospel text itself.

Mark presents the most human picture of Jesus, featuring obtuse disciples, intense confrontations with religious authorities, a lack of understanding by Jesus' audiences, and portents of the end of the age. The meaning of Jesus' ministry and his identity are actively concealed, typically at his own direction, and are only fully understood at the crucifixion where God's son is aligned with suffering, not power. Prior to the crucifixion, Mark tells of exorcisms and healings and the preaching of the kingdom of God. Jesus combats and is victorious over the dark and demonic forces that oppose the kingdom. He enters into a series of conflicts with scribes and Pharisees and temple authorities who, unable either to win their battles against him, or to preserve their control lock on the faith lives of the people, resort to plotting his murder. They seem to have gotten their way when Jesus is killed. But the tomb is found empty just before the gospel abruptly ends. We are left, along with the original witnesses, to chart the course of future events for ourselves.

The author's purposes for telling his story may have included strengthening a local community under persecution. That community consisted both of those Christians coming out of the Jewish tradition, and those who were Gentile converts. The Gospel According to Saint Mark quite intentionally includes the Gentile world, as we will see in the later volumes of this work.

Alternative theories exist about the Markan community. Some say the original audience was in northern Galilee or southern Syria, which is supported by the fact that these particular areas were the locus of many of the critical events that Mark reports around the life of Christ. In fact, Mark itself ends with a young man in the empty tomb directing the women who had come to anoint Jesus' body to send the disciples to Galilee to meet the risen Lord.

There is no actual resurrection appearance in the two oldest existing copies of Mark. This omission has led many to believe that there was a "lost ending" of Mark—perhaps a single papyrus scroll separated from the remainder of the work. The weight of modern scholarship is against the idea of there being a lost ending, and argues that the story was intentionally

Mark's World
Mark written in Rome, Syria or Galilee (64–75 C.E.?)

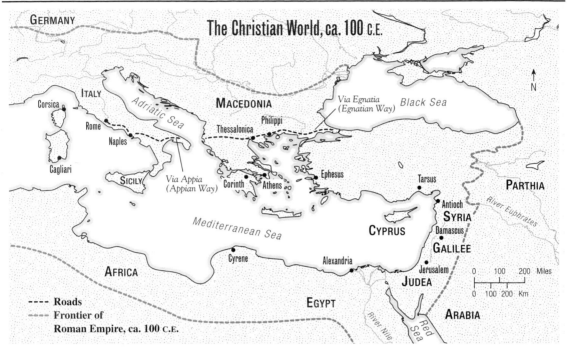

stopped where it was, with the women leaving the empty tomb in terror and amazement, even disobedience. The canonical ending of Mark, found in most copies of the Bible, does not fit well with the rest of the story and is considered to be an editorial add-on written for purposes of including a resurrection appearance.

Despite its central place in the Christian story, Mark's gospel could have been lost to us entirely, as the early Church's study was more keenly focused on the other canonical gospels. In recent decades, Mark has emerged as a major focal point for scholarly research, in part because it is the basis for so many other early Christian writings. In this series, it provides the core narrative. When we encounter Mark's version of any story, and the same story is recorded in a comparable place in Matthew's or Luke's sequence of events, we will typically look at Mark first. That way, we can see what the original story tells, and reflect on its meaning and purpose, before exploring the uses to which Matthew and Luke have put this source.[4]

---

[4]Because Mark contains no birth narrative, we will go some way into this series before that particular pattern becomes visible.

Mark at a Glance

† Written 64–75 A.D.

† A response to persecution

† Active, fast-paced, and to the point

† Written in Rome, or perhaps northern Galilee or southern Syria

† Apostolic Authority attributed to Peter

† Mixed Jewish and Gentile Christian audience, but more heavily Gentile

† Begins with Jesus' ministry

† Most human picture of Jesus

The Galilean Journey of the Q Community

The other shared source in the Synoptics is the sayings gospel, Q. It was probably written even earlier than Mark, perhaps around 50 A.D. We do not possess an actual copy of Q. In fact, scholars have only inferred its existence, pointing primarily to the contents of Matthew and Luke, which display a considerable amount of common material between them that is not found in Mark. The thesis is that the writers of Matthew and Luke also relied on a shared source other than Mark, which they edited and incorporated into their own gospels.

Recently, scholars have marshaled the available resource materials to craft and publish comprehensive re-creations of the Q document. In these works, the shared material in Matthew and Luke has been separated from the remainder of the narratives, then catalogued and reproduced in a format thought to approximate the contents and structure of Q. The resulting organization reflects how the Q material is presented in the canonical gospels, particularly in places where the shared sayings are similarly sequenced or clustered in Matthew and Luke. Where differences exist in how the sayings are presented, the Q scholars have followed certain methods to try to reconstruct a work as closely approximating the original as possible. For instance, a simpler version is generally given priority over a more complex version, which is considered to be a revision. This comparison between sayings is readily seen in Luke's and Matthew's versions of the Beatitudes. Luke's Beatitudes are stated in the second person, and are the more direct and immediately tangible of the two sets of sayings—"Blessed are you who are poor, for yours is the kingdom of God." Matthew's Beatitudes are in the third person and are more elaborate and spiritual—"Blessed are the poor in spirit, for theirs is the kingdom of heaven." The pattern that most frequently appears in the Q material, both within and outside the Beatitudes, is one of Lukan simplicity and Matthean complexity, suggesting to scholars that Luke more closely approximates the contents of the Q source and Matthew more intentionally develops or revises it.

A variety of theories exist about the origins of Q. One is that it was originally written in Aramaic—the predominant language used in Palestine at the time of Christ—but had been translated into Greek by the time Matthew and Luke used it. Other theories suggest that Q was compiled in layers, with certain sets of characteristics being unique to each period of the compilation. Still other theories hold that Q was an organic document, with sayings made by, or attributed to, Jesus appended over time to an original, short compilation. There is even some thought that several versions of Q were in circulation, and that Matthew and Luke possessed different ones. As most of these theories are complementary, rather than mutually exclusive, we need not be too restrictive in how we work with, or harmonize, the Q theories.

The Q source is distinct in a number of ways from narrative materials. For example, Q contains little or no miracle-oriented material, and is focused most heavily on the wisdom sayings of Jesus. Q does not mention his passion, death or resurrection. Some scholars believe the community of Q had relatively limited knowledge of the precise events that transpired at the end of Jesus' life. Their information was, at best, secondhand. Taking this view, the people of Q were probably from Galilee, where Jesus' early success in ministry occurred, and where a legacy of teaching would have been left. The final stages of his earthly ministry, involving opposition by his most powerful adversaries and resulting in his crucifixion, occurred far to the south, in Judea.

Historically, one major objection to the validity of the Q theory was that we had no direct evidence of any gospels being written with any structure other than a narrative one. For the better part of two millennia, the Church and archaeologists had neither preserved nor discovered any gospels that consisted solely of collections of sayings. This objection evaporated in the late 1940s, when a fairly complete copy of an ancient sayings gospel, The Gospel of Thomas, was unearthed in Nag Hammadi, Egypt, near the Nile River. Thomas was in codex form, with papyrus pages bound in leather. The fact that Thomas is a sayings gospel, and that it contains a considerable amount of shared material with the Synoptics, supports the Q thesis. It proves that this particular genre of literature was used in the early Church to preserve sayings of Jesus. Moreover, it was common in antiquity to compile sayings of great sages in one book, an example of cross-cultural data that also supports the Q theory.

Major excerpts of Q are found in Matthew's Sermon on the Mount and Luke's Sermon on the Plain; others are scattered or grouped throughout these Gospels. There is a certain degree of consonance in how these two canonical Gospels arrange their Q material. This pattern suggests that Matthew and Luke used their common source materials in a similar order to the way in which they had been received, but made such changes as were needed to serve the authors' narrative purposes.

The Rabbi's Journey

The next canonical gospel written after Mark was likely The Gospel According to St. Matthew, composed between 75 and 90 A.D. Tradition attributes it to the apostle Matthew, though no objective and independent evidence exists for his authorship. Based on this tradition, some hold that it reflects Matthew's apostleship and teaching, which were eventually condensed into writing by members of his community, even if not by the apostle himself. The first record of this book being associated with Matthew is found in the second century.

The attribution of the book to Matthew, even if it were actually written by someone else, would not have violated the literary conventions of the time. Prevailing practice allowed a leader's disciples, and also later adherents to his school of thought, to write literary works or compose speeches in character that were attributed to the leadership figure. Nor would Matthew's revision of Mark and Q during the process of creating a new story of Jesus run afoul of established literary standards within the Christian community. Some scholars hold that early Christians acted with editorial freedom in the development of sacred texts, believing themselves to be guided by the Holy Spirit and in communion with the risen Christ. In light of these circumstances, and unless context indicates otherwise, the word "Matthew" will be used in this series primarily to refer to the work or its author, whomever that might have been, rather than specifically to the apostle Matthew.

The best theory for where The Gospel According to Saint Matthew was written is Antioch of Syria, a prosperous, urban area that was the foremost city in the eastern regions of the Roman Empire. A large Jewish community lived there, and some aligned themselves with the Jesus movement. Among the reasons that Matthew is believed to have arisen out of Antioch is that it is the most Jewish-oriented of the Gospels, reflecting a heavily Jewish culture. It frequently cites the Old Testament, recognizes continued application of Jewish law and practices, and reports certain events in a fashion that suggests it was written against a backdrop of conflict between an early church congregation and a local synagogue—a conflict often believed to be a precipitating crisis for the composition of Matthew. The circumstances of that composition would not have involved so much a confrontation between two clearly distinct religions as a conflict between two groups of faithful Jews who differed in how they answered the question of whether Jesus was the Messiah. A prevailing scholarly opinion is that Matthew was written after these early Christians were thrown out of "the synagogue across the street" in Antioch, and that it was composed, at least in part, in reaction to this event and in order to assert the proper place of the Church in unfolding Jewish history. For this reason, *The Four Witnesses* calls Matthew "The Rabbi's Story."

Matthew's World
Matthew written in Antioch of Syria (75–90 C.E.?)

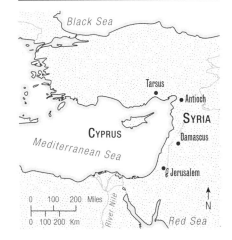

Matthew's emphasis on Jesus' conflicts with scribes and Pharisees may be a result of an increased concentration of Jewish authority toward the local synagogues after the Jerusalem Temple was destroyed. The Romans crushed the bloody Jewish rebellion and destroyed the Jerusalem Temple, the center of Jewish religious practice, in 70 A.D. With their temple destroyed, the Jews might have abandoned their faith; or, they might have taken an alternate or new direction. They chose the latter. What had been a religious system based primarily on observance of animal sacrifice and other rites in the temple was transformed into community-based religious observance in the synagogues. Wherever enough Jews were resident to establish a small worshiping community, a synagogue was built.

After the Jewish rebellion was crushed (and, perhaps, in light of a lengthy history of persons who claimed messianic status and started uprisings, only to end in disaster), the emerging group of Jewish religious authorities took a decidedly conservative bent. They demanded a more rigid orthodoxy that, on the one hand, would protect the people from following false messiahs and the disastrous consequences that went with them; but, on the other, would stifle more serious non-traditional attempts to experience a right relationship with God. So, groups at the margins or fringes of orthodox Judaism of the day, such as the Christians who were proclaiming Jesus to be the Messiah, fell out of favor with the religious authorities. As a result, Matthew's community, not wavering from the proposition that Jesus was the Messiah, may have been recently excommunicated from that "synagogue across the street," and so lived in a state of woundedness and isolation at the time the book was composed.

It is in this setting that we look at the negative depiction of the Jewish leadership, and, sometimes, even of the Jewish people in Matthew. When Jesus is on trial before Pilate and the people call for Barrabas to be freed and Jesus to be crucified, they state that Jesus' "blood [shall] be on us and our children"—a verse unique to Matthew. This phrase may more reflect a conflict occurring in 75–90 A.D., than one occurring around 30 A.D. The Pharisees held greater power in the period of Matthew's authorship than at the time of the crucifixion of Christ. So, as part of a community familiar with Mark's gospel, but lacking guidance as to how to deal with new hostility from the emerging Jewish religiopolitical leadership, Matthew may have composed this verse himself to reflect his own community's conflicts.

This gospel, written after excommunication of the Christians, has a tough edge to it. It has sometimes been abused in attempts to justify centuries of persecution of the Jews at the hands of Christians who had become more powerful and numerous than those whom they understood to be their adversaries. These tough edges should not be treated as declarations that Christian relationships with Jews should be hostile. That understanding would not be much of a gospel at all. Instead, the negative treatment of the Jewish leadership should be viewed in light of the likely historical context of Matthew. The harsher-sounding texts directed against segments of the Jewish population in Matthew reflect a dispute between loyal and devout Jews who disagreed about whether Jesus was the Messiah; they are not a continuing anti-Semitic diatribe giving Christians the right to persecute. These passages are not normative for our faith today.

One effect of the separation from the synagogue may have been the opening of Matthew's church mission to the Gentiles. Clues are found fairly early in the text, such as references to a light in Galilee of the Gentiles, and to the healing of a Syro-Phoenician woman. The expansion of the mission to Gentiles reaches its conclusion in the post-resurrection Great Commission of Jesus: to make disciples of all nations. As the Christians distinguished themselves from the Jewish rebellion against Rome, their separation from the mother faith grew. Unfortunately, a rift, which had historically presented itself in the form of Christians persecuting Jews, grew with it.

Even with such historical misuses and abuses of Matthew, it remains supremely the teaching gospel. Ancient lectionaries cite it more than any other gospel. It incorporates large quantities of Mark and Q, as well as independent materials to which the author had access. It organizes its sources in a manner conducive to being communicated orally, remembered, and repeated. For instance, Matthew often groups sayings and parables in clusters that could serve as memory aids to the people of an oral culture who communicated their sacred stories more in the telling than in the reading. Groupings are often in sevens or threes (this theme of numbers will be further developed during the course of this series). For example, the woes unto the "scribes and pharisees, hypocrites," are grouped in sevens. Likewise, there are three parables against the Jewish leadership in Holy Week.

Matthew's Jesus is depicted as a kingly figure of power, an identity disclosed from the very beginning of the gospel as his genealogy places Jesus in the direct line of descent from Abraham and David. Matthew frequently cites the Old Testament to establish that Jesus is the Messiah, the Anointed One.

In the early chapters of Matthew's gospel, we find a number of imperfect citations to the Old Testament, and, in one case, a non-existent citation. If Matthew is a steadfast Jew (who simply differs from some of his contemporaries on the question of whether Jesus is the Christ), we might ask: How can he make such "errors" when drawing on the Old Testament, the source above all sources for understanding the relationship between God and Matthew's own historically Jewish people? We should first note that, if we characterize these divergences or discrepancies as errors, we are feeding a literalistic prejudice on how the Old Testament should be used. There is nothing in Matthew's own usage of these stories to suggest that he was any sort of literalist. Rather, as we shall see, Matthew borrows liberally from Old Testament descriptions of ancient events in order to reinterpret them as prophecies about the Messiah, which were fulfilled in Jesus. For instance, we will encounter Matthew's statement about Rachel weeping for her children, an Old Testament lament over the Babylonian exile, which occurred many generations after Rachel's death. The prophet who described the exile in such terms drew on past events to provide a sense of meaning about what was occurring in his own time. Matthew's story follows a similar practice as he reinterprets Rachel weeping over her children as a prophecy of the Slaughter of the Holy Innocents, reported from Jesus' infancy. Similar uses of Scripture are found elsewhere, as Matthew relates the events of ancient Israel to the more contemporary events in the life of Christ.

One who is easily plagued by a need for absolute congruity in Scripture could fret over uses Matthew makes of the Old Testament. But it is much more helpful to interpret these passages in a symbolic or metaphorical way: as a mystical chord connecting the Old Testament to the New Covenant in Jesus. It is also helpful to examine Matthew's literary practice in the context of other Judaic practices dating around that time. The Rabbinic discipline of *midrash* involved study of texts from the Hebrew Bible, and relating them to one's particular situation. The Scriptures were searched and verses found that could speak to what was being experienced in the moment. *Midrash* represented, in essence, an "echo effect": the resonance between past and present, ancient Scripture and contemporary crisis, which provided true prophetic connection. This somewhat abstract approach to interpreting Scripture contrasts with the more concrete method found in literalistic prophecy/fulfillment thought patterns, where one presumes that an Old Testament author has, in his own time, intentionally used veiled language to point to the Christ event some centuries hence. Or, to cite a more modern version of this approach, a concrete method is found where one presumes that a New Testament work, such as Revelation, with its vivid references to angels and beasts and horsemen and a dragon and a whore, should be understood as specifically pointing to events that are being "fulfilled" two millennia later, rather than as describing what was occurring to the author's own people.

Many Christians from the post-Apostolic era to date have claimed that the events of Revelation or other apocalyptic literature were being fulfilled before their eyes, and that the end of the world was at hand. To some degree, all of them have been wrong, as the same world exists now as it did then. However, that does not mean that the authors of Revelation, or of the "Little Apocalypse" found in Mark 13 and its parallels, were "wrong." The writers of these apocalyptic works often used fantastic imagery to conceal the meaning of their words from those who were oppressing them—to wit, the Roman Empire. Their core message was that keeping faith in times of trouble would allow the Church to survive, and even prevail. This true prophetic purpose has repeatedly been fulfilled through the ages, and is the solid core of apocalyptic literature, though often missed as generations of Christians have sought to identify some contemporary tyrant as the Antichrist. Matthew's consonance with the Old Testament, and his practices in the nature of *midrash*, are abstract and mystical. They invoke the Old Testament witness in a way that better fits within the purposes of his gospel, including to establish continuity between the Old Order and the new Jesus movement, than would be found if he used a concrete prophecy/fulfillment pattern that we might try to fit into a tidy little box.

Matthew at a Glance

† Written 75–90 A.D.

† A response to Jewish Christians being thrown out of "the synagogue across the street"

† Methodically written, with sayings and stories grouped as a memory cue

† Written in Antioch of Syria

† Apostolic Authority attributed to Matthew

† Predominantly Jewish Christian audience, particularly with respect to:
(1) Old Testament references; (2) antagonism with contemporary Jewish leadership; and (3) coming to grips with extending mission to Gentiles

† Begins with Jesus' Jewish lineage and contains royal imagery

† Most king-like picture of Jesus

The Chronicler's Journey

The Gospel According to St. Luke was probably written next, around 85–95 A.D. Early tradition attributes its authorship to Luke, the beloved physician, and a companion of Paul in his missionary work. The tradition of Lukan authorship exists in part because Luke was believed to be a Gentile, and thus also a member of the group which appears to be the intended audience. Moreover, Luke himself was not so prominent a figure in the early Church that one would have been as inclined to write in his name as, for instance, in Matthew's, Paul's, or John's names. Other data supporting the theory of authorship by Luke himself is that the same person who wrote The Gospel According to Saint Luke also wrote Acts of the Apostles. Latter parts of Acts are told in the first person, suggesting that the author (or the author's primary oral source) stepped onto the stage at around the time Luke is believed to have accompanied Paul.

However, the idea of authentic Lukan authorship is not unanimous. There is some thought that Luke-Acts may have been produced by someone (or even a group) that was a part of a Pauline tradition, with the name "Luke" being attached to the work, much in the same way as the author of the first gospel may have been a member of a Matthean community, and the author of the second gospel a member of a Petrine community. If so, the association with Paul reflects an effort to connect this gospel to a particular line of apostolic authority, much in the same way that the other canonical gospels are connected to apostles. Given the circumstances described above, and unless context indicates otherwise, the word "Luke" will be used in this series primarily to refer to the work or its author, whoever he might have been, rather than specifically to the beloved physician and companion of Paul.

The prologue or introduction to Luke tells us something of the author's methodology for composing his work. It builds a bridge, connecting the past with the future. It goes back to earlier traditions to formulate a new written account of the story of Jesus. It also connects to the future, as the second part of Luke's work, Acts of the Apostles, ends with Paul in Rome.

A key attribute of Luke-Acts is the extension of the gospel to all peoples. Luke is a gospel of the universal grace and salvation of God. It favorably depicts Gentiles, despised Samaritans, occupying soldiers, women, the poor, and other groups that were marginalized in first-century Jewish thought and elsewhere in the Mediterranean world. Where one pericope or segment of Luke tells of a man's encounter with Christ, another will likely involve a woman in a similar setting. According to most NT scholars, Luke is the best piece of Greek writing in the New Testament, with the possible exception of the Letter to the Hebrews.

In composing his story, Luke incorporates much of Mark and Q, but moves their constituent parts around to follow more a literary than a chronological arrangement. He undertakes this task for purposes of writing a new account to "your excellency" Theophilus, a title of honor typically ascribed to somebody in the Roman administrative or governmental hierarchy. There is some theory that Luke's purpose in writing his gospel was to reassure Roman authorities, particularly those in some Hellenistic cities in the eastern Mediterranean, that members of the emerging Christian community were not political revolutionaries, and that they posed no threat to the empire. This point makes one wonder: What did Rome have to fear from the Christians in order that a Christian author felt compelled to reassure Rome of the movement's peaceful nature?

Luke's World

Luke written in Southern Greece, Northern Egypt, or Asia Minor (85–95 C.E.?)

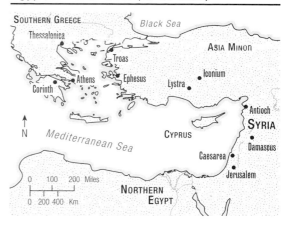

An answer may be that the early Christian movement was closely associated with the Jewish community. Many of the earliest Christians were observant Jews who went to Jerusalem for Passover and worshiped in the synagogues. Jesus himself was typical of an observant Jew in many ways, though a radical in others. Rome may have viewed the Christian movement as a sect within Judaism. This impression had some collateral effects. The Jewish revolt against Rome began in the mid-60s A.D. and largely ended with the destruction of the temple in Jerusalem in 70 A.D.[5] The temple had been the critical worship center, not only for Judaism, but also for early Christianity, as described in Luke-Acts. So, to the Roman Empire, the Christians were often regarded as being aligned with Judaism.

However, at some point, breaches occurred between traditional Judaism and the new Jesus movements. Circumstances surrounding one particular break can be inferred from the Gospel According to St. Matthew, as described above at pp 28–30. Luke addressed ways that Christians could be understood as loyal subjects of Rome, despite some perceived associations with Jewish revolutionaries, as seen in Luke's kingdom concept of Christianity. He explicitly understands that the kingdom of God is an inner kingdom, not a militaristic one. The founder

---

[5]The Jewish stronghold at Masada did not fall until 73 A.D.

of the movement practiced prayerful and compassionate deeds toward the poor, the sick, the disenfranchised, and the downtrodden. He was not in the desert sharpening battle axes. Luke wants his audience, Theophilus, to know that Jesus' followers are not out there, either, generations later.

Even with the apparent identification of one Theophilus as the addressee, there are other theories about who comprises Luke's audience. For instance, it may be that "Theophilus" is not used as an individual's name, but as a description. The word means "lover of God." It may be that "Theophilus" is intended to describe members of a group audience. Perhaps it includes Gentile Christians who had been among the seekers after the great Jewish monotheistic God, or proselyte converts to Judaism, who took the next step to become early Christians. If Luke-Acts is not specifically addressed to one person, it may be addressed to a community of people. While such a community is not as clearly defined geographically as are the possible locations of Matthew's and Mark's audiences, some scholars believe Luke was written to a Gentile Christian community in southern Greece or Asia Minor, while others believe Syria or northern Egypt to be more likely locations. Some scholars believe that Luke-Acts was written to assist in missionary efforts by providing a sound outline of the Christian story.

Many wonderful aspects of this gospel are unique to it: the stories of the prodigal son; the good Samaritan; the repentant thief on the cross. Luke's gospel contains great hymns, such as the *Magnificat* and the *Benedictus*. Luke tells his birth narrative from Mary's perspective, in contrast to Matthew's focus on Joseph's perspective. In Luke, Jesus' identity is disclosed at his birth, not to Eastern Magi, but rather to the shepherds and the simple folk. The gospel's pattern of featuring women and the poor prominently and favorably is foreshadowed from its earliest passages.

The Lukan genealogy of Jesus extends all the way back to Adam, and so encompasses the whole of humanity, instead of simply going only to Abraham, as does Matthew's genealogy. By going back to Adam, and then tracing the story forward through the founding of the Church in Acts, the writer prepares a sweeping sacred history, leading the author of *The Four Witnesses* to call it "The Chronicler's Story."

Luke is the most explicitly purposeful of the Gospels in attempting historical accuracy. Yet, like the others, it should not be read as a biography. All the Gospels are one-to-three generations removed from Jesus' earthly ministry, based on oral tradition, and written in response to community crises and concerns. They are records of God's revelation in human history, not transcripts from court proceedings, The authors expend more effort in expressing religious truth than historical fact.

Luke at a Glance

† Written 85–95 A.D.

† A response to the emerging Christian movement expanding in the Gentile world, and so affecting Rome

† Artistically written, with many great stand-alone stories

† Written in southern Greece, northern Egypt, Asia Minor, Syria, or some other populous part of the Gentile world in the eastern Mediterranean

† Apostolic Authority attributed to Paul (particularly as relates to Volume II of Luke's work, Acts of the Apostles)

† Predominantly Gentile Christian audience, but also honors Jewish roots

† Begins with strong historical context and humble imagery

† Most inclusive picture of Jesus, with special emphasis on women, the poor, and the outcast

In this broad overview, we have seen the canvases on which our evangelists placed their paint. We are now prepared to grapple more fully with the story of Jesus. With a discerning mind and open spirit, we can begin to peer through a prism not so cluttered by the passions, presumptions and prejudices of our own time. By embarking on this journey, we can hope to understand the story in a new way that helps us see Jesus more clearly; follow him more nearly; love him more dearly.

CHAPTER THREE

Out of Ur in the Chaldees and into Occupied Israel

The history of Israel is the history of covenant. In a dark and tumultuous time, God called Abram out of his ancestral land, Ur in the Chaldees, to a new land, called Canaan. It was a land of promise, a land flowing with milk and honey. Abram responded by faith, a concept better understood as trust in God's power and purpose and love and care for us, than as "intellectual assent to a certain set of propositions."[1]

By faith, Abram and Sarai, his beautiful and barren wife, left their homeland on an absurd journey in response to God's promise that they would

---

[1] The quoted phrase is how religious historian Karen Armstrong describes what "faith" came to mean after the dominant mode of religious thinking became doctrinal rather than rooted in a direct, personal and community experience of God. The tendency to equate faith with adherence to doctrine was expressed in the formulation of the creeds and in the settling of the canon. It culminated in the fourth century A.D. Arian controversy.

have descendants as numerous as the stars and the sands. They went to Canaan, tarried there for a time, but still continued to wander elsewhere, living as nomads. And yet, Canaan remained a place of covenant, both for Abram (later called "Abraham") and for his progeny. The "barren" Sarai (later called "Sarah") was well past child-bearing years when her baby, Isaac, drew his first breath. God honored his covenant with Abraham against all odds.

Over the next few generations, the connection established among God, the family of Abraham, and the land of Canaan, followed a tortuous course. Abraham and Sarah's grandson, Jacob (later called "Israel"), had left Canaan early in life to escape the wrath of his brother, Esau (*See Gen 35:10*). Jacob had cheated Esau out of Isaac's blessing and the birthright properly due him. Jacob returned to Canaan many years later, after making a fortune in the world, and achieved at least a partial reconciliation with Esau.

But Jacob, in his old age, once again left the Promised Land. He and his family traveled to Egypt in search of relief from a severe famine. There, they found refuge, and even temporary prosperity and comfort, due in no small part to the fact that Jacob's older sons had many years earlier sold his favorite son, young Joseph, into slavery. Overcoming great adversity, Joseph eventually rose to become a trusted advisor to Pharaoh. This placed him in a position

Abraham's World
Ur in the Chaldees to Canaan (2000–1900 B.C.E.)

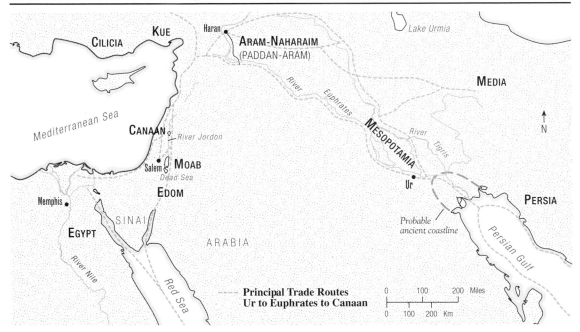

to provide for his father, along with his now-forgiven brothers and extended family, in their time of distress.

But the powerful people of Joseph's generation died and gave way to the next. The political winds shifted, and new powers emerged. The temporary refuge in Egypt was followed by enslavement.

Then Moses, also a descendant of Abraham and Sarah, led his people out of Egypt in a dramatic escape that became the core story of the Jewish people, or "primal narrative" as scholar Marcus Borg, of Oregon State University, calls it. Their Exodus is still commemorated annually at the Passover celebration.

Abraham's descendants then went back to Canaan as a free people, where they claimed and conquered the land and made it truly their home. Joshua, Moses' successor in leadership, was the triumphal general. He led the people into the Promised Land, where they renewed their ancestral covenant with Yahweh. In exchange for receiving such blessings, they pledged that they would eschew other gods and serve only him. And so, the Hebrews took tenuous control over the Promised Land that continued for generations.

Their civilization reached its peak during the reigns of King David and of his son, King Solomon, who built a great temple in Jerusalem to Yahweh. But, weaker successors lost the land. The northern part of the now-divided kingdom, still called Israel, fell to the Assyrians in 722 B.C. The southern part, now called Judea, was destroyed by the Babylonians in 587–586 B.C. Many of the Hebrew people, particularly the leaders, were sent as exiles to Babylon, located in present-day Iraq.

The political winds again changed, and upon Persia's conquest of Babylon, the children of Israel enjoyed restoration of many of their ancestral rights. Jews living in exile were allowed to return home, rebuild their temple, and reclaim something of their lands. But only a relatively small percentage seized the opportunity; most stayed in Babylon and blended into the surrounding culture.

Those who did return learned, to their dismay, that the land was not their own in the way Abraham had once envisioned, or as had been realized during the United Monarchy of the Davidic and Solomonic eras. Instead, the land had become subject to successive occupation by one powerful kingdom or another—the Assyrians, the Babylonians, the Greeks, and then, the Romans. Nothing, though, quenched the desire of the Israelites to govern their own affairs. Theirs was a divine mandate to be discharged by force (or so many thought) if not freely conceded by the occupier. Abraham had been called to this land, the reasoning went, and to this land his descendants had once again returned. They were not going to tolerate it being forever occupied by foreigners.

A common Jewish belief was that the Messiah—God's anointed—would come and restore Israel to its former greatness. During Roman occupation, many Jews had the expectation of deliverance by a military conqueror, a warrior carrying Yahweh's banner, as in the time of Joshua. With such days a thousand years in the past, and no tangible hope of a peaceful restoration, could anyone other than a conquering hero like David be the Messiah? It is in this setting—haunted by memories of greatness and sparked by hopes of restoration, during an age of Roman occupation and Jewish ambition—that we begin to read the story of Jesus.

†††

Mark's spare introduction is this: "The beginning of the good news of Jesus Christ, the Son of God." It is a succinct start to a succinct gospel whose brevity and simplicity often hide its depth. With simple clarity, Mark sets forth the purpose of the gospel: to proclaim the good news of God's saving action in Jesus Christ.

The Divided Kingdoms of Judea and Israel
(922–722 B.C.E.)

Matthew and Luke have introductory material, with much the same purpose as Mark's, but with different approaches. The introductions, along with the birth narratives that follow shortly on their heels, communicate critical information quite early in each story about the identity and mission of Jesus. We will visit the birth narratives later in this volume. In this chapter, we will examine how both Matthew and Luke use their introductions to set the stage for the birth of the Messiah, and, ultimately, for his mission and ministry.

With an understanding of the spirit of the times, we now turn to Luke's prologue.

☩ LUKE 1:1–4 The Prologue

¹Since many have undertaken to set down an orderly account of the events that have been fulfilled among us, ²just as they were handed on to us by those who

from the beginning were eyewitnesses and servants of the word, ³I too decided, after investigating everything carefully from the very first, to write an orderly account for you, most excellent Theophilus, ⁴so that you may know the truth concerning the things about which you have been instructed.

1. What is Luke trying to communicate to his audience, "Theophilus," in his prologue?

2. In the language of the prologue, what communicates something about the author, the audience, the story, or the subject matter?

The prologue to Luke is an explicitly conscious effort both to set a serious tone about the author's undertaking, and to describe what he has done. By using a formal style of Greek, the author shows himself to be scholarly, and his subject matter to be of utmost importance. The first four verses of the gospel form a single sentence. While editors of our day might consider Luke's opening to be rather windy, in antiquity, the ability to compose a lucid sentence of this type was considered evidence of the author's skill. Luke possessed a descriptive style that was highly prized among the lettered people of his day.

Having set the *tone* in this fashion, Luke makes the *substance* seem almost elusive by comparison. There is no mention of precisely what events have been fulfilled, but only that they have been. Jesus of Nazareth is not named, as he is in Mark and Matthew, though we will see in due course that the book is about him. The prologue is tantalizingly written, and leaves the reader asking for more.

The prologue also says something about methodology. Luke ties his work to the work of those who preceded him. He discloses that a number of people have attempted a similar undertaking, a written composition about the events he will describe. We have already seen what a substantial body of work that meets the definition of "gospel" has come down to us in some form. We might infer from Luke's description that he is giving credit where due, presumably to Mark (from whom Luke takes his narrative structure) and to the people of Q (where Luke gets much of his teaching material). The prologue also provides a clue about there being an L source, containing material unique to Luke, including such gems as The Prodigal Son, the Good Samaritan, and the Road to Emmaus.

The prologue also says something explicit about Luke's more remote sources. The author is dependent, not only on written materials, but also ultimately on the oral tradition "handed on to us by those who from the beginning were eyewitnesses and servants of the word." Rather than claiming personal authority, Luke puts himself within the tradition and province of the Christian community.

And yet for Luke, uncorroborated heresay will not suffice. His research has been painstaking, having investigated "everything carefully from the very first." It is important that he attempt to be accurate in what he tells. Luke is the most comprehensive of the gospels. Taken in conjunction with his second volume, Acts of the Apostles, his literary legacy forms the lengthiest body of work by any New Testament author.

But, the organization of Luke is not strictly sequential, nor is the content entirely accurate to the finest detail.[2] In the course of his gospel, the author makes some historical and geographic mistakes, and displays some chronological inconsistencies with the other Synoptics. He also modifies some of his Jewish-oriented sources to resonate better with his Gentile audience. Being more theological than literal-minded, Luke intends, through his organization, to group critical religious themes in ways that add to the quality of the presentation, if not to its factual continuity.

In recognizing the process Luke has followed, it is important that we not impose our own modern sensibilities concerning the proper relationship between historical precision and literary cohesion. The fact that he has researched extensively, but still taken some literary license, does not reflect negatively on the quality of his research or on the general reliability of his account. We must remember that he was writing a half century or more after the fact. He based his version of the story of Jesus on the information he had available, which was not identical to the information other writers may have had. And, consistent with the responsible interpretation of Scripture, we must also remember the importance of balance among the historical, literary, theological, and communal aspects of his work.[3]

So, we might ask: How, precisely, did Luke's investigatory work result in a gospel displaying such a balance? Can we see the hand of God present in this process? Are there models to assist us in coming to grips with what his work ultimately means, and why Christians consider it to be "Scripture"?

Among Reformation-based churches, Scripture is traditionally interpreted in light of its overarching themes and within a community of faith. Professor David Hester, of Louisville

---

[2] For more information, *see* chapter 2, under the subheading "The Chronicler's Journey."
[3] This concept is explained in greater detail in the Introduction.

Presbyterian Theological Seminary, asserts the importance of this approach to interpretation, especially with difficult texts.[4] Another model showing this tradition is found in "An Outline of the Faith, Commonly Called the Catechism" of *The Book of Common Prayer*, which is used in the Episcopal Church. The Prayer Book articulates one denomination's collective understanding of how the authors of the Bible composed their works. The version of the Prayer Book that has been in use in the United States since 1979 is the latest in a series dating back to the Elizabethan era. In contrast to some ideas about biblical authorship, which more or less understand the Bible as a flawless transcription of divine dictation, the Episcopal catechism describes a more subtle process:

Q: Why do we call the Holy Scriptures the Word of God?

A: We call them the Word of God because God inspired their human authors and because God still speaks to us through the Bible.

Q: How do we understand the meaning of the Bible?

A: We understand the meaning of the Bible by the help of the Holy Spirit, who guides the Church in the true interpretation of the Scriptures.

Note that the catechism does not describe the Bible as being inspired in and of itself; rather, its *human authors* were acting under divine inspiration when telling their stories. They retained their humanity, instead of becoming inerrant scriveners of divine words. Stated differently: God did not possess Luke; he guided him.

The Holy Spirit is also involved in the interpretive, as well as the compositional, process. Because of this presence, we are not to fear grappling with the meaning of difficult texts. The Spirit is there to help us in our interpretation. Again, drawing on the Catechism from the Prayer Book:

Q: How do we recognize the presence of the Holy Spirit in our lives?

A: We recognize the presence of the Holy Spirit when we confess Jesus Christ as Lord and are brought into love and harmony with God, with ourselves, with our neighbors, and with all creation.

---

[4]*See Interpretation Bible Studies: First and Second Samuel* at pp. 38–39, interpreting God's command to Saul to destroy every living thing among the Amalekites.

Q: How do we recognize the truths taught by the Holy Spirit?

A: We recognize truths to be taught by the Holy Spirit when they are in accord with the Scriptures.

Finally, it is the Church (meaning us) which the Spirit guides; not only individuals, but also communities. It is not up to any single person to declare definitively how to interpret the Bible. Each has the right to bring his or her own understanding and conscience to bear as part of a larger community. The work of the Spirit is accomplished through both individual and group study and reflection. It is through both methods that theological matters are explored in the marketplace of ideas and "the spirits tested," as 1 John 4:1 urges.

God will not provide an authority figure to give us *the* answer. We need to be willing to struggle with the meaning of biblical texts. Perhaps more importantly, we need to struggle with how they are to be lived. In the process, we just might encounter the divine presence.

In this sense, the Bible is to be taken seriously as a record of God's revelation in human history. The Bible is a collective work of people who, for more than a millennium, grappled to proclaim something uniquely important about the relationship between God and a tribe, then God and a people, then God and all humanity. It was written by those who felt called to speak for God to the people of their own time, and who still speak to us on his behalf. We can glimpse something of the divine through the written word scrupulously drafted by people like Luke.

To whom is this Luke writing, and why? The addressee is called "Theophilus," a Greek name. He is described as "most excellent"—or, "your excellency." Given the salutation, it may be that Theophilus is an administrator of the Roman Empire. Perhaps Luke is writing this book for an important official to establish that the Jesus movement, which proclaims the gospel in royal terms and describes its purpose as inaugurating a "kingdom," is not an earthly threat to Rome's political sovereignty. Much of what Jesus is reported as saying has to do with right living and relationships, and proper priorities, not royal or political prerogatives. It is a new mode of living that is more about the kingdom within and among his followers than about earthly lines of authority and succession. While the loyalty of Christian to Lord is absolute and resolute, it is not a sort of loyalty that necessarily interferes with the followers being law-abiding subjects of the empire.[5] In the late first-century milieu, with the land of covenant

---

[5]Inevitably, there have been times when duty to God and being a law-abiding citizen of an earthly realm have conflicted. But, as a rule, the two roles, in a civilized and humane society, need not be mutually exclusive. The

under occupation, and the Jewish rebellion having occurred and been quashed, this message might well have been necessary to ensure the survival of the young Christian community to which Luke belongs.

But perhaps the name "Theophilus" is used more generally. It may connote someone other than our hypothetical official, such as an individual, or a group, recipient of the letter. The word "Theophilus" means "lover of God." As both Luke and Acts are addressed to Theophilus, it may be that the audience is a group of Gentile seekers or converts, in Alexandria or Antioch, for instance, rather than an individual representative of the Roman imperial system.

Regardless of whether the audience is an individual with certain authority in the Roman Empire, or a Gentile Christian community, there is much to be gleaned from what Luke communicates here and shortly hereafter. Luke-Acts provides a sweeping context to understand Christian beginnings. It is primarily through Luke's description of leaders and events within the Roman Empire that we have information about the time and circumstances of Jesus' life and ministry and the birth of the Church.[6]

✝✝✝

Having completed our first scriptural reading in this volume and having reviewed the related commentary, we will now take the opportunity (as we will often do in this book) to reflect on what we have just studied:

1. Does Luke's acknowledgment of his indebtedness to the work of others affect your understanding of the way the Bible was composed and compiled? If so, how? And how might it affect your understanding of what it means to say that the writing of Scripture is "inspired"?

Apostle Paul (the primary actor in Acts of the Apostles), was simultaneously the most influential Christian in the world of Gentiles and a good citizen of the Empire. Chapter 13 of his Letter to the Romans strongly calls for submission to, and respect of, civil authority. Following his principles, when tried on contrived charges brought by some of his Jewish opponents, Paul did not despair of the Empire's system of justice, but exercised his right as a citizen to appeal to the emperor (*See* Acts 25). The misfortune of Paul and other Christian leaders is that the mad Nero was in power at the time a huge fire consumed much of Rome. He was ready to affix blame, and the Christians were convenient scapegoats. According to tradition, Paul and Peter were among those who lost their lives in the immediate fallout from Nero's lethal whim. The Neros of history call for a pragmatic, rather than legalistic, interpretation of Romans 13 and other texts addressing questions of civil authority. Sometimes, as in the case of Dietrich Bonhoeffer, that approach can cost you your life at the hands of people like the Nazis.

[6]While Matthew will also provides some clues, Luke-Acts gives the more comprehensive account.

2. Do you think the precise identity of the audience is critical to Luke's story? As you continue with your study, consider whether you might interpret passages of Luke differently if you view his primary purpose as being: (a) a defense of the Christian movement under Roman scrutiny; or (b) teaching material addressed to a community of the faithful, largely for purposes of religious instruction? How might this understanding affect the way you present this gospel to others?

†††

If we think back to the King James Version of the Bible, we will remember how its translation of Matthew 1 says that Abraham begat Isaac, who begat Jacob, who begat Judah and his bothers, and so on, down the line through the generations until the genealogy culminates in the birth of Jesus. For many decades, Sunday School children have called this passage "the begats." No doubt, one reason is that "begats" is a funny word, a piece of mischief that would make Tom Sawyer himself proud.[7]

But the childish desire to give the passage a funny name might also imply something more instructive about it. Countless children may have been reacting, subconsciously, at least, to the fact that there is precious little to explain why Matthew starts out his gospel with a lengthy "snoozer," having no apparent purpose other than to give a demonstration of the author's knowledge about a family tree. In this regard, the "begats" could not be more different from, say, the story of Jesus and his disciples feeding 5,000 hungry and exhausted people. There, human need is sufficient justification for abundant and compassionate grace, which is always a story worth telling.[8] But, having said that, Matthew has a vantage point as well, and it is time for us to look at it.

♱ MATTHEW 1:1–17 The Genealogy of Jesus

[1]An account of the genealogy of Jesus the Messiah, the son of David, the son of Abraham.

---

[7]The NRSV replaces the verb "begat" with the more familiar phrase, "was the father of."

[8]The feeding of the five thousand is the only miracle of Jesus that all four canonical Gospels report. This comprehensive treatment speaks to the universal appeal of the story.

²Abraham was the father of Isaac, and Isaac the father of Jacob, and Jacob the father of Judah and his brothers, ³and Judah the father of Perez and Zerah by Tamar, and Perez the father of Hezron, and Hezron the father of Aram, ⁴and Aram the father of Aminadab, and Aminadab the father of Nahshon, and Nahshon the father of Salmon, ⁵and Salmon the father of Boaz by Rahab, and Boaz the father of Obed by Ruth, and Obed the father of Jesse, ⁶and Jesse the father of King David.

And David was the father of Solomon by the wife of Uriah, ⁷and Solomon the father of Rehoboam, and Rehoboam the father of Abijah, and Abijah the father of Asaph, ⁸and Asaph the father of Jehoshaphat, and Jehoshaphat the father of Joram, and Joram the father of Uzziah, ⁹and Uzziah the father of Jotham, and Jotham the father of Ahaz, and Ahaz the father of Hezekiah, ¹⁰and Hezekiah the father of Manasseh, and Manasseh the father of Amos, and Amos the father of Josiah, ¹¹and Josiah the father of Jechoniah and his brothers, at the time of the deportation to Babylon.

¹²And after the deportation to Babylon: Jechoniah was the father of Salathiel, and Salathiel the father of Zerubbabel, ¹³and Zerubbabel the father of Abiud, and Abiud the father of Eliakim, and Eliakim the father of Azor, ¹⁴and Azor the father of Zadok, and Zadok the father of Achim, and Achim the father of Eliud, ¹⁵and Eliud the father of Eleazar, and Eleazar the father of Matthan, and Matthan the father of Jacob, ¹⁶and Jacob the father of Joseph the husband of Mary, of whom Jesus was born, who is called the Messiah.

¹⁷So all the generations from Abraham to David are fourteen generations; and from David to the deportation to Babylon, fourteen generations; and from the deportation to Babylon to the Messiah, fourteen generations.

1. What is the point of Matthew's genealogy?

2. Why are matters of pedigree found in the Bible at all, and then displayed with the prominence that Matthew gives to the Jesus genealogy?

3. More simply put: Why does it matter?

4. Why does the genealogy list a few women, but omit most? Why does it list the particular women that it does?

5. How does Matthew's genealogy differ from Luke's? See Luke 3:23–38.

†††

From a modern perspective, it would be easy not to dwell on a genealogical account. We could simply make a passing reference to it and move ahead. Yet, succumbing to this temptation would not serve us in reaching a deeper understanding of its meaning. An informed Jewish mind of the first century would react to the genealogy in a much different way. If Matthew were writing to such an audience (which we assume he was), it would have quickly grasped that his gospel starts, not with a whimper, but a bang.

At the outset, Jesus is identified with two of the most critical figures of Jewish history. He is called the son of David, the son of Abraham. He is also called the "Messiah," which literally means "Anointed One," and was used historically to describe the ritual setting apart of kings and priests for their unique functions. But by the time of Jesus' birth, the term "Messiah" had come to mean something beyond "anointed"; it had come to mean something central to the hopes of occupied Israel.

Jewish ideas around the Messiah had reached explosive expectations by the first century: The expected Messiah was associated with the promise to Abraham of a mighty people; with Moses' promise of God sending another man to fulfill his prophetic and protective role; and with the promise of David's throne in David's city being the seat of Jewish power and the locus of the preeminent people of the world. The Messiah was regarded as a long-awaited, ideal king who would restore the fortunes of Israel and usher in an era of greatness. To call Jesus the Messiah, as Matthew does in his first verse, is to project an aura of incomparable expectation around him.

But that greatness was not, in Matthew's view, conferred by happenstance. Jesus' role as Messiah was an inevitable fulfilment of God's plan, foreshadowed by his lineage in a way that gives the reader confidence about the credibility of Jesus' destiny. He is not a pretender to the throne, as so many false messiahs who led the Jewish people on the road to destruction had proven to be. Rather, he is specifically tied to Abraham and his covenant with God about a promised land, and descendants as numerous as the stars and the sands.[9] He is tied to King David by descent, and so is rightfully heir to the throne. He is also linked, through David—the greatest king of his people—to a certain grandeur.

Unlike Luke's genealogy, which starts in the beginning with Adam, Matthew's genealogy begins with Abraham and God's covenant.[10] In this way, Matthew's genealogy implies that Jesus is to have some unique role within historical Judaism. Matthew defers until later any specific description of a broader role Jesus might play for the balance of humanity. More universal ideas are hinted at all along, but only come to complete fruition at the close of his gospel, when the risen Christ commissions his followers to make disciples of all nations.

There is other symbolism that we might miss as well, but which a first-century Jew would have noticed. In the Bible, the mention of particular numbers is symbolically significant. We see a lot of twelves: twelve tribes of Israel; Twelve Apostles; twelve books of the minor prophets. Sevens are also used with frequency: the days of the Genesis creation story; the number of times Elisha ordered Namaan the Syrian to bathe in the Jordan to be cleansed of his leprosy; the number of woes to the scribes and the Pharisees. Forty is also common: Noah's forty-day voyage over the waters; the children of Israel's forty years of wandering in the desert; Jesus' forty-day struggle with temptation.

In this genealogy, there are fourteen generations from Abraham to David, fourteen generations from David to the deportation (commonly called the "exile"), and fourteen generations from the exile to the coming of the Messiah.

Before looking at how repetition of the number fourteen fits within the framework of this passage, let us first look at what each demarcation point along the genealogical path signifies. The first period, from Abraham to David, encompasses the time from the founding promise of covenant until the zenith of the Israelite kingdom. It is the period of ascent by the covenant people, from bare beginnings, through slavery and escape and wandering in the desert and conquest, to the time that the kingdom reached its height. In the days of David, the kingdom of Israel was filled with potential. Its hope was to continue on an upward trajectory and take its place among the powers of the world.

---

[9]The Jewish people generally traced their ancestry to Abraham. In this sense, Jesus would not have been unique. But, in the context of the rest of the genealogy, and what it suggests about Jesus' identity, Matthew's decision to trace the lineage back to Abraham at the outset of his gospel is critical to the story he tells his predominantly Jewish-Christian audience.

[10]We will focus more on the other differences in the two genealogies when we read Luke's version in a later volume.

Instead, the United Monarchy of Israel and Judea was divided after the death of David's son and heir, King Solomon. David's later descendants abandoned the grand and wonderful, if flawed, ways of their ancestors. Despite David's failings—the most notorious of which was his adulterous union with Bathsheba and the murder of her husband—he was, at his core, beloved of God and struggled to be true to the purpose set before him as the leader of the covenant people.

These first fourteen generations, from Abraham to David, whose net result was a remarkable ascent, were not to continue. The divided kingdom fell into disarray—first the northern kingdom of Israel, then the southern kingdom of Judea. Fourteen generations after the Davidic apex, the ancient Jews hit rock bottom in the Babylonian exile. It was an experience of incomparable suffering to a people so identified with place as were the children of Abraham. The sound of their lament is preserved in beautiful and painful Psalms, which have inspired music more than twenty centuries later:

> **By the rivers of Babylon, where we sat down on**
> **and there we wept, when we remembered Zion**
>
> **Oh the wicked carried us away to captivity, required of us a song;**
> **but how can we sing of Zion in a strange land?**
>
> **So may the words of our mouths, and the meditations of our hearts**
> **be acceptable in thy sight, Oh Lord!**[11]

The exile was such a catastrophic event that it was included in the genealogy as a time against which to measure all other events. All that had been worked for was lost. The people of God were gone from the Promised Land. Their fate appeared to be in the hands of their tormentors.

Then, the genealogy ascends. It recounts fourteen generations from the exile to the coming of the Messiah, during which a return home of sorts had occurred. In the advent of the son of Abraham, the son of David, there is restoration and redemption for Israel. The genealogy culminates in the true return from the Babylonian exile; not just physical, but spiritual as well. The Messiah has come, and God's will for his people is in the age of completion.

It would not serve us to understand the genealogy as being completely literal. Even allowing for the *general* accuracy of Matthew's genealogy (an issue we will revisit with Luke's

---

[11]These words, put to music, combine aspects of Psalm 137 and Psalm 19.

Babylonian Exile
The Rivers of Babylon and the Land of Zion (587–539 B.C.E.)

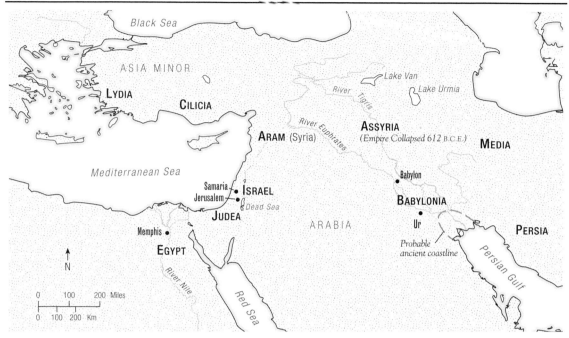

genealogy) we can still see how he works selectively with his material to ensure that there are fourteen generations in each of the three stages of history of the covenant people. He leaves out several generations that can otherwise be reconstructed from the Old Testament.[12] This deviation from a strictly historical understanding of the Old Testament record suggests that the author has an important theological purpose in mind when separating, by equal spans, each major milestone along the genealogical trail: the call of Abraham; the reign of David; the Babylonian exile; and the coming of the Messiah.

According to Professor Boring's commentary on Matthew in *The New Interpreter's Bible* series, patterns of fourteen are often found in Jewish writing. There are fourteen periods, or eras, of Jewish history. There are records of fourteen rabbinical links to Moses. Fourteen is the numerical value of David's name in the Hebrew alphabet. Repeated use of the number

---

[12]For example, if we look at a genealogy from the Old Testament book of 1 Chronicles, at chapter 3, we see much the same lineage. However, several generations between Joram and Uzziah are omitted from Jesus' genealogy. Also, Mannesseh's successor in Chronicles was Amon, not Amos, as in Matthew. There are several other omissions and misnomers in Matthew's genealogy as well.

fourteen, while having mystical overtones, also had the practical effect of serving as a memory aid for teaching in a predominantly oral culture with no printing press.

The fourteen generations in each span are also multiples of seven. Seven is considered to represent completeness in Jewish thought. God created the world in seven days. Elisha told Namaan of Syria to bathe in the river Jordan seven times to complete his cure for leprosy. The dream world images that Joseph of the Old Testament interpreted were often grouped in sevens. In the New Testament, Jesus declared that we are to forgive our offending brother for seventy times seven offenses. Using a multiple of seven to measure the generations is in keeping with the Jewish pattern and practice of acknowledging that certain numbers reveal something about the sacred.

There is another profoundly important aspect to Matthew's genealogy that could easily be overlooked, but that would not have been lost on a person of the first century. Most Jewish genealogies describe a male lineage. Matthew deviates markedly from that practice as five women, more than one of whom are Gentiles, are mentioned in his genealogy of Jesus. They include a woman who disguised herself as a prostitute to have an heir (Tamar); a spying harlot (Rahab); a despised Moabite (Ruth); a woman who had been in an adulterous union with the King (Bathsheba, simply called Uriah the Hittite's wife in Matthew's genealogy); and an unknown girl named Mary.

To stir the pot even more, the names of the great matriarchs—Sarah, Rachel, Rebecca, and Leah[13]—the very women who we might expect to be identified if any deviation from the all-male genealogical norm is to occur—are absent. Why would they be omitted, and an assorted group of marginal characters be listed? Let's look at the circumstances of each and see if a pattern emerges.

Tamar

The first-named female ancestor of Jesus is Tamar. Her story is found in Genesis 38. We are told that Tamar was the daughter-in-law of Judah, a son of Jacob. Her first husband was stricken down for his evil ways. In keeping with familial duties, Judah provided another son to marry Tamar so that she might have a child. Naturally, we might assume, her heir would be able to care for her in her old age. But, more important to the patriarchal society, any child would be considered the deceased man's son, rather than the biological father's son, and the

---

[13]Leah was the first wife of Jacob and mother of Judah, who is named in the direct lineage of Jesus. Her younger sister, Rebecca, was Jacob's favorite wife. She was the mother of some of "Judah's brothers" referenced in the genealogy as a group (*See* Gen. 29–30).

deceased's lineage would continue.[14] This son wished to deprive his deceased brother of an heir, and carried out his marital relations with Tamar accordingly. His deeds were wicked in the sight of the Lord, leading to this brother's death as well.

For reasons unbeknownst to us, but likely grounded in the superstitious fear that Tamar was "bad luck" and fatal for his sons, Judah failed to honor his promise to have yet another son marry Tamar. Running out of options, Tamar disguised herself as a prostitute and sat outside a local pagan temple where she succeeded in soliciting Judah's business. When she turned up later, pregnant but unmarried, Judah made preparations to have her burned at the stake, presumably for bringing shame on the family by her unwed pregnancy.

But Judah repented of this intent when she provided him with evidence that he was the man responsible for her condition. On reflection, he considered himself to have greater fault in the affair than Tamar. And so, through her efforts at self-preservation and by asserting her just claims to become a mother to children, she and her posterity survived.

Rahab

The next woman on the list is Rahab, who seems to have been a career prostitute, rather than a situational one like Tamar. Her story is told in chapters 2 and 6 of Joshua. When the Jewish armies were moving toward the conquest of Canaan, the City of Jericho was a key objective. Joshua sent scouts to conduct reconnaissance. They received aid from an unexpected source— a local gentile whore, Rahab, who first hid them, then assisted their return to Joshua's army as a preparatory step for the invasion.

Ruth

Ruth was a Moabite. Her story is told in the book of the Bible bearing her name. It is a beautiful and faithful story. When Ruth was widowed as a young woman, her mother-in-law, Naomi, prepared to return home to Israel. In doing so, she encouraged Ruth to stay in her own land. Ruth's response was from the heart:

---

[14]We will read more about this topic in a later volume in this series when we examine the legal and cultural customs around the ancient Levirate law—the practice of a man marrying his dead brother's wife, with offspring being considered the progeny of the dead man. Ideas behind this practice included perpetuating the decedent's line, orderly transfer of his property, and, to some lesser degree, care for the widow in her old age. Jesus was involved in a controversy with the Sadducees about this topic during Holy Week.

[16]But Ruth said, "Do not press me to leave you or to turn back from following you! Where you go, I will go; where you lodge, I will lodge; your people shall be my people, and your God my God. [17]Where you die, I will die—there will I be buried. May the Lord do thus and so to me, and more as well, if even death parts me from you!"

[18]When Naomi saw that she was determined to go with her, she said no more to her.

This devotion (*See* Ruth 1:16–18) came from a woman born to a gentile tribe the Israelites detested. The Moabites were rumored to be the offspring of the incestuous union between Lot and one of his daughters after his wife had been turned into a pillar of salt for looking longingly back at burning Sodom (*See* Gen. 19). In her own story, the Moabite Ruth is reported to have uncovered the feet of Boaz at night on the threshing floor—a step along the way toward winning his love and having a son and heir (*See* Ruth 3–4).

Bathsheba

The next woman mentioned is "the wife of Uriah," none other than the beautiful Bathsheba. She is not mentioned by name in the genealogy, perhaps to emphasize to the reader that she was someone else's wife when her relations with David began. Her story is told at 2 Sam. 11–12. King David saw her bathing on the roof and, smitten, took her in an adulterous union.[15] In a way that only lustful and possessive kings can do, David soon set up her husband, a mercenary named Uriah the Hittite, to be killed in battle. The prophet Nathan denounced David for his actions, and the child of the illicit relationship with Bathsheba died. However, like Judah before him, David repented of his misdeeds. David married the widow of Uriah, and she again became pregnant and gave birth to the baby later known as King Solomon (2 Sam. 12:24–25).

Mary

And this brings us to Mary. Where will she fall in the history of the scandalous, unconventional, yet remarkably resourceful women? Will she be seen as something other than a paragon of virtue? And what will her story be?

---

[15]Some scholars argue that David raped her. Certainly, his power and title as king was an intrinsically coercive one.

Matthew has listed an unseemly group of women to illustrate how God has worked unexpectedly in the course of human events through imperfect yet extraordinary people, rather than just through the "respectable" and the commonplace. The women of the Old Order prepare the reader for the unusual circumstances of Mary giving birth to Jesus. Some of them bring to mind a bumper sticker, very popular in and around Asheville, North Carolina: "Well behaved women rarely make history!" With such an ancestry, will Jesus, too, be great? Will he, Son of Abraham, Son of David, be a renowned descendant of the famous men and singular women whom Matthew has honored to name in the genealogy of the Messiah?

✝✝✝

1. Oftentimes, Judeo-Christian morality is associated with traditional ideas about what constitutes sexual purity. Yet, we see substantial departures from these norms in Jesus' genealogy. How does the fact that Matthew chose to identify certain of Jesus' more sexually unconventional female ancestors by name fit alongside traditional ideas about sexuality? About divine providence? About the way that people who are not stereotypically considered "role models" can, in fact, fulfill that function? Have you known people like that?

2. Matthew's genealogy of Jesus left out a number of people who can be identified as part of the same lineage in the Old Testament. Why was it so important that he achieve spans of fourteen generations between each major signpost that he failed to name identifiable people in the genealogy? Would such literary license be acceptable today? How does that sort of treatment affect your understanding of the Bible?

3. Matthew's genealogy of Jesus is explicitly and symbolically Jewish. How (if at all) does that affect your understanding of Jesus' earthly mission? The practices of the early Church? Because the Christian movement soon encompassed Gentiles in far larger numbers than Jews, what does it suggest about reaching out beyond our normal community boundaries? How can we do so?

4. We will later see that Luke's genealogy traces Jesus' lineage back to Adam. Had Matthew followed a similar line, would that have diminished the force of his immediate identification of Jesus as the explicitly Jewish Messiah, by both word and pedigree?

5. How do you react to Jesus being associated with Abraham? David?

6. Does the word "Messiah" have different connotations than you might have thought? Is it a more worldly title than you generally considered it to be? Does the expected role of the Messiah to first-century Jews differ from what you might have thought?

✝✝✝

Having covered some of the sweep of Jewish faith history from Abraham's call out of Ur in the Chaldees, through the expectation of the Messiah's birth in occupied Israel, we can again reflect on how each evangelist has placed his story within the culture of the time.

Luke introduces his gospel as being told to one who is, ostensibly at least, an influential official in the Roman Empire. The story he is about to tell is worthy of the highest level of attention. The information to be communicated is meticulously researched and sound. The Roman Empire is being introduced to a figure of such greatness that his arrival can only be heralded with the most solemn of introductions. And yet, the figure is not described in a way to make him inherently a threat to the Peace of Rome. We will see his incomparable wisdom and thirst for compassion and justice communicated peaceably. It is, in some ways, a circumspect introduction, not launching directly into the royal identity of his subject, but simply foreshadowing something great in a different realm.

Matthew, by contrast, uses a thoroughly Jewish genealogy (except for the fact that some gentile and nonconformist women are named) to place Jesus within the line of the great figures of Jewish history. He is a child of the covenant. He is descended from kings. He represents the final and complete return from the Babylonian exile. He is the Messiah expected to come and reign anew in the land of the covenant. He is the ideal king at the end of the age.

Roman and Jewish.

Philosopher and King.

Could two introductions to the story of the same person be any more different?

From the Jerusalem Temple to the Judean Hill Country

Jesus was not born in a vacuum. He entered life in a religious, cultural and political amalgamation. His world teemed with energy and served as a breeding ground for change. The march of history had created a volatile mix in first-century Palestine, begging many questions that could only be answered with the passage of time. Would the converging forces remain discrete? Would they blend? Would they clash?

In these early days of the Common Era, *Pax Romana*, or the Peace of Rome, prevailed.[1] The destructive battles for control of the Roman

---

[1] The term "Common Era," or "C.E.," is a way to denote the years since the ancient estimate of the date of Christ's birth. To say that Jesus was born is 1 C.E. is the equivalent of saying

Republic—now an empire—had already ended. The Roman system of roads allowed for safe and speedy travel as had never before been experienced. With people so much better able to go from place to place, the Greek thirst for knowledge and change, and the Roman passion for order and action, encountered not only each other, but also different cultural influences with an increased frequency and intensity. The times provided a fertile ground for assorted philosophies and religious movements to meet and strive for preeminence.

The Greek love of philosophy had pulled many of the more sophisticated and educated people of the day away from their ancient polytheistic religious traditions, where great and petty gods had once vied for advantage in all too human settings. The movement, which was a shift in the intellectual and spiritual centers of gravity, was now toward the idea of one God. Still, there remained many facets to the emerging Greek notions about God. One particularly influential idea was of a remote Deity associated with pure reason. On one level, this concept bore little resemblance to a personal God who was intimately involved in the messy stuff of human history. But on another level, when compared to pagan polytheism, it was still a step in the direction of the place that the Jews had long occupied.

Amid this eclectic world, many people of the Greco-Roman culture found the ancient Jewish faith fascinating and appealing. It was filled with spiritual and ethical ideas, more complete than that which the pagan world provided. And, its idea of God was more tangible and accessible than what Platonic or Aristotelean thought provided. This God was understood to have revealed himself in personal and intimate ways. He visited with the ancients, telling Noah to build an ark; calling on Abram and Sarai with news that made Sarai laugh about the birth of a child in their old age; and meeting in close confines with Moses in order to declare the law. It was meaty stuff.

Ancient origins and powerful traditions added to the prestige of the Jewish faith among Romans. The earliest Jews had embraced the concept of one God long before Plato was born. This was no emerging mystery religion with its secret cultic practices, dying and resurrected fertility gods, and elaborate initiation ceremonies. Its roots went back to time immemorial.

The time and place of Jesus' birth were filled with ideas and possibilities. Something altogether new might emerge from this heady mix, something that makes a quantum leap out of the prevailing systems of the past, and into a new era. Yet, with all this rational and philosophical influence, it was an age still open to the mystical. In the first century, there was

---

he was born in 1 A.D. The letters "A.D." are an abbreviation for "Anno Domini," or "the year of our lord." Likewise, the letters "B.C.E.," or "before this common era," mean the same thing as "B.C.," or "before Christ." This series uses both forms of notation.

a ready willingness to see omens and portents and to attune oneself to heavenly messengers and dreams, and the telling of stories in the stars.

Our evangelists understand this preternatural world. When they tell the beginnings of the story of Jesus, they surround it with celestial signs, angelic messengers, and mysterious visitors. And yet, simple folk in a rustic setting also have roles to play, especially in Luke's story. We will now step into this complex web of ideas and cultures, and let Luke tell us about an event foreshadowing the coming of Jesus: the expected birth of John the Baptist.

✝ LUKE 1:5–25 The Expected Birth of John the Baptist

[5]In the days of King Herod of Judea, there was a priest named Zechariah, who belonged to the priestly order of Abijah. His wife was a descendant of Aaron, and her name was Elizabeth. [6]Both of them were righteous before God, living blamelessly according to all the commandments and regulations of the Lord. [7]But they had no children, because Elizabeth was barren, and both were getting on in years.

[8]Once when he was serving as priest before God and his section was on duty, [9]he was chosen by lot, according to the custom of the priesthood, to enter the sanctuary of the Lord and offer incense. [10]Now at the time of the incense offering, the whole assembly of the people was praying outside. [11]Then there appeared to him an angel of the Lord, standing at the right side of the altar of incense. [12]When Zechariah saw him, he was terrified; and fear overwhelmed him. [13]But the angel said to him,

"Do not be afraid, Zechariah, for your prayer has been heard. Your wife Elizabeth will bear you a son, and you will name him John. [14]You will have joy and gladness, and many will rejoice at his birth, [15]for he will be great in the sight of the Lord. He must never drink wine or strong drink; even before his birth he will be filled with the Holy Spirit. [16]He will turn many of the people of Israel to the Lord their God. [17]With the spirit and power of Elijah he will go before him, to turn the hearts of parents to their children, and the disobedient to the wisdom of the righteous, to make ready a people prepared for the Lord."

¹⁸**Zechariah said to the angel,**

"How will I know that this is so? For I am an old man, and my wife is getting on in years."

¹⁹**The angel replied,**

"I am Gabriel. I stand in the presence of God, and I have been sent to speak to you and to bring you this good news. ²⁰But now, because you did not believe my words, which will be fulfilled in their time, you will become mute, unable to speak, until the day these things occur."

²¹**Meanwhile the people were waiting for Zechariah, and wondered at his delay in the sanctuary. ²²When he did come out, he could not speak to them, and they realized that he had seen a vision in the sanctuary. He kept motioning to them and remained unable to speak. ²³When his time of service was ended, he went to his home.**

²⁴**After those days his wife Elizabeth conceived, and for five months she remained in seclusion. She said,**

²⁵*"This is what the Lord has done for me when he looked favorably on me and took away the disgrace I have endured among my people."*

Let us reflect on the following questions before we comment on the text:

1. Why does Luke tell the story of John's birth as a precursor to the story of the birth of Jesus?

2. John is featured prominently in all three synoptic Gospels after the birth narratives. What about John's story is critical to the story of Jesus? Are there parallels between the two stories that help us better understand each?

This passage is so packed with living out Old Testament edicts, reliving Old Testament patterns, and foreshadowing the dawn of the New Covenant, that it is hard to know where to

The Jerusalem Temple

(circa 4 B.C.E. – 33 C.E.)

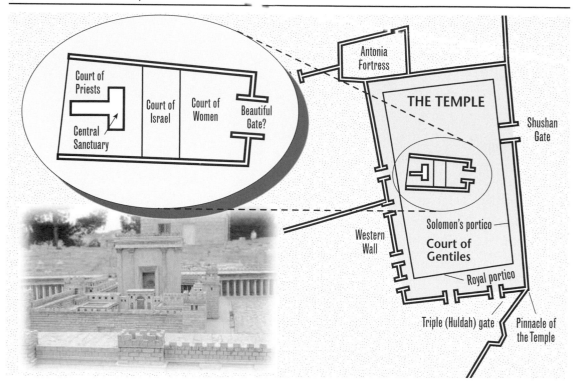

begin our discussion. Let's just follow Luke's lead and go step by step, starting at the beginning, but also jumping around a bit as suits our purposes. We start with why a priest named Zechariah is to be found in a given place at a given time.

The Time

This passage provides Luke's first signpost that helps us, as modern readers, to estimate the date of Jesus' birth. The story opens during the reign of King Herod. This Herod, often called "Herod the Great," was a Jewish strongman who served under Roman authority as the provincial king. He enjoyed a greater degree of autonomy than did some of his contemporaries and successors who claimed a similar title in occupied lands. We will have considerably more to say about him in Matthew's story of the slaughter of the Holy Innocents. We will also have some things to say about his delightful family as we progress through our studies of the synoptic Gospels.

For now, though, our reference to Herod will be for the same purposes as Luke's—to mark a point in time. The reign of Herod the Great was from 37–4 B.C. It is in this time of relative Jewish stability within the empire that Zechariah enters the temple sanctuary.

The Occasion

Zechariah is a member of a priestly order; one of twenty-four groups of that class who serve on a rotating schedule at the Jewish temple in Jerusalem. Each group serves approximately two weeks per year. The roles one or two of them might play in a particular service within the temple sanctuary are chosen by lot on a given day.[2] The sanctuary was a small area at the heart of the temple where the most solemn of rituals occurred, and where incense was offered to Yahweh. On this day, it is Zechariah's duty to enter the sanctuary and offer that incense.

In the Jerusalem Temple at the time of Herod, the priests entered the sanctuary twice each day to offer incense. If a priest had served in this capacity once, the chances of him ever doing so again were extremely limited to non-existent. The lots for incense duty were cast among the priests who had not yet served in this capacity. On this day, the lot fell to Zechariah. He climbed to what he doubtless considered to be the pinnacle of his priestly career as he entered the sanctuary. What he found on the other side was beyond belief.

The Players

Luke tells us that, when Zechariah entered the sanctuary, the whole assembly of the people was praying outside. It was not a moment to be taken lightly. But on the inside, it was all the more profound. Zechariah, already short of breath, and likely to have had a slight tremor in his hand

---

[2]Selection by lot was a time-honored method for choosing a person for a particular calling. It was not a practice restricted to religious Jews. There was a time when the men of Athens chose their leaders for a term by lot. In the earliest days of the Christian era, this method was also used to discern God's will, particularly in the Lukan world. For example, it was used in Acts when Matthias was chosen to take the place of the fallen and deceased apostle, Judas Iscariot.

as he entered the realm of the holy, was confronted by the Archangel Gabriel. This Gabriel is none other than the one who appeared to the Old Testament prophet, Daniel, in the book bearing the latter's name (*See* Dan. 8). Christian tradition also links Gabriel with heralding the coming kingdom by blowing his horn at the end of the age. In Islamic tradition, he is associated with having appeared to Mohammed in his visions. If Gabriel is on the scene, you can bet that the news is going to be extraordinary.

And what is his news? It is something of a highly personal nature that leaves Zechariah confounded. He has lived a blameless life before God, as has his wife, Elizabeth, who herself is a descendant of Aaron and so within a priestly line. They have no children, but are among the prayerful and reverent people in the land. To get a sense of what they might have been like, we could imagine a favorite older couple at church or in our neighborhood. What is not as easy to form is an image of why their contemporaries may have held some negative opinions about the couple's virtue, even against the evidence of their own eyes.

The News

This old, childless couple is somehow to have a child. But he is not just any child (if "just any" is ever a fair way to characterize any youngster). He is to be great in the sight of the Lord. People will rejoice at his birth. He will turn the hearts of many in Israel back to the Lord. He is set aside for a particular purpose, a mission in God's saving action. With the spirit of Elijah, he will restore natural affection within estranged families, lead the foolish into wisdom, and prepare people for the Lord.

The Reaction

Zechariah is not easily satisfied. Like Abram and Sarai before him, he is skeptical about the prospects of the blessed event actually occurring, grounding his objections in his and his wife's old age. This skepticism is not a good idea. Zechariah has no doubt seen the Old Testament witness where, time and again, an aging family is blessed with the news of an unexpected birth. Not only Abram and Sarai, but also Isaac and Rebecca in the very next generation, had such an experience. And, most similar to what is at hand, the aged Hannah received an announcement that even she would have a child. Her boy, young Samuel, was later consecrated to the Lord, as Gabriel indicates John will be. Samuel served the judge, Eli, as a youth, and went on to be judge over Israel himself as a man. In that capacity, he anointed Saul, then David, as king.

Zechariah's unbelief results in a peculiar sanction being imposed. He is dumbstruck until the predicted events reach their fulfillment. We might view this as a punishment, though it is not crystal clear that this is the case. His involuntary silence may be a holy one, allowing him to come to grips, not only with the nature of his own experience, but also to serve as a mute witness to those around him that the sanctuary experience was not of this realm. He returns to the outside world transformed by the experience and comes back into the company of an expectant audience.

What of Elizabeth?

We now turn to his wife. The word spoken by Gabriel is to be fulfilled. Zechariah returns home and she becomes pregnant, but remains in seclusion. It is almost as if a holy shroud has descended around both husband and wife as they enter a new and unexpected chapter of their lives.

While we can share readily in their joy, we may not as easily be able to understand their prior shame. We can concede that God's favorable gaze appears to have been cast on an old couple. But what of the notion Elizabeth expressed: that before this pregnancy, they had been disgraced? Jewish thought of the time tended to associate childlessness with God's disfavor. On a practical level, the status could be life threatening, as an aged generation relied on their grown children for support. With such a dire outcome, the argument went, could there be any reason for childlessness other than God's disfavor?

Someone fond of drawing attention to the misfortunes of others could point to the "sinful" life of a childless couple, whether known or unknown, and affix blame on them for their condition. It was an era when people had not yet come to appreciate the complex nature of the human reproductive system and the many things that can go wrong with it. In the case of Zechariah and Elizabeth, an explanation that blamed them for their unhappy state would approach the insidious. "They act so nice, but they must be terrible sinners or God would not have inflicted childlessness on them. Serves them right!" But Zechariah and Elizabeth will escape this unjust accusation and the grief they have borne due to their childless status. They have turned the corner; Elizabeth will not only give birth, but the child will be remarkable.

1. Do we, like Zechariah's and Elizabeth's peers, tend to blame others for their misfortunes? Will the New Testament witness permit us to continue to do that?

2. Does it seem Zechariah was being punished for his unbelief? Or was there a blessing there, too? Keep this tension in mind as we continue with the rest of his story.

3. There is a tendency to associate the late blessing of parenthood with God's favor in the Bible. Are there occasions where the opposite—lack of children—is seen by responsible biblical characters (rather than by naysayers) as containing a message of God's disfavor?

4. What do you make of Angelic appearances generally? In this story? We will explore some modern stories later in this chapter.

†††

We have seen the promise of an unusual birth made to an old and childless couple. Now, we will turn our attention away from them for the moment, and see what occurs in a similar, but distinct, story.

☩ LUKE 1:26–38 The Annunciation

²⁶In the sixth month the angel Gabriel was sent by God to a town in Galilee called Nazareth, ²⁷to a virgin engaged to a man whose name was Joseph, of the house of David. The virgin's name was Mary. ²⁸And he came to her and said,

"Greetings, favored one! The Lord is with you."

²⁹But she was much perplexed by his words and pondered what sort of greeting this might be. ³⁰The angel said to her,

"Do not be afraid, Mary, for you have found favor with God. ³¹And now, you will conceive in your womb and bear a son, and you will name him Jesus. ³²He will be great, and will be called the Son of the Most High, and the Lord God will give to him the throne of his ancestor David. ³³He will reign over the house of Jacob forever, and of his kingdom there will be no end."

³⁴Mary said to the angel,

"How can this be, since I am a virgin?"

³⁵The angel said to her,

"The Holy Spirit will come upon you, and the power of the Most High will overshadow you; therefore the child to be born will be holy; he will be called Son of God. ³⁶And now, your relative Elizabeth in her old age has also conceived a son; and this is the sixth month for her who was said to be barren. ³⁷For nothing will be impossible with God."

³⁸Then Mary said,

"Here am I, the servant of the Lord; let it be with me according to your word."

Then the angel departed from her.

1. What similarities do you see between the story of the promised birth of John the Baptist and the annunciation to Mary? What differences? Do they suggest something about the relationship between John and Jesus?

2. Virgin birth stories are twice told in the Gospels, though from different perspectives. The idea of the virgin birth is also mentioned in the ancient creeds. Do you understand the concept literally? Symbolically? In some other way? Does it make a difference for your faith life? We will also examine this topic when studying Matthew.

3. Does Mary's response to Gabriel's announcement suggest something about her character? About her understanding of a call or mission?

Luke has taken us to a new place. We have left the Jerusalem Temple behind, and now find ourselves well to the north in Nazareth of Galilee. Gabriel appears, once again as the bearer of remarkable news. As with Zechariah's story, the Annunciation is so packed with a sense of the sacred that we will need to break it down into smaller pieces for consideration.

The Time

Six months have passed since Gabriel's appearance in the sanctuary of the temple when he left Zechariah dumbstruck.

The Occasion

There is nothing auspicious about the occasion of his appearance, at least on the surface. Mary is not in the sanctuary of the temple. She is not at the pinnacle of an established career. We can fairly assume that, when he appears, she is about the ordinary business of the day—or, more likely, settled down for the night with her mental faculties more open to mystery than when preoccupied with cooking a fish or cleaning a pot. We are given no advance sign that a significant event is about to occur, except that the proverbial elephant now appears in the room; it is Gabriel, and pretending he isn't there won't make him go away.

The Players

Again, we have Gabriel. Also, for the first time in Luke, we meet Mary.[3] No one else is physically present, but the spiritual presence of the Lord God hovers, and bears along with it the announced coming of the Son of the Most High. It is here foretold that he is one who will reign over the house of Jacob and will follow in the steps of his ancestor, David.

---

[3]Our previous introduction to Mary in this book was Matthew's gospel, where she made a surprise appearance in a Jewish genealogy.

The News

As with his appearance to Zechariah, Gabriel is not on some mundane chore. He revealed to Zechariah that his wife, already an old woman, would give birth. Here, Gabriel reveals the more surprising news that a virgin, too, will give birth.[4] And this will not be "just any" child; he will be "great and will be called the Son of the Most High, and the Lord God will give to him the throne of his ancestor, David. He will reign over the house of Jacob forever, and of his kingdom there will be no end." The forecast of the child's future is beyond the wildest dreams that Mary, an engaged but as of yet unmarried woman, might have entertained. It also exceeds what is foretold about Zechariah and Elizabeth's son, even though John will be called "great." Yet, there is a strong connection between the two anticipated births, as we learn here that Elizabeth is Mary's relative, and has already been pregnant for six months.

It is so easy to get caught up in the wonder and tradition of the story and miss some of its symbolic significance. The relationship between John and Jesus tells us something about what is taking place in a changing world. John the Baptist is a great figure drawing an end to the age of Israel's past, and also providing a transition to Jesus as the figure ushering in a new age for the world. When we see how Luke draws attention to Elizabeth's advanced age, and to Mary's presumed youth, we see the foreshadowing of a new era.

The Reaction

As with Zechariah before her, Mary does not know what to do with the remarkable news that a child will be born to her. She questions the prediction and, reasonably enough, cites her virginity as a barrier to any imminent motherhood. It does not seem to be an altogether different response from Zechariah's. However, Mary's reaction does not leave her dumbstruck.

It may be that some subtle differences between their reactions underlie their disparate treatment. When Zechariah raises the question about prospective parentage, he states his objection in a more declarative way, almost laying the groundwork for his own disappointment.

---

[4]The idea of the virgin birth contains some Old Testament connotations to which Matthew specifically refers. Luke makes no reference to the Old Testament, a fact that should not surprise us, as he is a gentile author writing to a gentile audience. When we reflect on Matthew's version, we will explore how the idea of the virgin birth was important in the early Church, and how that significance has come down to us.

"I am an old man and my wife is getting on in years." Gabriel sees unbelief in him, and he is left speechless. Even in the course of "living blamelessly," he was not ready to trust fully in God's graciousness.

Mary, however, simply raises an obvious question, making no declaration about why God cannot accomplish what the angel has said. It is as if Zechariah had momentarily forgotten the Old Testament witness to that graciousness, whereas Mary says what she says in a spirit of youthful wonder. Gabriel's response to Mary contains a cursory explanation, but no sanction.

There is a subtle statement about God's relationship to his people in her final words, "Here am I, the servant of the Lord; let it be with me according to your word." While Gabriel's statements confidently express what will come to pass, Mary's reply shows that the setting does not involve coercion. Mary declares herself to be God's servant, and consents to the way put before her. It is a response from faith, not from mandate.

What of Joseph?

There remains a named, but still silent, party. We are told that Mary is engaged to one Joseph, a member of the household of David. While the ancestral line is specifically noted, and a royal career for the coming child is forecast, there is little more for us to see on such topics right now. Later, Luke will show us precisely what sort of royal reign we are to expect from the new occupant of David's throne, along with many other surprises. And we will see something about how Joseph perceives the mysterious circumstances of the phase of life he is entering when studying Matthew's birth narrative, which is not told from Mary's perspective (as in Luke), but from Joseph's perspective.

John and Jesus: Shared Patterns and Paths

The lives of John the Baptist and Jesus of Nazareth follow parallel courses. The paths that await them will include adult calls to radical ministry, and will lead them both to lose their lives at the hands of the powerful. But the patterns begin much earlier, as seen here and in the next chapter.

Below, we set out parallel courses in the Lukan infancy narrative between John and Jesus, which a number of scholars identify:

1. Both John's and Jesus' expected births are announced by an angel. John's father, Zechariah, is told in the temple that his son will be great before the Lord. Jesus' mother, Mary, is told by Gabriel that her son will be great and will be the Son of the Most High.

2. Both children have publicized births. In John's case, as we shall see, it is publicized by his parents to neighbors and relatives. In Jesus' case, it is to be publicized by a multitude of the heavenly hosts to the shepherds keeping watch over their flocks by night.

3. Both stories will report on the circumcision and naming of a child. Zechariah's tongue is loosed at John's naming amid a local celebration. In Jesus' case, the circumcision takes place at the temple, the center of Jewish worship and a place often favorably portrayed in Luke-Acts.[5]

4. Both John and Jesus will have public presentations as infants where prophecies are made about them. The public presentation of John's is at his parents' home, made to the neighbors in the hill country, where Zechariah tells the child, John, that he will go before and prepare the way of the Lord. Jesus' public presentation and the accompanying prophecies occur at the temple. We will see that two aged holy people who worship there, Simeon and Anna, foretell what lies ahead for Jesus' grander mission.

5. Finally, there will be a description of both children's growth. John grows, strong in spirit, in the wilderness. Jesus grows, filled with wisdom and the favor of God; and, when an adolescent, leaves those at the temple amazed at his words.

Luke goes to some pains to trace these parallel stories and to set the stage, both for the commonalities and for the distinctions between John and Jesus, and the movements each

---

[5]Mark and Matthew often portray the temple unfavorably.

founded. Luke emphasizes that John's role was to announce the coming kingdom. Jesus, however, fulfills the kingdom's advent.

There may have been an important issue to the early Church that explains Luke's particular emphasis on the relationship between John and Jesus. If we look at Acts 18–19, we see that Paul and some of his colleagues encounter John's disciples in their mission work with the early Church. Though it was a number of years later, these disciples of John did not yet know the gospel message in its fullness. After it is told to them, they are brought into the fold. By starting here, in the earliest pages of Luke-Acts, we see how the followers of John can be taught that his unique place in God's saving plan was not to create a free-standing movement, but rather to point to the way of the Lord, a trend which was carried forward in the Pauline mission of Acts.[6]

1. Luke tells the story of a unique birth from a man's perspective, and then a story of an even more unique birth from a woman's perspective. This is the first installment in Luke's pattern of pairing related stories involving one gender, then another, throughout his gospel. It is an inescapable conclusion that he is doing so intentionally. Why might Luke establish this pattern? In your experience, what gifts and graces do men and women bing togther that might not be present if they were separate?

2. There are no accounts of the virgin birth in the oldest New Testament writings, which are by Paul, or in the oldest gospel, Mark. Nor are such accounts found in the latest gospel, John. Do the omissions of any account of Jesus' birth by Paul, Mark and John imply something about their information? What about their practices and priorities? Might it be that these authors had no knowledge of the reported circumstances of Jesus' birth? Or, might it be that recounting anything that they may have heard was outside their purposes?

3. Like Zechariah and Mary, do people of today have experiences of angels? Before we are too quick to answer in the negative, or to discount such claims, consider the following:

---

[6]Apparently, the early Church was not entirely successful in its mission to John's disciples. The Gospels themselves report some encounters with them but do not relate the conclusions. Even today, there are small enclaves of people who follow the John movement in what is present-day Iraq.

Of Men and Angels

A number of books have been written over the last generation or so telling about modern experiences of angels. The television series, "Touched by an Angel," was highly rated for an extended period of time. Such a proliferation of cultural references to angels suggests that there is a deep longing to experience an encounter with the spiritual realm, perhaps through contact with a messenger of God. In fact, "Messenger of God" is the most basic definition or understanding of the word "angel."

Yet, we are somehow ill-equipped to handle ideas of angels in any systematic fashion. We have no objective way of judging the validity of what people describe as their experiences of God's messengers. Nor do we even have an objective way to evaluate our own experiences that might involve angels.

Even ill-equipped as we are, we still may perceive enough ourselves, or through others' stories, that touch a deep spot or resonate within us so that we consider, and perhaps believe, that there are angels among us. Here are two such stories.

The first involves a man from Alabama suffering from cancer in the prime of life. He had been out of town for treatment and was on a return trip, eating with his child at a cafeteria-style table. A presence, whom he later described winsomely as an unattractive black woman, came and cleaned a table near him. They had never met before. She asked how he was doing, and he said that he was doing well. The visitor replied that he appeared to be at peace. He said that yes, he was at peace. She told the man she would be praying for him. Stepping out of a personality shell prone to religious reserve, the man replied that he would pray for her, too. Then she was gone. When the man spoke of her to his child, there was a puzzled response. The child had seen and heard no one. Cancer later took the man's bodily life. His mother, a prominent professional with a vocation in music ministry, has acquired two beautiful artistic renderings of black angels. To this day they occupy a place of honor in her living room.

Another man found himself in the wrong place at the wrong time. An armed bank robbery was occurring and shots were fired outside the building. He was hit. An overweight black woman wearing a white uniform crawled across the parking lot to his assistance and took off an item of her own clothing to treat his bleeding until the danger passed and more conventional help could arrive. She saved his life in the process. The story was repeated on the news and she was asked to come forward and identify herself. No one ever did. Nor does the man know of anyone who could identify her. Some years later, while he was the pastor of a sizeable suburban Presbyterian church in another Southern city, the man told his congregants that he had once seen an angel. She was an overweight black woman wearing a white uniform.

Two white Southern males experienced black women giving God's love to strangers as angels. Is this image surprising? Nobel Prize winning author William Faulkner, a Mississippian and America's greatest twentieth-century writer, was so inspired by some of the black women of his acquaintance that he embodied them in the strongest, wisest and kindest characters he developed. Foremost among them is Dilsey of *The Sound and the Fury*, who, in a twentieth-century setting, held both her own family and the crumbling white aristocracy they served together by force of love and will.

What do your angels look like?

††††

Our paired stories of surprising angelic visits and expectations of new life now converge, as Mary makes her way to see Elizabeth.

☦ LUKE 1:39–56 Mary Visits Elizabeth

39In those days Mary set out and went with haste to a Judean town in the hill country, 40where she entered the house of Zechariah and greeted Elizabeth. 41When Elizabeth heard Mary's greeting, the child leaped in her womb. And Elizabeth was filled with the Holy Spirit 42and exclaimed with a loud cry,

"Blessed are you among women, and blessed is the fruit of your womb. 43And why has this happened to me, that the mother of my Lord comes to me? 44For as soon as I heard the sound of your greeting, the child in my womb leaped for joy. 45And blessed is she who believed that there would be a fulfillment of what was spoken to her by the Lord."

46And Mary said,

"My soul magnifies the Lord, ⁴⁷and my spirit rejoices in God my Savior, ⁴⁸for he has looked with favor on the lowliness of his servant. Surely, from now on all generations will call me blessed; ⁴⁹for the Mighty One has done great things for me, and holy is his name. ⁵⁰His mercy is for those who fear him from generation to generation. ⁵¹He has shown strength with his arm; he has scattered the proud in the thoughts of their hearts. ⁵²He has brought down the powerful from their thrones, and lifted up the lowly; ⁵³he has filled the hungry with good things, and sent the rich away empty. ⁵⁴He has helped his servant Israel, in remembrance of his mercy, ⁵⁵according to the promise he made to our ancestors, to Abraham and to his descendants forever."

⁵⁶And Mary remained with her about three months and then returned to her home.

1. What prompts Mary's visit to Elizabeth? Is there significance to the fact that she departs Galilee "with haste" to see her?

2. Elizabeth is reported to be filled with the Spirit as the child, in her sixth month of pregnancy, leaps in the womb upon Mary's arrival. Is there something Luke is trying to communicate in this interchange about the respective roles of John and Jesus? Note that Elizabeth refers to Mary as the "mother of my Lord."

3. Do you see anything in Mary's speech (or, more properly, her song, commonly called "The *Magnificat*") that surprises you? If not, reread it as if it were for the first time.

Elizabeth's and Mary's paths now meet. As Mary presses southward from Galilee to a Judean town in the hill country, then to Zechariah's house, and on to her kinswoman Elizabeth, we sense she is on a purposeful journey. Likewise, in recognition of some crucial purpose, Elizabeth's response is immediate and strong. Luke uses Elizabeth's voice to set the events in proper perspective for his audience. She recognizes aloud that Mary is the mother of her Lord. Elizabeth's son, John, is implicitly subordinate to Jesus, as Elizabeth's mission is implicitly subordinate to Mary's. It is a role Elizabeth embraces.

We have already seen in this chapter how the story of Samuel and his mother, Hannah, foreshadows the story of the Baptist's expected birth. Hannah praised God for being given a child in her old age. In 1 Samuel 2:1–10, when she consecrated her son to the Lord, Hannah described a world turned upside down. God would make the poor become rich and the well-fed become hungry.

Given the close connection between Hannah's and Elizabeth's stories of late blessings, it may not surprise us that some ancient manuscripts place the *Magnificat* on the lips of Elizabeth rather than Mary. It is as fitting a song for Elizabeth, in light of the events that have transpired, as was Hannah's song at the consecration of Samuel. But, with Jesus to be the greater agent of change than John, the song is even more fitting coming from Mary than from Elizabeth. For these and other reasons, when scrutinizing the ancient manuscripts to see which ones are deemed more reliable, the greater scholarly inclination is to conclude that those manuscripts in which Mary sings the hymn are closer to the original.

It is widely thought among scholars that the *Magnificat*, along with other major pronouncements or proclamations in Luke's infancy narrative, actually started out as hymns in the early Church. Luke has people singing these hymns in his story, using their voices to incorporate the emerging musical trends into a narrative structure, marrying the liturgy and the proclamation of the Word.

Regardless of whether we use a version of the Bible where Mary is the singer of the *Magnificat*, or one where Elizabeth is the singer, the words and music are the same, as are the implications for what is taking place. Proclaimed by either Mary or Elizabeth, we see an early indication of the destiny of the expected child. His role will not be to preserve the status quo.

Jesus' disruption of the status quo is found in all three synoptic Gospels, but takes different forms. We can liken the perspectives of our three evangelists to three different philosophical traditions. Luke is a liberal. He is ready to throw open the gates of the kingdom of God, immediately and unreservedly, to Gentiles, women, the poor, the outcast. The wealthy and the powerful have no special claim to retain their privileges, and, in fact, those privileges are often seen as a barrier to living as citizens of the kingdom of God.[7] Luke fears radical change not in the least. He is egalitarian, open, and inclusive.

Matthew is a conservative. We will see repeatedly, even in the birth narratives, that Jesus is tied firmly to historical Judaism. The changes in store are profound, but arise out of a specifically Jewish context, and are sometimes more evolutionary than revolutionary. While

---

[7]Much of the message of the synoptic Gospels concerns the kingdom of God being at hand and its establishment on Earth. We will visit this topic time and again, particularly in parables of Jesus and his major teachings.

the Kingdom of Heaven (the term Matthew generally uses instead of the Kingdom of God) is inclusive, it moves more incrementally, from the Old Testament, to the New Covenant, to the Great Commission in the closing verses of Matthew: the gospel is to be preached to all nations.

Mark is a populist. He doesn't trust Big Business or Big Government. Particularly, he does not trust Big Business when it is masquerading as Big Religion in the Jerusalem Temple power structure, whose system is based on accumulating power and wealth rather than on promoting justice and mercy. The Big Government he has no use for is Rome, along with its local collaborators, whose combined forces occupy and oppress the people. If Mark was written in response to the persecution of early Christians in the city of Rome itself (assuming that was his community), or in response to the suffering in Palestine at the hands of the Romans as a result of the Jewish rebellion (under the alternative assumption that the Markan community was somewhere in Palestine), he has every reason to loathe the concentration of worldly power and believe it to be inimical to the power of the Kingdom of God.

Luke's liberal bent in general—or even his radical one—and that of the *Magnificat* in particular, have served to scare despots right down to the twentieth century. Something about Mary proclaiming how God has "brought down the powerful from their thrones, and lifted up the lowly" and how he has "filled the hungry with good things, and sent the rich away empty," made right-wing dictators of Latin America squirm. They outlawed the use of the *Magnificat* on the grounds that it was advancing "Marxist" purposes.

1. Does the *Magnificat* speak to you in any particular way? Does its reversal of expectations and disruption of the status quo make you feel invigorated? Fearful? Perplexed?

2. Mary is often perceived as reserved and quietly compassionate. Does her vigorous trip to see Elizabeth suggest another side to her? What about her proclamation of a new reign that will entirely disrupt the status quo? Are we still surprised today to see multiple facets of our own personalities, or of others that we think we know well?

3. It seems that Mary, arriving during Elizabeth's sixth month of pregnancy and staying with her for about three months, would have been present until right around the time of the Baptist's birth. What might she and Elizabeth have talked about (especially since Zechariah was dumbstruck!)? What might they have done together? Does this sort of idyll suggest something about how we might experience certain phases of the

Christian life that we regard as being particularly blessed? For instance, should we take time from our busy-ness and live as "human beings," rather than the more common American way of living as "human doings"?

4. This segment argues that Luke is a liberal, Matthew a conservative, and Mark a populist. Do these labels help in looking at the three stories from different angles? Are they oversimplifications? Do such labels help us examine our own assumptions and ideas? Do they assist in studying the biblical texts, or tend to divide us "along party lines"? Hopefully, they can at least provide some food for thought and prompt reflection or discussion.

†††

CHAPTER FIVE

From Denial to Acceptance: Two Journeys to Fatherhood

We have spent some time with the story of Zechariah, told in the Gospel According to Saint Luke. We have also been introduced to Joseph, though only in passing. Now, we will join each of them in transitional journeys where they move from an initial denial of the fatherly roles to which they are called, toward accepting, then even embracing, these roles. In the case of Zechariah, the transition will involve moving toward living into the message Gabriel has already delivered. In the case of Joseph, told in the Gospel According to Saint Matthew, we will see how he first receives unsettling news, then responds to an unexpected explanation of it. Both journeys go from false starts to faithful responses.

✝ **LUKE 1:57–66 The Birth of John the Baptist**

⁵⁷**Now the time came for Elizabeth to give birth, and she bore a son.** ⁵⁸**Her neighbors and relatives heard that the Lord had shown his great mercy to her, and they rejoiced with her.** ⁵⁹**On the eighth day they came to circumcise the child, and they were going to name him Zechariah after his father.** ⁶⁰**But his mother said,** *"No; he is to be called John."* ⁶¹**They said to her,** *"None of your relatives has this name."* ⁶²**Then they began motioning to his father to find out what name he wanted to give him.** ⁶³**He asked for a writing tablet and wrote, "His name is John." And all of them were amazed.** ⁶⁴**Immediately his mouth was opened and his tongue freed, and he began to speak, praising God.** ⁶⁵**Fear came over all their neighbors, and all these things were talked about throughout the entire hill country of Judea.** ⁶⁶**All who heard them pondered them and said,** *"What then will this child become?"* **For, indeed, the hand of the Lord was with him.**

1. When last we saw Zechariah, his lack of trust had left him mute. Here, the passage implies that he was left deaf as well, given that relatives and neighbors motioned to him in order to seek his input about the naming of the child. Do his physical condition (whatever it was) and the circumstances of its alleviation say something about the meaning of the story?

2. After Elizabeth says the child's name aloud, the visitors argue with her based upon there being no one in the family named "John." How do their opinions and involvement in this issue strike you? How do you feel about the importance of passing down family names?

3. Zechariah's muteness (and possible deafness) are alleviated when he responds to the visitors' questions about the boy's name by writing "John." Does his written declaration of the name of the child, consistent both with Gabriel's earlier instructions and with what Elizabeth has already said, suggest something about Zechariah's silent journey from the time of Gabriel's revelation to the time of the child's birth?

This section of Luke also overflows with information that we can better address when it is broken into smaller pieces.

The Circumcision and Naming

Elizabeth's withdrawal from the community comes to an end with the birth of her son. We will remember that, when her retreat into seclusion began, it was accompanied by a reflection on the disgrace she felt among her people due to her childlessness. The withdrawal was a step in the process that transformed her from having a self-image grounded in barrenness, to one grounded in thanksgiving flowing from the "great mercy" the Lord had bestowed upon her. She takes her place among those in the Old Order who had received late blessings and raised great leaders for the people. Elizabeth's late blessing is a major link in the unfolding chain of God's saving action, as is the case with Sarah and her son Isaac, Rebecca and her sons Esau and Jacob, and, most similarly, Hannah and her son Samuel. Emboldened by Mary's recent companionship and a shared sense of destiny, Elizabeth shed an identity that she had come to hate and embraced one which reflected her belief in a better standing with her community and with God.

The same people who had once defined her as barren, and so had fostered a sense of superiority over her, now appear and rejoice with Elizabeth on the occasion of the child's circumcision. Jewish law prescribed a boy's eighth day as the one on which to perform the circumcision rite. This aspect of Judaic ritual practice distinguished the male members of that race in a visible way from the Gentiles around them.[1] In his commentary on Luke's gospel, William Barclay compares the significance of Jewish celebrations around circumcision to that of Christian celebrations around infant baptism.

---

[1]In fact, circumcision was so important in the Judaic tradition that it came to express something about purity and defilement, inclusion and exclusion, honor and shame. It could also be used opportunistically to gain an advantage or assert a claim of preference. Jacob's daughter, Dinah, was ravaged by a Gentile, a member of a ruling family in Canaan. The man was so smitten with her that he soon also sought her hand in marriage—a step that became a requirement of the Mosaic law. Thereupon, Jacob's family insisted that all male members of the "suitor's" clan be circumcised if he were to marry Dinah. Their insistence on circumcision was not for purposes of religious observance, but was an artifice. While the Canaan tribesmen were recovering from the circumcision procedure, Jacob's sons slaughtered all the menfolk and took the good things of the land as spoils, also bringing the women and children along as their own (*See* Gen. 34). In a less barbaric setting, Saint Paul used the words "circumcision" and "uncircumcision" as metaphors, respectively representing matters of heavenly and earthly concern (*See, e.g.,* Rom. 2).

This passage, set in a celebratory moment, reveals some of the complexity in human relations. Those whom Elizabeth felt had held her in low regard now rejoice with her. Yet, even though they participate in the celebration, and are apparently both joyful and sincere about it, they are not altogether perfect companions. They have what seem to be some pretty nervy expectations about what the child should be named and why—a notion of entitlement that would offend many a modern parent. And they are more than willing to state their opinions strongly, arguing with Elizabeth about the child's name and appealing to Zechariah to intervene. In legal terms, these folks seem to be "officious intermeddlers," the type of people who step in and "help" without being asked, and who confer little, if any, value on the objects of their magnanimity. We do not have any evidence that they are people who, by wisdom, judgment, or position, have demonstrated some special capacity to help John's family solve this problem.

Mixed blessing though they may have been to Elizabeth, they provide a little comic relief for the audience. After all, we have recently spent some extended episodes in which the players on the stage have hovered in the "thin places" between Heaven and Earth. A little benign grounding in the here-and-now—such as arguing about what a baby should be named—helps relieve some of the tension.

We should also allow ourselves a cheer for Elizabeth, who has firmly asserted her parental prerogatives in the face of nosy neighbors, and without much help from Zechariah, at least early on. While Gabriel directed Zechariah to name the child "John," we are not told how it came to pass that Elizabeth knew to announce it. Did the mute Zechariah communicate the substance of the angel's directions to her in some way? Or, is it something she knew independently, whether intuitively or by divine revelation? Either way, Elizabeth will not let this mixed blessing of opinionated family members and neighbors (who do, of course, care enough to show up at the circumcision) dictate who she and her family are to be, especially in a time when much more was associated with the name of a person than merely being a form of identification. Someone's name was also thought to disclose something important about his character.

Zechariah Speaks

For nine months, Zechariah has been silent. But now, things change. The crowd is motioning to him to seek his input, implying that he is deaf as well as mute. Are they asking him, as the "man of the house," to overrule Elizabeth's refusal to call the child anything but John? Unlike the Zechariah we met in the sanctuary of the temple—who was set in his ways and unwilling to trust in God's graciousness—the Zechariah of the Judean hill country is positive in his response to the situation now at hand. He confirms what Elizabeth has spoken, strongly and unequivocally. Somehow, in the period of muteness Gabriel has prescribed, Zechariah has made the silent journey from denial through acceptance to positive affirmation. He is father to a child with a clear calling. He is no longer some timid priest unwilling to believe that God has something great in store, even for his household. He knows the hand of the Lord is upon the child.

And the child's name, once written, allows words to flow again from his father's lips. Zechariah gives praise to the Almighty. The silence is broken.

The Friends and Relations Respond

Zechariah's words unleash a response. We see an audience filled with amazement and fear. What has happened? What is this child to become? Word travels through the hill country, the status quo is disrupted, and the community becomes aware that something extraordinary is happening.

Zechariah Sings

We now reach the second canticle from Luke's birth narrative, called the *Benedictus*. As in the *Magnificat*, word and liturgy meet. Another of the hymns of the early Church springs forth, this time from Zechariah's mouth. With his song, something about what the child's birth means begins to take form.

✝ LUKE 1:67–80 Zechariah's Song: the *Benedictus*

67Then his father Zechariah was filled with the Holy Spirit and spoke this prophecy:

68"Blessed be the Lord God of Israel, for he has looked favorably on his people and redeemed them. 69He has raised up a mighty savior for us in the house of his servant David, 70as he spoke through the mouth of his holy prophets from of old, 71that we would be saved from our enemies and from the hand of all who hate us.

[72]Thus he has shown the mercy promised to our ancestors, and has remembered his holy covenant, [73]the oath that he swore to our ancestor Abraham, to grant us [74]that we, being rescued from the hands of our enemies, might serve him without fear, [75]in holiness and righteousness before him all our days.

[76]And you, child, will be called the prophet of the Most High; for you will go before the Lord to prepare his ways, [77]to give knowledge of salvation to his people by the forgiveness of their sins. [78]By the tender mercy of our God, the dawn from on high will break upon us, [79]to give light to those who sit in darkness and in the shadow of death, to guide our feet into the way of peace."

[80]The child grew and became strong in spirit, and he was in the wilderness until the day he appeared publicly to Israel.

1. How does Zechariah's song foreshadow the life of John the Baptist? Does it also set the stage for Jesus' coming?

2. Does the *Benedictus* speak to you of a historical deliverance? A spiritual one? How might it fit into the life of the early Church?

✝✝✝

Twentieth-century scholarship has discovered a particular strand of thought dating back to first-century Israel that may underlie the *Benedictus*. That strand comes to us today, not as an ongoing movement, but in the form of an archeological remnant. In *The Good News According to Luke: Spiritual Reflections*, Richard Rohr—a Franciscan monk, spiritual director, and retreat leader—ties the ideas in the *Benedictus* to a movement among a group of first-century Israelites called the Essenes. Our knowledge of the Essenes is relatively recent, as much of it comes from the Dead Sea Scrolls that were discovered in the 1940s in the desert lands east of Jerusalem, at a place called Qumran.[2] The Essenes of Qumran established a sort of

---

[2]The ties between the Essenes and the Qumran community are not absolutely clear, though the weight of scholarly authority appears to support the connection. This book assumes the connection does exist.

protest movement and developed their own liturgies, theologies, and practices. The movement was largely eschatological, meaning that much of its focus was on an expectation of the coming end-times. That expectation was fueled by a belief that God would restore Israel, which had been suffering at the hands of its enemies for centuries.

Life in the Qumran community was ascetic, prophetic, and strict. It was not a place for the faint of heart. The Essenes, disenchanted with the Jerusalem power structure—and attributing much of the suffering of Israel to the failures of its soft, materialistic, and compromising leadership—arose early every morning to observe the possibility of the coming of the Messiah with the rising of the sun. This morning wait was a liturgical community observance. The Essenes were anticipating God's direct intervention to transform the corrupt and decaying world; to restore the fortunes of Israel; and to bring judgment to those who had soiled its purity. This judgment also extended to those who presided over the temple cult and religious control systems. The Essenes withdrew to Qumran to establish a setting where God's mercy would be received by them, even as his judgment was rendered against the evils found in Jerusalem and the wider world.

From time to time, there has been speculation among Christian scholars that John the Baptist, and perhaps Jesus, were Essenes who eventually broke from the movement to rejoin and reform a world that those who dwelled at Qumran had, in their isolationist fervor, rejected. If it is true that John has left Qumran to attempt a wider cultural reform, then he—despite all of his wrath-talk that we will later study—was a figure representing greater hopefulness for the world than what he had previously believed to be the norm.

However, much of this association between John and the Essenes is conjecture. Even though Luke speaks of John going into the desert until he appeared publicly in Israel—and we do see a certain compatibility between his and the Essenes' harsh judgments on the world—scholars have not developed an evidentiary record compelling the conclusion that either John or Jesus were part of the Qumran community. Regardless of the conclusion, the Qumran movement did exist, and there is no reason to rule out the possibility that its spirituality has at least some parallels with early Christian spirituality in the Lukan community.

The Benedictus

Understanding that the ideas of desert dwellers, awaiting the Messiah's arrival and God's judgment on the world, may underlie the *Benedictus*, let us examine it more closely. Toward the end of the passage, we see a strong connection to the Qumran spirituality that Richard Rohr describes. In the words of Zechariah, God's "tender mercy" will break upon us like the dawn from on high. The expectation of divine intervention within the Qumran community was connected to daybreak. The Essenes, through observance of their morning rituals, greeted each new day as the day that the Messiah might come and set things right. The faithful would receive relief and reward, even as the wicked were judged.

Qumran thought is to be distinguished from other strands of first-century Judaic thought, which also had Messianic expectations. In other places and within other movements, the Messianic ideas revolved around the arrival of a conquering military figure, such as the Davidic one that the Zealots expected. In the period of occupation, various would-be "messiahs" sought to lead the people against Rome in one way or another, and to restore Israel's sovereignty through force of arms. The Essenes did not subscribe to this formula, as their expectations were about God's direct deliverance by other means. To them, God, acting through the Son of Righteousness, was to break into the world with transformative powers in a supernatural way.

We also see strong connections to historical Judaism in the *Benedictus*. Zechariah makes favorable references to Abraham, the house of David, and the prophets of old. Luke ties John the Baptist's birth to the Old Testament tradition through Zechariah's hymn, which is filled with allusions to God's saving action in Israel's history. Luke connects the Old Covenant to the New, using John as the pivotal figure who goes before to prepare the way of the Lord.

But what is the nature of that saving action? The deliverance, or salvation, first promised in the text is a deliverance from enemies. It is not deliverance from our own sinful nature, or from Hell, or from any of the other notions that have sometimes occupied Christian thought as believers contemplated the eternal with fear and trembling. We see in the first chapter of Luke that God is intimately concerned with the here and the now. His deliverance is from the immediate suffering and oppression experienced by the weak at the hands of the strong. It is more like the Old Testament liberation from slavery in the Exodus, or the return from the Babylonian exile. In this respect, Zechariah's theology differs little from Mary's theology, which is reflected in the *Magnificat*.

Yet, the deliverance is not *only* from the oppressor. As many stories in the Old Testament show, Israel associates its misfortunes with its sinfulness. When it falls away from the good way God has set before it—falls into sin, so to speak—it experiences calamity. This is the priestly line of OT thought, where God forgives and restores. But how is a right relationship with God restored?

Unlike the apocalyptic scenarios the Essenes envisioned, Zechariah sees a different reality. He, who at first could not believe God's graciousness would be bestowed upon him, now accepts and proclaims it. He addresses John as a prophet who goes before to prepare the way of the Lord. "And you, child, will be called the prophet of the Most High; for you will go before the Lord to prepare his ways, to give knowledge of salvation to his people by the forgiveness of their sins. By the tender mercy of our God, the dawn from on high will break upon us, to give light to those who sit in darkness and in the shadow of death, to guide our feet into the way of peace."

While the influence of the Essenes is present, it is not the last word in Zechariah's song. Israel need not beat itself about the head and neck ceaselessly over its misfortunes. It need not despair that it is unacceptable to God. The knowledge of salvation—deliverance, healing, being made whole—is grounded in its direct relationship with forgiveness of sins. Indeed, the text implies that the forgiveness is already complete, and that John's duty is to expand the people's knowledge of it. It will be the infant John's job in due time to proclaim that message in a manner that sets the stage for the coming Messiah in the "dawn from on high." That dawn will shed light on those in darkness, and by its light, guide people on the path of peace.

We will see how John lives out that call when we meet him again as an adult. For now, we are simply told that he grew and became strong in spirit. Like the Essenes, and maybe even with them, he is a child of the wilderness. And when he reappears in the Synoptics, he will make an impression that is impossible to forget.

1. How does the *Benedictus* prepare the audience for the coming message of Jesus? Is Luke's early focus on Zechariah, Elizabeth and John more about similarities to Jesus, or differences?

2. Zechariah uses the term "salvation." What is your understanding of salvation? To deliver from oppression? To heal? To make whole? What are we saved from? And what are we saved for? Often, understandings of this term in contemporary culture reflect the idea that the convert is saved from death or Hell—extreme states of unhappiness. Does this understanding encourage more of a fear-based theology or a hope-based one? To what does God call us? How do we know? We will revisit the term "salvation" from time to time, and look more closely at its meanings.

3. John is set apart in ways we find very difficult to comprehend. Most parents don't allow their children to go live in the wilderness. Most people don't seclude themselves until they are adults, then suddenly reappear when the time is right for them

to fulfill some mission. Does this separation of John from a normal upbringing portend something about his life? Is it a formative experience that prepares him to proclaim the coming of the Lord? Or, is it a metaphorical return to the desert of repentance, where the Israelites wandered with Moses for forty years as they journeyed from faithlessness to covenant? Have you experienced a formative time of separation and preparation?

We now turn to The Gospel According to Saint Matthew to witness the experience of another man who will find himself disconcerted by news of impending fatherhood.

✝ MATTHEW 1:18–25 The Birth of Jesus, from Joseph's Perspective

18Now the birth of Jesus the Messiah took place in this way. When his mother Mary had been engaged to Joseph, but before they lived together, she was found to be with child from the Holy Spirit. 19Her husband Joseph, being a righteous man and unwilling to expose her to public disgrace, planned to dismiss her quietly. 20But just when he had resolved to do this, an angel of the Lord appeared to him in a dream and said,

"Joseph, son of David, do not be afraid to take Mary as your wife, for the child conceived in her is from the Holy Spirit. 21She will bear a son, and you are to name him Jesus, for he will save his people from their sins."

22All this took place to fulfill what had been spoken by the Lord through the prophet:

23"Look, the virgin shall conceive and bear a son, and they shall name him Emmanuel," which means, "God is with us."

24When Joseph awoke from sleep, he did as the angel of the Lord commanded him; he took her as his wife, 25but had no marital relations with her until she had borne a son; and he named him Jesus.

1. What does it mean to say Joseph is a "righteous" man?

2. What do you make of Joseph's dream encounter with an angel?

3. How do you understand the idea of prophecy as used in this setting?

In this segment of Matthew, we see both some similarities to Luke's gospel, and some differences. The similarities include an angelic messenger bearing remarkable news about a virgin giving birth. The differences include the audience to whom the angel gives this news and the perspective from which it is heard. As we shall see, Matthew's birth narrative is told from Joseph's perspective, while Luke's birth narrative is told from Mary's. Another major difference is that Matthew contains no references to the birth of John the Baptist.

While containing some of the same subject matter, Luke's and Matthew's birth narratives are not actually parallel stories; the texts do not show any signs of having flowed out of a common stream or tradition. They share no specific material, wording, or even perspective. Thus, they are not parallels that begin with a shared literary source that each evangelist uses when telling his narrative, and that end with the form taken in the synoptic Gospels. However, we consider them together here because they fall in the same general time frame and involve similar subject matter.

Preliminary Matters

The first verse of The Gospel According to Saint Matthew declares, in the context of his genealogy, that the Messiah has come and his name is Jesus. At the end of that seventeen-verse pericope, the genealogy returns to the coming of the Messiah as a defining moment in the history of the Israelites. Having prepared the reader for the nature of the topic he is to address, Matthew now returns to the identity and birth of the Messiah in chapter 1, verse 18. By bracketing the genealogical detail within these Messianic references, Matthew invites the reader to pay close attention to what the material might be saying about Jesus, and how certain issues about his identity are to be addressed in the birth narrative as a whole.

Joseph's Dilemma and his "Righteous" Response

Before we begin to explore an array of ideas about the virgin birth through historical, literary, theological, and communal lenses—those tools that we aspire to use to engage in the responsible interpretation of Scripture—let us consider this: Matthew tells us that Joseph has learned his fiancé, Mary, is pregnant. And he knows he is not the father. Nor can he conjure up an acceptable explanation about how she came to be in this condition. He receives this painful information in first-century Jewish culture, a society not known for permissiveness. Even in the wider Greco-Roman world, which, on balance, was not as particular about matters of sexual behavior, it is difficult to imagine that an engaged woman being pregnant, and her fiancé knowing he is not the father, would ever be acceptable.

But, it is not difficult to imagine Joseph going through stages of grief and anger at the knowledge of Mary's pregnancy, maybe even plunging into despondency for a time before arriving at a decision about what to do. He will dismiss Mary, put her quietly aside so she won't be disgraced. Joseph makes this decision even though he has been dealt a great blow, not only in matters of the heart, but also in ways that can affect virtually every aspect of his life. Then, as now, marriage involved serious personal, emotional, familial and financial considerations. It involved issues around family life, lineage, procreation, care for the elderly, economics, companionship, and property management and distribution. Particularly in the Mediterranean world of the first century, there were also questions of honor and shame. The camp in which Joseph finds himself is painfully apparent.

In Joseph's decision to put Mary aside quietly rather than to disgrace her publicly, we see evidence of spiritual love, desiring someone's highest good despite what they might have done. Also remember that people in similar circumstances to Joseph's do not always act compassionately and that the consequences can be anything but just.

Take, for instance, a literary example. In the Shakespearean comedy, *Much Ado About Nothing*, young Claudio has been forced to confront a rumor that his lady love, sweet Hero, has been seen in the arms of another man on the eve of their planned nuptials. Claudio does not forgive, and does not even follow Joseph's example of deciding to quietly break the engagement. Rather, Claudio responds in hot anger and humiliates Hero in the presence of the wedding party, leaving her in a state of disgrace. We soon learn that Claudio's rash behavior is based on a canard. Yet, in his ignorance, he had insisted on believing it, beating a pathway leading all toward tragedy. The unbearable situation is redeemed only by good fortune revealing the true facts, and Claudio tasting more than a touch of hard-earned and much-deserved humility.

And so we have Joseph, who, like Claudio, is confronted with a circumstance of the most wrenching nature. How will he answer?

1. Joseph's character is described as "righteous." It is a trait that guides him toward a humane response to Mary. How, precisely, does Joseph display righteousness?

2. What is the quality of that character trait? Can you give modern-day examples of this same quality of righteousness?

3. Could you respond to a serious personal wrong with the kind of spiritual love that Joseph displayed toward Mary?

†††

The state of betrothal in first-century Judaism carried many more legal entanglements between bride and groom than our modern-day practice of engagement. Betrothal was more formalized and the financial involvements more complex. The gravity of this bond suggests that deviations from expected behavior would have more serious consequences than those that occur in modern engagements. Hence, the Judaic law imposed extremely serious punishments for certain sexual conduct, including by an engaged woman. The OT law is declared in Deuteronomy 22:13–29:

> [13]**Suppose a man marries a woman, but after going in to her, he dislikes her** [14]**and makes up charges against her, slandering her by saying, "I married this woman; but when I lay with her, I did not find evidence of her virginity."** [15]**The father of the young woman and her mother shall then submit the evidence of the young woman's virginity to the elders of the city at the gate.** [16]**The father of the young woman shall say to the elders: "I gave my daughter in marriage**

to this man but he dislikes her; [17]now he has made up charges against her, saying, 'I did not find evidence of your daughter's virginity.' But here is the evidence of my daughter's virginity." Then they shall spread out the cloth before the elders of the town. [18]The elders of that town shall take the man and punish him; [19]they shall fine him one hundred shekels of silver (which they shall give to the young woman's father) because he has slandered a virgin of Israel. She shall remain his wife; he shall not be permitted to divorce her as long as he lives.

[20]If, however, this charge is true, that evidence of the young woman's virginity was not found, [21]then they shall bring the young woman out to the entrance of her father's house and the men of her town shall stone her to death, because she committed a disgraceful act in Israel by prostituting herself in her father's house. So you shall purge the evil from your midst.

[22]If a man is caught lying with the wife of another man, both of them shall die, the man who lay with the woman as well as the woman. So you shall purge the evil from Israel.

[23]If there is a young woman, a virgin already engaged to be married, and a man meets her in the town and lies with her, [24]you shall bring both of them to the gate of that town and stone them to death, the young woman because she did not cry for help in the town and the man because he violated his neighbor's wife. So you shall purge the evil from your midst.

[25]But if the man meets the engaged woman in the open country, and the man seizes her and lies with her, then only the man who lay with her shall die. [26]You shall do nothing to the young woman; the young woman has not committed an offense punishable by death, because this case is like that of someone who attacks and murders a neighbor. [27]Since he found her in the open country, the engaged woman may have cried for help, but there was no one to rescue her.

[28]If a man meets a virgin who is not engaged, and seizes her and lies with her, and they are caught in the act, [29]the man who lay with her shall give fifty shekels

of silver to the young woman's father, and she shall become his wife. Because he violated her he shall not be permitted to divorce her as long as he lives.

The Judaic law does not bode well for an unmarried pregnant woman, especially one who is engaged. If Joseph weds Mary, and she is found to have been pregnant prior to the marriage — and, therefore, not a virgin—then her penalty under religious law is death.[3] To make matters worse for Joseph, the term "righteous," as used in first-century Judaism, related more closely to compliance with the Jewish law than it did to faithfully observing a sense of justice that arose, not only out of that law, but also out of wisdom and practicality and compassion and how human happiness is affected by the direction one chooses. These more complex notions about justice—that are not dependent solely on the written word—involve balancing principles and priorities while developing a righteous response.

In deciding to dismiss Mary because of her condition, Joseph is choosing a course that strays from a strict application of the Judaic law. This approach to the problem might well expose Joseph to the accusation that he is something quite other than "righteous." Stoning Mary—not setting her quietly aside—was the obvious way to observe the law. After all, who would believe her defense?

What are we to make of this decision? First, Joseph has diverged from a wooden, or literal, interpretation of Scripture and ventured into the cloudy and hazy world where the religious law is respectfully considered, but matters of personal judgment are also taken seriously. This is an approach to decision-making that literalists, legalists and authoritarians through the ages have not encouraged. Joseph has decided to do something other than strictly apply the law to what he believes to be the facts, and is still called a righteous man, so we must assess what this concept of righteousness is coming to mean. In this passage, we see for the first time the new righteousness that the Gospel According to Saint Matthew advocates. We see a certain honor paid to the Old Covenant, but the New Covenant emerges in a way that goes to the core intent underlying the written legal precepts. Matthew leaves some old understandings of the law behind and embraces new ones, particularly as Jesus declares them in the Sermon on the Mount.[4] And, as we shall eventually see in Matthew, that new righteousness is measured by the human need for both justice and mercy. Jesus himself will declare that the new law is the law of love.

---

[3]We do not know the extent to which this law was enforced. Even if the standards were more lax in practice than as written, the codified penalties are so harsh that it is safe to assume people did not lightly brush them aside when pondering prohibited conduct and its potential consequences.

[4]Matthew, unlike Mark, will not advocate for radical breaks with some aspects of the Judaic law.

A Change of Direction: An Angelic Message

Having reached a resolution to his predicament that begins to establish the new righteousness, Joseph hopes to find some relief in sleep. It is in a dream state that he receives news from an unnamed angel about the circumstances underlying Mary's pregnancy. The circumstances are not what he had reasonably assumed. The hand of God is in the mix as the angel describes that Mary's condition has been created by the Holy Spirit. Joseph is told only of poignant and mysterious circumstances, but given no concrete explanation about how it has occurred. He is also told to take Mary as a wife, and to name the son "Jesus" because he will save his people from their sins. The name "Jesus" is derived from the Hebrew word "savior," and so is descriptive of the role the child will play in God's saving action. We are not told, though, how this saving action is to occur.

Matthew's declaration about prophesy and fulfillment are not given to Joseph, only to the reader. We also see that Joseph, who speaks nary a word (unlike his more talkative wife-to-be, whom Luke describes), follows the directions given him, and the will of God is carried out.

In this preternatural atmosphere, it is easy to assume that Joseph had some special knowledge about the mysterious, and equally easy to overlook that he was acting largely on faith. There is no objective way Joseph can verify that his dream involved a revelation of God through an angel. It might have been "an undigested bit of beef, a blot of mustard, a crumb of cheese, a fragment of underdone potato," as Dickens' Ebenezer Scrooge would say, that caused this and Joseph's other odd dreams. The ideas about taking Mary as his wife, and naming the child Jesus, might easily have dissipated with the morning light and a return to the "normal" events of the day. Joseph could simply have rationalized his way right out of the mystery. But fortunately for all involved, including Joseph and his place in history, he followed the path put before him.

The Virgin Birth

Let us now address the virgin birth in a more comprehensive way. It is not a topic without controversy. To some people, a literal understanding of the story is a matter of fundamental importance to Christian faith. To others, the whole notion of a virgin giving birth sounds so much like superstition, and displays such an aversion to human sexuality, that it undermines the credibility of at least part of the Christian story. To still others, it is considered a matter of considerable consequence on a symbolic or theological level, regardless of whether a biological miracle has occurred. We will start with the historical and theological setting, and proceed from that point toward a fuller understanding of the story's significance for contemporary Christian faith. In the process, we will seek to interpret this story, and the related theories and doctrines, in light of literary composition, theological meaning, historical context, and the concerns of the community of the faithful to whom Matthew's gospel is addressed.

The virgin birth appeared fairly late among the Christian writings that found their way into the canon. The letters of Paul, which comprise the oldest works in the New Testament, contain no reference to a virgin birth. Nor does the Gospel According to Saint Mark, the oldest of the canonical gospels. The fourth gospel, which most scholars concur was the last one to be written, also contains no mention of a virgin birth. Only in Luke and Matthew do we read these stories. Why did these two evangelists choose to tell their stories in this way, while the other New Testament writers either knew nothing of the tradition, or chose not to include it?

Luke and Matthew tell the story because it adds something to their compositions. We have already seen how the Lukan birth narrative sets the stage for the rest of that gospel. For Luke, John and Jesus are paired figures, with John representing the grand tradition and culmination of the Old Order, and Jesus representing the dawning of the New. In the remainder of Luke's birth narrative, we will also see how parallels are drawn between Jesus and Augustus Caesar, as the reader is called to grapple seriously with the relative priorities of the claims of the Kingdom of God, and the claims of a worldly empire.[5]

Matthew also asks his audience to make a similar comparison. If anything, his contrast is considerably stronger then Luke's, as he displays a "conflict of kingdoms" theme throughout his work that Professor Boring, in his commentary on Matthew, shows is critical to the gospel story. For instance, the Herodian royal line in Matthew is uniformly portrayed in a negative light, beginning in the birth narrative. Jesus is presented as a royal figure to whom true homage is rightfully paid, whereas Herod is depicted as an evil monster. In this way, Matthew's beginnings invite (or even compel) the reader to see immediately a conflict of kingdoms, much as Luke's beginnings invite one to observe a change from the Old Order to the New, and a contrast between the Kingdom of God and the Kingdom of Men. Both birth narratives provide a foretaste of what the rest of their Gospels will hold.

In telling of a virgin birth as part of their larger infancy narratives, these two evangelists add considerable weight to their gospels. Luke and Matthew have both chosen to underscore

---

[5]Even though Luke makes clear how we are called to set our priorities along these lines, he judiciously avoids using loose words that might call the Jesus movement into disrepute.

the infancy narratives by telling of a virgin birth, surrounded by angelic visitations, celestial signs, and other symbols forecasting an historical turning point and communicating something about the life of Jesus. It was the Greco-Roman practice to look back upon the events surrounding the birth of a great figure in order to find clues about his destiny. When the Christian movement ventured beyond its primarily Jewish beginnings, and made headway into the predominately gentile culture, the story of Jesus took on different hues so that the new audiences could understand its import and participate in it properly.

By the last quarter of the first century, when the gospels of Matthew and Luke were being written, Jesus was being proclaimed in the gentile world as a figure worthy of worship. It was a world accustomed to stories of divine births attended by unique signs. It was also a world that demanded credentials. Were there any such signs and credentials to be found in the story of Jesus? How could the Church establish for the surrounding culture the idea that the figure of Jesus was one worthy to follow, to worship?

The pagans told myths of their gods coupling with human women to sire demi-gods and heroes (witness Hercules and a plethora of other mythological figures). Yet, the trappings of the holy were not limited to remote figures of a mythological past. Relatively recent figures were the subjects of larger-than-life stories. Julius Caesar was thought to be the offspring of a god and a mortal woman. And after death, in the case of both Julius and Augustus Caesar, the Roman Senate declared them to be gods. So, the culture held, when one looked back upon the lives of the "divine" figures of the era to their beginnings, one could see the presence of divine actors on the stage.[6]

This line of tradition, at least in its popular Greco-Roman form, would not sit easily in Jewish thought. To the Jews, God was transcendent and pure, qualitatively different from the flawed deities of the classical world. Could there be a peaceful co-existence between the Jewish conception of God and a Roman one? The Romans expected to see supernatural signs dating from the beginning of one's life that set destiny's patterns. Could the Christian movement meet this expectation without straying into pagan ideas that suggested a certain physical intimacy in the relations between gods and women?

Luke and Matthew showed that the answer was yes. There was considerable Jewish tradition around God blessing aged and childless patriarchs and matriarchs with children. These blessings also said something about the children's extraordinary destinies. We have seen

[6]We should not be too quick to scoff at these traditions. The Greco-Roman conception of deities was not necessarily grounded in literalism. Practitioners of ancient faith-rites often took mythological stories as symbolic accounts about the great issues of life, regardless of whether the events reported actually occurred in history.

this in Abraham and Sarah, Isaac and Rebecca, Elkenah and Hannah. The children of all turned out to be great leaders of the Jewish people. Symbols could also be found around these earlier births, such as the fact that, while Esau was born first, his twin brother Jacob entered the world grabbing at Esau's heel. (Jacob eventually overtook Esau in birthright, blessing, and success.) In this tableau, the Jewish people, like the Romans, connected the circumstances of one's birth with his future greatness. When it came to studying Jesus, the Old Testament tradition set the stage for the New Testament story.

The early Christians, according to Professor John Dominic Crossan, of the University of Chicago, used the works of the Old Testament as "foundational . . . texts to understand Jesus, his movement, his destiny, and the lives and hopes of his first followers."[7] Could the Hebrew Bible serve as such a foundational text and prophetic tool to describe the destiny of Jesus as the Messiah in a way that spoke, not only to the Jews, but to the Gentile world as well? Could it validate the identity of Jesus as Son of God to those in the Gentile world that were proving to be increasingly receptive to the Christian message?

When searching the Scriptures—meaning, the OT, as the NT had not yet been compiled— Matthew settled on Isaiah 7:14 to provide a sign of the divine purpose in Jesus' beginnings. This passage of Isaiah 7, with emphasis added, is part of a longer saga during the reign of King Ahaz when the southern kingdom of Judea was under threat by two enemy kingdoms in 734–733 B.C.:

> [10]Again the Lord spoke to Ahaz, [11]"Ask a sign of the Lord your God; let it be deep as Sheol or high as heaven." [12]But Ahaz said, "I will not ask, and I will not put the Lord to the test." [13]And he said, "Hear then, O house of David! Is it too little for you to weary men, that you weary my God also? [14]**Therefore the Lord himself will give you a sign. Behold, a young woman shall conceive and bear a son, and shall call his name Immanu-el.** [15]He shall eat curds and honey when he knows how to refuse the evil and choose the good. [16]For before the child knows how to refuse the evil and choose the good, the land before whose two kings you are in dread will be deserted. [17]The Lord will bring upon you and upon your people and upon your father's house such days as have not come since the day that Ephraim departed from Judah—the king of Assyria."

---

[7]This statement is found on page 16 of *Jesus: A Revolutionary Biography*, in a chapter that addresses in some detail, from an historical perspective, a number of aspects of the birth narratives.

First note that this prophetic utterance did not address the eventual coming of the Messiah, but Ahaz's immediate dangers. Also note, from the emphasized verse, that the New Revised Standard Version does not use the word "virgin" at Isaiah 7:14 (as the King James Version does), but instead uses the phrase, "young woman." The NRSV's phrase is, in fact, the better translation of the Hebrew word, *"almah,"* which is broad enough to encompass a young woman of marriageable age, and even a woman who had married but not yet had her first child. The word was not restricted to women who had never had sexual intercourse.

When the Hebrew Bible was translated into the Greek Septuagint, which was widely used in Jesus' time, the Hebrew word *"almah"* was translated as the Greek word *"parthenos."* There seems to be some disagreement among scholars over how closely the two words relate. Some think the Greek *"parthenos"* to be more synonymous with the Hebrew *"almah"* while others seem to think it more synonymous with our English word "virgin." Both the Hebrew and the Greek versions relate to events transpiring at the time of Ahaz, and make the point that the enemies he fears will themselves have their kingdoms laid waste. It is not, strictly speaking, a Messianic prophecy, and does not mean an actual virgin giving birth, but only alludes to the fact that before a young woman does give birth, and the child learns to choose, the opposing kings will fall.[8] The prophecy was, in fact, fulfilled and Ahaz's kingdom was delivered from imminent peril.

What, then, are we to make of it? Matthew takes the text quite seriously. But perhaps he does not use it to display a concrete prophecy/fulfillment pattern. We have already discussed how Matthew takes Old Testament passages and ties them to his own community's experience. This practice is in keeping with the Jewish idea of *midrash.* To tell an old story and a similar new story together creates an echo effect.[9] Just as the OT prophecy about a young woman giving birth foreshadowed relief from the oppressor in her time, the NT story about a young woman—called a "virgin" in the Septuagint and in Matthew—who will be giving birth to the Messiah, also speaks of relief from the oppressor then and now. The story honors Jewish perspective and simultaneously makes sense to Gentile audiences, as it affirms their expectations that extra-ordinary events will occur in connection with the birth of God's Anointed.

But some more literalistic ideas may also have been at work in the idea of the virgin birth. In antiquity, the belief was that semen contained *all* the material needed to create new life. The womb merely served as the good soil where that life could form. A child conceived by the Holy

---

[8]There is even some thought among scholars that Isaiah was in the presence of a particular young woman when he spoke, and that the reference was to the completion of events before she gave birth and her child learned right from wrong.

[9]*See* chapter 2, The Rabbi's Journey, *supra,* at page 31, for a more detailed discussion of the echo effect.

Spirit, the argument goes, would be one for whom God provides all the material for the fetal development and ultimate birth in a unique way.[10] As such, God's creative work is found here in the conception and birth of the New Adam, much as God's creative work first occurred in Genesis, when the first Adam and Eve were formed out of dust.

This approach to the virgin birth makes Jesus become God's son in a more or less biological way, though by means other than the Greek and Roman gods were said to have practiced. But, this narrow biological understanding founders in a scientific age. While the ancients "knew where babies came from" in a general sense, they did not know of the respective functions of sperm and egg and the combination of chromosomes and other materials. We now know that genetic material is provided by both parents, not just the father. So, the idea that the birth of the New Adam was solely God's creative work, with no human contribution to the child's biological design, does not persevere in this era, even though its symbolic import remains.

Finally, there was an ancient idea spread to malign the circumstances of Jesus' birth. The Matthean and Lukan communities both preserved a tradition that Jesus was the Son of God in a way that involved unique conception. This tradition led opponents of the Christian movement to argue that, if "God" was Jesus' father, Jesus must have been illegitimate, and this sort of God-talk was just a way to dodge the issue. A Roman philosopher of the late second century, Celsus, who was particularly nasty toward Christians, claimed that the story of the virgin birth was a cover-up of Jesus' actual illegitimacy, a status shameful in antiquity to both parent and child. There was even an idea that Mary had been raped, and Jesus was the rapist's son. As Crossan relates, "The illegitimate father was, [Celsus] claims, a Roman soldier named Panthera, in whose name we catch a mocking and reversed allusion to *parthenos*, the Greek word for the young woman from Isaiah 7:14." This idea about Jesus' birth was intended by the Church's opponents as a vicious attack, not as an objective theory.

Any approach to the virgin birth creates problems that need to be addressed. In light of modern scientific understanding, Mary's contribution of genetic material moots the argument that the unique creation God was making in Jesus was required to have a divinely pure biological basis. Ideas around illegitimacy also present problems, particularly in light of their speculative nature and the fact that they arose out of an attack intended to discredit the early Christians.[11]

---

[10]Judeo-Christian tradition holds that all material, genetic or otherwise, is grounded in God as creator, or in God as Being Itself.

[11]The idea does offer a redemptive aspect, though: *if* Jesus is shamefully illegitimate, but is uniquely loved and valued by God so as to be called his son, then we are forced to conclude that God is the God of the disadvantaged, the despised, and the devalued. He is the father of last resort and, hopefully, we experience him also as the father of first priority.

If we are looking for a third way, we could consider a simpler alternative to speculative ideas of illegitimacy or notions of a strictly biological miracle. Luke Timothy Johnson is a Roman Catholic scholar teaching at a Methodist institution, Candler School of Theology at Emory University. In his book *The Real Jesus: The Misguided Quest for the Historical Jesus and the Truth of the Traditional Gospels*, Professor Johnson criticizes the Jesus Seminar (of which Crossan is a leading member), and others who seek to reconstruct an historical picture of Jesus by using cross-cultural anthropology and other tools.[12] While Johnson is not himself a literalist, he does see the current trend toward historical research as misplaced. He suggests that, "[i]f the virgin birth seems historically unlikely, one would think that a normal birth would be the logical alternative."[13] Johnson discourages following some writers down a speculative or overly hypothetical path and implicitly suggests that, from the standpoint of historical probability, it is more likely that Joseph is the father than some unknown and unnamed character. While he does not argue for this point, it is consistent with other Roman Catholic scholars, such as John Meier and Raymond Brown, who do not believe the tools of the historian can answer the question definitively.

And so, the questions remain: What is the virgin birth, and what does it mean? Those who embrace a literal view can freely continue to do so; they have their own right to interpret. Those who have problems with a literalistic approach to this story have some options to explore when formulating their own understanding of what the story is about.

Whether literal fact or symbolic statement, the truth and importance of the story remain. It is about God's power to create and to make a new creation. It is about Jesus' greatness being foreshadowed in the circumstances of his birth. It is about identifying Jesus as the Son of God in a way that you and I do not claim, even though we, too, are children of God. It is about remarkable beginnings, with a re-creation of the human race along a line different from that sinful one that the first Adam followed. It is about God being among us, and within us, and our responding faithfully to that reality, just as Joseph responded faithfully to the news that was given him. These are the truths that underlie a major strand of our Christmas stories and celebrations, regardless of whether the virgin birth is to be understood literally or symbolically.

---

[12]C.S. Lewis also criticized searches for the historical Jesus. (See *The Screwtape Letters*, ch. xxiii).
[13]*The Real Jesus*, at 33.

1. Does Joseph's initial decision to dismiss Mary strike you as kind? Cruel? Weak? Humane? Righteous? Why?

2. What does the transformation of "righteousness" from observance of the written law to practicing justice and mercy say about our relationship to God? About how we should interpret Scripture? How do we practice "righteousness"?

3. Do we still, in present times, look at beginnings as foreshadowing the events of one's life? Think of stories about George Washington and Abraham Lincoln.

4. This chapter suggests that there is more about the meaning of the virgin birth to be found in its symbolic significance than in its strict, literal interpretation. But, does that rule out literalism? Are we called to believe that God's exercise of power and dominion over the natural order—including deviation from the norms he has established—is a place where we can find the holy? Are we also called to find the holy in the ordinary workings of the world? Where have you found it?

†††

CHAPTER SIX

From Nazareth to Bethlehem

Matthew's infancy narrative has little to say about the events immediately surrounding the birth of Jesus. Its larger themes are found preceding and following the birth itself, covering a vast expanse of time and distance. A wealth of interpretive material is found in Matthew's genealogy of Jesus; Joseph's dreams; the author's mystical links to Old Testament prophecy; and the coming of the Magi. Each offers a lense through which to view the unfolding story of the Messiah. At the same time, Herod's evildoing is embedded in the material, as circumstances foreshadow Matthew's "conflict of kingdoms" theme. Later in this chapter, we will see just how these events begin to play themselves out.

For now, we will return to a more tranquil, even pastoral, setting in the Gospel According to Saint Luke. Here, the events describe, more immediately, the birth of Jesus. Even in their sparsity, they tell us something about what his ministry and mission will ultimately encompass. Luke builds upon the foundation he has already laid in the *Magnificat* and the *Benedictus*. He marshals pieces of the story that draw attention toward a powerful concern for the poor and the outcast. By this process, Luke, like Matthew, foreshadows much of the rest of his work.

✟ LUKE 2:1–7 The Census and the Journey

¹**In those days a decree went out from Emperor Augustus that all the world should be registered. ²This was the first registration and was taken while Quirinius was governor of Syria. ³All went to their own towns to be registered. ⁴Joseph also went from the town of Nazareth in Galilee to Judea, to the city of David called Bethlehem, because he was descended from the house and family of David. ⁵He went to be registered with Mary, to whom he was engaged and who was expecting a child. ⁶While they were there, the time came for her to deliver her child. ⁷And she gave birth to her firstborn son and wrapped him in bands of cloth, and laid him in a manger, because there was no place for them in the inn.**

Here are some thoughts about the biblical text to consider while reviewing the commentary that follows:

1. Luke provides points of reference concerning the time and circumstances of Jesus' birth. What might be his purpose?

2. The situation that confronts Mary and Joseph is difficult. Is Luke trying to tell his audience something when making this point?

✟✟✟

As we have already seen, in each passage of his birth narrative, Luke tells the careful and informed reader much more than meets the eye. To better understand his narrative, it helps to limit the number of verses we consider at a time. It also helps to integrate what we have examined minutely with the rest of the work, so that it becomes part of a more unified whole.

The Kingdom of Herod the Great
(37–4 B.C.E.)

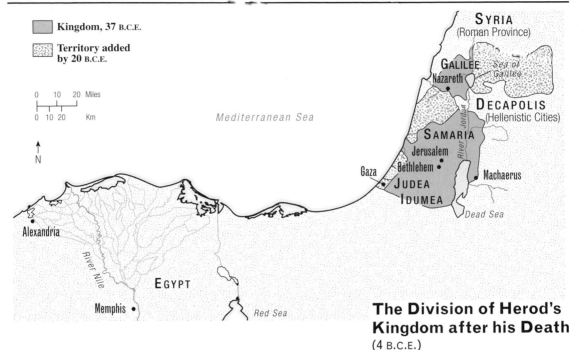

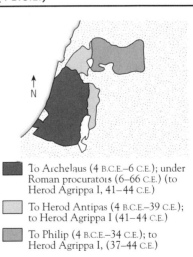

The Division of Herod's Kingdom after his Death
(4 B.C.E.)

To Archelaus (4 B.C.E.–6 C.E.); under Roman procurators (6–66 C.E.) (to Herod Agrippa I, 41–44 C.E.)

To Herod Antipas (4 B.C.E.–39 C.E.); to Herod Agrippa I (41–44 C.E.)

To Philip (4 B.C.E.–34 C.E.); to Herod Agrippa I, (37–44 C.E.)

An Occasion for a Trip to Bethlehem

Luke tells us that Mary and Joseph's trip to Bethlehem was required by a Roman registration. This type of mandate was more than a census for administrative purposes; it also provided tax-collecting data. Rome periodically used such means to fund its vast empire, which Luke calls "the world." Yet, historical records dating back to the days of the empire itself have presented serious, even insurmountable, problems to those scholars who have attempted to date the birth of Jesus by using such secular tools.[1] The point of Luke's story, though, is not to write a detailed

[1] Professor R. Alan Culpepper, who is affiliated with the Southern Baptist Convention, is the dean of the Mercer University School of Theology. He outlines these problems at pages 62-63 in his commentary on Luke in *The New Interpreter's Bible* series.

history of Roman bureaucracies, but an "orderly account" in which he proclaims a gospel: good news of God's saving action. The historical accuracy of the details he gives are not as critical to the birth narrative as is their theological meaning. It would be a mistake to rush straight to a solely theological interpretation without first exploring what the historical setting has to tell us, and recognizing in the process the shortcomings that arise when taking an entirely historical approach to the Bible.

First, let us consider the broad historical context. Augustus, having emerged victorious from the struggles to control the vast expanse of Rome's domain, reigned over the empire from 27 B.C. to 14 A.D. Quirinius, a comparatively minor figure to whom the pericope also makes reference, became governor of Syria in 6 A.D. The great administrative province of Syria included Nazareth of Galilee, which was in the northern part of Palestine, and Bethlehem of Judea, which was in the south. The year 6 A.D., then, serves as one reference point from which to attempt to date the birth of Jesus.[2]

There are other reference points, as well. Earlier, Luke told us that his narrative begins "in the days of King Herod," when Gabriel appeared to Zechariah in the temple. Within a few months of this appearance, both Elizabeth and Mary became pregnant. Herod's reign ended in 4 B.C. Matthew's story also places the birth of Jesus during the time Herod was king.

These historical markings, grouped together, have created a puzzling problem for scholars. It is impossible that Jesus was born both while Herod was king of Judea, and while Quirinius was governor of Syria, as there was a ten-year lapse between the end of one's administrative period and the beginning of the other's.[3]

To resolve this issue, scholars tend to give the greater nod of historical accuracy where Matthew and one of Luke's reference points agree, dating the birth of Jesus at around 4 B.C.,

---

[2] The traditional Christian calendar was revised in 525 A.D. by a Roman abbot. In it, the Church designated its estimate of the year Jesus was born as "1 A.D."—the first year of our Lord. It has since been determined that this early estimate was erroneous. The estimates described in this chapter more closely approximate when Jesus' birth occurred, given what later scholarship has disclosed about the Roman and Jewish political situations which mark the time around his birth, his death, and the gospel accounts of his age at the beginning of his public ministry.

[3] Some scholars attempt to resolve the discrepancy by dating Luke's reference to Quirinius at an earlier time during which he had served Rome in the province of Syria as viceroy, rather than as governor. However, that approach does not "correct" other historical problems, and therefore merely substitutes one error for another. Either way, the gospel account contains a factual misapprehension.

Yet, this observation does not suggest, much less require, that we toss Luke's birth narrative into the dustbin of religious history on the grounds of technical error. Rather, it requires us to examine the texts as works that are not *primarily* historical. Such references have, at most, a secondary significance. They are intended to put us in some general chronological time frame in order to follow the narrative. *Primarily*, the purposes of the birth narratives are to tell us of something remarkable, and to invite us to draw some theological inferences about Jesus' identity from the circumstances they describe.

very late in the reign of Herod the Great. As Luke and Matthew both attest to the birth taking place during that reign, it is that time period which draws our attention and casts light on the story of Jesus. We see that, from the beginning, the shadows of Romans and Herodians are present, projecting danger over the gospel stories. God's action, even in their presence, is of greater importance than the details about exactly when the story begins.

Having established that complete factual accuracy is less important to Luke than theological meaning, we now need to address other historical problems with his birth narrative so we can read how his story develops with more of a literary than a literal eye. The Gospel According to Saint Luke contains our only record of a census having been taken in Syria during Augustus' reign. Such censuses became fairly regular events in Syria and other provinces ten to twenty years after the birth of Jesus. But Luke, writing as much as 100 years after the birth, composes a setting that includes a Roman census. Over the years preceding the composition of his gospel, the L tradition likely developed a certain set of ideas around Jesus' birth being in Bethlehem that eventually came down to Luke in some form. In this book, the "why" of that Bethlehem tradition is discussed later in connection with Matthew's story of the visit of the wise men. The "how" of it is found, at least for Luke, here in the story of the census.

The logistics of the Roman census were different from Luke's description. For instance, people were not sent to ancestral homes to be registered. That process would create an administrative nightmare, involving travel to places one's family might have occupied only in the distant past. The productive time lost during such travels would not advance the empire's agenda. It would add to administrative burdens while diminishing the agricultural and commercial activity that supported the economy. That, in turn, would impair the tax base Rome was trying to enhance. Moreover, requiring such travels would pose risks to the *Pax Romana* as people resentfully moved away from the peaceable routines of life in their own locales, and toward places that might be charged with rebellious fervor grounded in religion and nationalism. Places like Jerusalem, for instance. Not surprisingly, historical records reflect that subjects of the empire registered in their current communities, rather than their ancestral lands.

One aspect of the registration process that may have influenced the oral tradition and Luke's composition is that it could, and did, involve travel of some distance in certain circumstances. When the people to be counted were tradesmen living in one place and working in another, they were required to return to their own homes to be registered. In this situation, both accuracy (getting people counted in their own home regions where their taxes were to be paid) and efficiency (requiring only a relatively small group to travel) balanced out and served to maximize revenue to the Imperial treasury. We might even speculate that Joseph fell in this camp. Perhaps, as a carpenter, he left his home in Bethlehem of Judea to work in the large metropolitan area of Sepphoris of Galilee, just a few miles from Nazareth. If so, he would have been required to return home to Bethlehem to participate in the census. But again, this idea is speculation.[4]

Yet, even with these historical problems, the story remains pertinent. We are studying faith documents, not trial transcripts. And in his Prologue, Luke has told Theophilus that he relied on the oral tradition to provide an orderly account, not a tedious report, of the grand story he imparts.

Luke's version also tells us something about the shadow Rome casts; its primary purpose is to serve itself. Even the *idea* of a pregnant woman and her intended being forced to travel, by foot at worst and donkey at best, over an eighty-some mile distance from Nazareth to Bethlehem, simply for purposes of satisfying the requirements of a bureaucracy bent on collecting money from the poor, is an indictment of the Roman power structure. Luke portrays Rome in its might as freely making people, such as Mary and Joseph, comply with the priorities of an occupying force, regardless of risk or cost to the peasantry. That arrogance will be brought to a sharp point in Holy Week.

1. Luke tells a powerful story, where the geopolitical forces converge to put Mary and Joseph in Bethlehem at the time of the child's birth. We will soon see characters in Matthew speaking of a prophecy that involves the Messiah coming from Bethlehem. If literally true, does the convergence of events leading to Jesus Messiah's birth in Bethlehem say something about God's will, power, and sovereignty? If figuratively true, but not historically accurate, does the story still say the same thing? How have you seen God's hand at work in your life, including the places you have traveled?

---

[4]Matthew's birth narrative seems *partially consistent* with this idea. Matthew has Joseph living in Bethlehem at the time of Jesus' birth, only later moving to Nazareth. If this were the case, theoretically, Joseph could have been working and staying temporarily in Nazareth earlier, at the time of a census, but been required to return to Bethlehem, his actual home, to register. That would also explain why, when the time came, Matthew's Joseph determined to move the family to Nazareth, instead of some other place. Yet, Matthew would be *inconsistent* with Luke's story to some extent as well. Matthew has no tradition of a journey to Bethlehem to be taxed, and no textual suggestion of a Nazareth residence prior to the birth of Jesus. Moreover, other chronological issues resist being reconciled. Matthew has Joseph wed Mary shortly after being directed to do so in a dream. The marriage is clearly before the birth of the child. Luke, however, at least implies they were merely engaged at the time of the birth.

No matter how we view the two versions, we cannot package them neatly together. Studying Scripture bears little resemblance to a controlled laboratory experiment. It is a little messier—like life itself.

2. In this segment, we see the political and economic priorities of an empire brought to bear for no greater purpose than its self-preservation. Does advancement of that agenda nonetheless serve the purposes of the Kingdom of God, at least indirectly? If so, what does that reality say about the relationship between our worldly striving and God's higher purpose? Can you think of times when meeting a secular requirement opened a spiritual door?

†ᵗ†

✝ LUKE 2:5–20 The Birth of Jesus

⁵[Joseph] went to be registered with Mary, to whom he was engaged and who was expecting a child. ⁶While they were there, the time came for her to deliver her child. ⁷And she gave birth to her firstborn son and wrapped him in bands of cloth, and laid him in a manger, because there was no place for them in the inn.

⁸In that region there were shepherds living in the fields, keeping watch over their flock by night. ⁹Then an angel of the Lord stood before them, and the glory of the Lord shone around them, and they were terrified. ¹⁰But the angel said to them,

"Do not be afraid; for see—I am bringing you good news of great joy for all the people: ¹¹to you is born this day in the city of David a Savior, who is the Messiah, the Lord. ¹²This will be a sign for you: you will find a child wrapped in bands of cloth and lying in a manger."

¹³And suddenly there was with the angel a multitude of the heavenly host, praising God and saying,

¹⁴"Glory to God in the highest heaven, and on earth peace among those whom he favors!"

¹⁵When the angels had left them and gone into heaven, the shepherds said to one another,

"Let us go now to Bethlehem and see this thing that has taken place, which the Lord has made known to us."

16So they went with haste and found Mary and Joseph, and the child lying in the manger. **17**When they saw this, they made known what had been told them about this child; **18**and all who heard it were amazed at what the shepherds told them. **19**But Mary treasured all these words and pondered them in her heart. **20**The shepherds returned, glorifying and praising God for all they had heard and seen, as it had been told them.

Let us first ponder the following:

1. These words are so familiar. We read them each Christmas and hear them recited in children's pageants. Consider rereading them, and see if anything new comes to mind.

2. The shepherds were terrified. Why?

3. The first words of the angel are, "Do not be afraid." In Scripture, angels speak words such as these time and again. What message remains for us, 2,000 years later?

An Old Story

There once was a child named David keeping the family sheep around Bethlehem of Judea. While he was away in the fields, a man named Samuel visited David's father, Jesse. Samuel was not just any man; he was a prophet, and judge over the Israelites. Samuel did not visit Jesse to pass the time of day with idle talk. He was there for a solemn, wonderful, and secretive purpose. He had come to anoint a future king who would replace the one that had fallen out of favor with Yahweh, the God of his people.

Samuel insisted on meeting each of Jesse's sons. Guided by the Spirit, he passed by the strong and tall older brothers. Finally, he settled on young David, handsome, ruddy and bright eyed—David, who had so little hope of being tapped by the prophet that he had been left in the fields near Bethlehem, tending the sheep, while his brothers were presented to Samuel. In the end, David was summoned. And it was young David that Samuel anointed. He became the shepherd who God raised up to lead his sheep, the people of Israel, to glory.[5]

---

[5]*See 1 Samuel 16.*

One shepherd was regarded in this manner 1,000 years before Jesus was born. If we leap over that span, and two more millennia as well, we arrive in our modern culture. We now regard shepherds (romantically, perhaps) as simple, humble, appealing folk with good, solid, salt-of-the-earth values. It is a favorable impression, albeit a different one than David left.

But if we focus on either the Davidic or the modern picture, it would lead us in the wrong direction when trying to understand this section of Luke's gospel. To Luke's contemporaries, living 1,000 years after David and nearly 2,000 years before us, the shepherds would not have enjoyed any sort of favorable reputation.

The God of the Lowly

In Luke's time, Israelite shepherds were virtual outcasts. They were ceremonially unclean because their job did not allow them to observe those standards of ritual purity which the power structure considered central to Jewish religious observance in the first century C.E.[6] For instance, if a sheep strayed on the Sabbath, might the shepherd be compelled to follow it, and so breach the regulations prohibiting work on that day? If a sheep came in contact with something "unclean," might the shepherd be defiled in retrieving it? Moreover, the ethics of the shepherds' vocation were questioned. They were frequently suspected of grazing their sheep on others' land. They were considered low-class, no-count scoundrels. We might compare them, at best, to day laborers on the fringes of American cities, working when they must in order to get by. At worst, they were more like petty criminals.

What is Luke telling us by having the birth of the Messiah announced to people such as these? As so often occurs in Luke, God identifies with, and reveals himself to, the simple, the outcast, the poor, the downtrodden. It is not the respectable people who receive the first news of the birth of the Messiah, but the reviled

---

[6]We will study this purity system throughout this series and examine its sharp contrast to the early Jesus movement. The gospel of Jesus Christ is not a purity system, with first, second, and lower-class tiers of citizens. It is good news of inclusion, where filthy Gentiles and other sinners are radically deemed acceptable to God despite their "sins" of genetics, environment, and behavior. They are recipients of a grace that abolishes religious ideas of virtue and vice, and embraces them in God's reconciling forgiveness and love.

A New Story

In my own church, we are challenged by a mission involving society's "unclean"—like shepherds of our day. We provide worship space for a homeless congregation, charging nominal rent, which is set in order to make our participation in that ministry more than simply a "handout." The worshiping community that gathers there is called the Church of the Advocate. Another parish pays the lion's share of compensation for the clergy who serve it. The Church of the Advocate is ultimately part of the greater Diocesan community and ministry.[7]

With some exceptions, our congregation does not know exactly how to approach these differently and difficultly situated people. It is much easier to minister to them, by providing dollars, than with them, by providing more personal contact and including them as ministers in our own mission. Yet, we take little steps in the direction of relationship. How will the faith community called the Church of the Advocate affect its members? How will it affect the broader community of Episcopalians and other Christians in Western North Carolina?

To Luke, it is clear that people such as these, people who were "living in the fields" (in the words of chapter 2, verse 8), are central participants in the gospel story. The shepherds are entrusted with the message of the coming of the Messiah. They proclaim it to others, and are the first evangelists.

When telling of the announcement to the shepherds, Luke makes some subtle points. There will be a "sign," the angel proclaims. We might expect that the promised sign of the Messiah would be the appearance of the heavenly host in the sky. Yet, these angels do not claim that role, instead saying that the sign the shepherds will "find [is] a child wrapped in bands of cloth"—"swaddling clothes" according to the King James Version—and "lying in a manger." Unlike receiving angelic visitations, the act of clothing an infant in this sort of garb was utterly *unremarkable*; it was the way most mothers of the time and place wrapped their newborns. In this "sign" we see humility on the occasion of the Savior's entry into the world. And it is that humility, not the choir of angels, toward which the shepherds must look for a

---

[7] I will also allow a footnote to brag on Judith Whelchel, who was ordained in my parish and later became the first vicar of the Church of the Advocate. Her vision and energy led to the formal founding of this worshiping community, which continues to be a vibrant ministry, even after she moved on to other callings.

sign. If we wish to find the presence of God in the world, we need to seek the small, the weak, the unremarkable, the ordinary.

And finally, there is the "where" of Jesus' birth to consider. Scholars are uncertain about the intended use of the word "inn" in this context. The place where there was no room may have been an area of someone's personal home, which was typically rented to travelers. The place may have been one where peasants could seek shelter while in transit, but happened to be occupied on this particular night. Either way, there is no room in the inn.

We are left with a phrase that has borne a powerful image throughout Church history: the closing of our hearts and lives to God. Instead of finding rest in the best—or even the most ordinary—of places, the Messiah finds it in the lowest: a trough, located in some crude stable or cave, where animals feed. His parents are strangers in the land. His attendants, marginalized characters that the culture considers unclean. His country, a place at a shabby fringe of the mighty Roman Empire.

1. If you envision the birth of the Messiah being announced first to the outcasts of society, do you gain a new perspective on Luke's nativity? On how God regards those we look down upon? Are there ways we can live our lives that help us overcome our prejudices?

2. Mary is said to treasure the words spoken to her and to ponder these matters in her heart. Is this an abiding image of Mary? We will later see her questioning the way Jesus lives out his mission. How does that later image fit with this early one?

3. The shepherds are explicitly depicted as following the angel's directive, and in proclaiming the good news they have been told. What on earth is God doing, selecting such poor role models as evangelists? Doesn't he know that he can't entrust the "good news of great joy" to people who wouldn't be invited even to a reception honoring a local luminary, much less a universal one? Doesn't God know he can't rely on people who would not be caught dead sporting some first-century equivalent of the bumper sticker: "Morals Matter, Character Counts"? And what does all this mean to you?

†††

We now return to Matthew's nativity.

✝ MATTHEW 2:1–12 The Visit of the Wise Men

¹In the time of King Herod, after Jesus was born in Bethlehem of Judea, wise men from the East came to Jerusalem, ²asking,

"Where is the child who has been born king of the Jews? For we observed his star at its rising, and have come to pay him homage."

³When King Herod heard this, he was frightened, and all Jerusalem with him; ⁴and calling together all the chief priests and scribes of the people, he inquired of them where the Messiah was to be born. ⁵They told him,

"In Bethlehem of Judea; for so it has been written by the prophet: ⁶'And you, Bethlehem, in the land of Judah, are by no means least among the rulers of Judah; for from you shall come a ruler who is to shepherd my people Israel.'"

⁷Then Herod secretly called for the wise men and learned from them the exact time when the star had appeared. ⁸Then he sent them to Bethlehem, saying,

"Go and search diligently for the child; and when you have found him, bring me word so that I may also go and pay him homage."

⁹When they had heard the king, they set out; and there, ahead of them, went the star that they had seen at its rising, until it stopped over the place where the child was. ¹⁰When they saw that the star had stopped, they were overwhelmed with joy. ¹¹On entering the house, they saw the child with Mary his mother; and they knelt down and paid him homage. Then, opening their treasure chests, they offered him gifts of gold, frankincense, and myrrh. ¹²And having been warned in a dream not to return to Herod, they left for their own country by another road.

As in Luke, we see a familiar story here in Matthew. Often, it is heard from pulpit and lectern, in pageants and in Sunday School class, interpreted in song, and infusing worship in the days surrounding Christmas and Epiphany. Yet, its familiarity can serve to hide the questions it raises.

1. Who are these wise men from the East? And, to where might the term "the East" refer?

2. Why do the wise men go to Jerusalem in their quest?

3. The reason Herod is disturbed is at least implicit. He considers himself the king. The announcement of someone else's claim to that title is unsettling. But why is "all of Jerusalem" frightened with him?

4. Why are the chief priests and scribes frightened if the one to be proclaimed king may also be the long-awaited Messiah? What does that say about their priorities? Their conscience, even?

✝✝✝

The wise men from the East come seeking one born to be king. The text does not suggest that they know who this person is, or upon what criteria he will base a claim to the throne. As far as they know at first, the mysterious child is a natural successor to the incumbent king, born within his family, who will ascend to the throne in a traditional way.

Given how the wise men appear out of the blue, with no apparent connection to Judaic faith or royalty, we should not be surprised that it is the local establishment, rather than the visitors themselves, who first speak of the kingly figure as "Messiah," God's anointed. Herod, who represents worldly rather than religious power, equates strangers searching for "the king of the Jews" with a quest for that Messiah. It threatens him that they are searching for a successor who is apparently outside Herod's own family. Herod's mind casts about in the pool of ideas for information he hopes he can use to ward off a termination of his own royal line.

To secure weapons to defend his throne, Herod calls on his henchmen: the chief priests—those charged with maintaining the temple as the center of worship—and the scribes—those charged with reading and interpreting the Old Testament. If he can find out where the Messiah is to be born, then maybe, just maybe, he can keep the danger at bay while the child is still a baby.

Out of Bethlehem

The priests and scribes answer that the Messiah is expected to come from Bethlehem. And herein lies a problem for the early Church. Not only the Church, but also its opponents, knew Jesus was from Nazareth in Galilee, not Bethlehem in Judea. Even Nathanael, who would become a disciple of Jesus, is depicted in the fourth gospel as questioning whether anything good could come out of Nazareth (*See* John 1:46). In chapter 7 of that same book, both the crowds, and those in authority, consider Jesus' association with Nazareth, rather than Bethlehem, an obstacle to him being the Messiah. If Jesus were the Messiah, the line of thought went, then he needed to have some connection with Bethlehem, the City of David.

Why did some people use this measuring stick when testing Jesus' credentials? The answer, as is often the case when exploring Matthew's birth narrative, is found in the Old Testament. In Matt. 2:5–6, the authorities, who Herod summons, declare that the Messiah is to come from Bethlehem. Their words paraphrase what the prophet Micah proclaimed in Israel during the eighth century B.C.[8] When the imminent prospect of being conquered by foreign powers confronted the children of Israel, and they were in fear of the worst, Micah promised them a deliverance that is now recorded in chapter 5 of the book bearing his name:

> Now you are walled around with a wall;
> siege is laid against us;
> with a rod they strike the ruler of Israel
> upon the cheek.
> ²But you, O Bethlehem of Ephrathah,
> who are one of the little clans of Judah,
> from you shall come forth for me
>
> one who is to rule in Israel,
> whose origin is from of old,
> from ancient days.
> ³Therefore he shall give them up until the time
> when she who is in labor has brought forth;

---

[8]The minor prophet, Micah's, era overlapped with that of a better-known prophet whose words we have already considered in Matthew's birth narrative: first Isaiah. The biblical designations of "major" and "minor" prophets refer to the length of their works, not to the importance of their words.

then the rest of his kindred shall return
to the people of Israel.
[4]And he shall stand and feed his flock in the strength of the Lord,
in the majesty of the name of the Lord his God.
And they shall live secure, for now he shall be great to the ends of the earth;
and he shall be the one of peace.

✝✝✝

The ancient Jews traditionally interpreted this text as a prophecy of the coming of the Messiah. In it, we witness Micah and his people looking toward liberation from oppression, and the dawning of an idyllic age. The passage evokes memories of the long ago Davidic era and an echo effect is present:[9] siege; deliverance; and a beacon of hope shining from David's town of Bethlehem. Its origin is in the Old, the ancient days. It is a prophecy of the re-gathering of the people of God; its images are of a secure flock, living peacefully on Earth. Micah offers a foretaste of a time when the divine presence dwells among us, and Israel beholds the day of her salvation.

In light of this text, the first-century Jewish institutional leadership that Matthew depicts expected the Messiah to come from Bethlehem. And so, it was important to the Lukan and Matthean communities to connect their own stories

David's Kingdom
(1000–961 B.C.E.?)

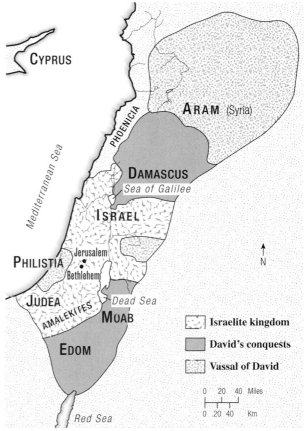

---

[9]For a fuller discussion of this concept, *see* chapter 2, The Rabbi's Journey, at p. 31.

of Jesus to Bethlehem.[10] Luke makes this connection in the journey of Mary and Joseph to Bethlehem. Matthew accomplishes it with the arrival of the wise men. Both stories reflect oral traditions placing the birth of Jesus in Bethlehem of Judea.[11]

But, even assuming that certain modern scholars, who place the birth of Jesus in Nazareth, are correct,[12] does that assumption require us to set aside the stories of a Bethlehem birth as flimsy oral tradition, written only to satisfy some "requirements" about the relationship between the Old Testament and the Messianic Age?

"Clearly not," as one of my favorite law professors was fond of saying. This conclusion would be inconsistent with how Matthew reinterprets ancient Scripture for use in his time. We have already seen him work wonders with a prophecy about a virgin giving birth. Can he make a similar connection for us here?

If we adopt Matthew's vantage point, we might see that a Bethlehem birth is more important theologically and literarily than historically. Matthew's approach aided his community, with particular Jewish-Christian sensitivities, to preserve a tradition of the Messiah coming from Bethlehem. This approach opens a literary door as much as a literal one. Micah's prophecy is that one from Bethlehem, a royal figure, would come from old to deliver Israel from

---

[10]Paul and Mark demonstrate no such need. John identifies the issue but, lacking a birth narrative, does not seek to resolve it. Consequently, the Bethlehem issue appears to have been more important to some communities within the early Church than to others.

[11]While some very serious biblical scholars treat these texts as accurately identifying Bethlehem to be the birthplace of Jesus, the historical verdict of most mainline scholars is that Jesus was born in Nazareth. The latter group's contention is that the somewhat different Bethlehem birth traditions, which Luke and Matthew report, reflect how early Christian communities, working decades after the fact, searched the Scriptures to mark the birth of the Messiah in Bethlehem as keeping with the Old Testament tradition. By reporting these traditions, Matthew and Luke tell us theological truths, regardless of what historical information was (or was not) available to them. *See, e.g., The Meaning of Jesus: Two Visions,* by Marcus Borg and N.T. Wright, at Part VI; *Jesus, a Revolutionary Biography,* by John Dominic Crossan, at chapter 1; and *Gospel Truth: The New Image of Jesus Emerging from Science and History, and Why it Matters,* by Russell Shorto, at chapter 2.

For different views, see generally Luke Timothy Johnson's *The Real Jesus: The Misguided Quest for the Historical Jesus and the Truth of the Traditional Gospels,* criticizing the scholarly movements that focus on reconstructing a historical picture of Jesus, and urging that the focus instead be on Jesus as depicted in the New Testament.

For a marriage of the historical and the traditional, we have N.T. Wright, formerly a professor at Oxford and Cambridge, and now canon at Westminster Abbey. Wright, a leading traditional scholar, looks at the convergence of the Matthean and Lukan birth narratives, and concludes that, while they are different, they are generally compatible, thereby supporting (or at least not undermining) the idea of a Bethlehem birth. *See* Borg and Wright, *supra,* cited in this footnote. Wright also views Luke's version as an effort to solve a puzzle about the Bethlehem birth he already understands to have occurred, rather than as a creative composition to connect Jesus to that place.

In considering *any* perspective on the synoptic birth narratives, remember that neither author would have had first-hand knowledge of the nativity; they were writing 75–100 years later. So, we can expect different strands of tradition to have arisen in the early faith communities and to have later been reflected in the different Gospels.

[12]*See* previous footnote.

the oppressor; to restore the people; to protect the flock; to make it secure; to preside over a reign of peace, and to be great to the ends of the Earth. Does the figure whom Micah foretells sound like anyone you know?

1. Does Micah's prophecy establish credentials for identifying the Messiah? How does Jesus fulfill them? Does the word "impeccably" come to mind?

2. We have spoken of Matthew's echo effect with the OT. Is that primarily what we see here? Do we see a comparable approach in Luke's gospel? How do we hear the same echoes today?

3. An overly zealous insistence on historical reliability can strip away much of the gospel story, leaving little in the arena of mystery to ponder. And, failure to study the Bible critically can leave us stranded in a literalism that doesn't always work. How do we strike a balance?

4. If we fail to raise questions that go to the heart of people's faith lives, would that somehow mean that they didn't really exist? And would we, in our unquestioning silence, miss the opportunity to engage others who do feel compelled to grapple with them?

✝✝✝

The connection of the Messiah with Bethlehem, and the reports of Jesus' birth there, whether they are literal or literary, tell us about his identity, as does other imagery in this passage.

An Ethereal Visit

On January 6th of each year, the Western Church observes the visitation to the Holy Family by wise men from the East. It is the Feast of the Epiphany, and follows the twelve days of Christmas. The term "epiphany" means spiritual revelation. It is a manifestation of God to humanity. In a more general setting, the word can be understood as a moment of sudden intuitive understanding, or a flash of insight. To the Christian Church, in particular, Epiphany is the celebration of the revelation of the Lord Jesus Christ to the Gentiles, represented by the wise men who had seen a star in the East.

The Religious Traditions of the Wise Men

The wise men, or Magi, were part of a pagan, priestly line, possibly from Persia or Arabia, the area in the "East" where the star was seen. In this context, the best translation of the Greek term used to describe them is "astrologer." A number of biblical words were developed to delineate among those with mystical or magical powers. Some practitioners of these arts were mere tricksters. They occupied the bottom rungs of the "magical" spectrum, both when considering their power and when considering the seriousness of their undertakings. At the upper end of the spectrum were the astrologers, or Magi, highly educated people who were able to discern spiritual and mystical truths.

The Magi are often associated with the ancient Zoroastrian religion, a movement that was already in flower at the time of the Babylonian exile of the Jews around the sixth century B.C. Before then, the Jewish people held a limited to non-existent view of the afterlife. During the exile, the Jews encountered Zoroastrian belief systems. Developing Jewish ideas of an afterlife bloomed following this religio-cultural exposure. In fact, the OT Book of Daniel, some portions of which were likely written during the Babylonian exile, contains the most fully developed concept of the afterlife found in the Hebrew Bible.[13]

The Zoroastrian system included dualistic aspects involving two gods. One's nature was pure good while the other's was pure evil. They were joined in cosmic battle in heaven. In keeping with religious ideas that prevailed in the area of the Tigris and Euphrates Rivers, conflicts among deities were believed to be mirrored by struggles among their human followers on Earth.

These struggles had eternal implications. At the end of life, one was to walk out upon a broad sword over a pit. If he had lived a life of good, he would cross safely to the other side. If not, the sword would turn edgewise and he would fall into a pit of fire and destruction.

The Jews who returned from the exile carried Zoroastrian imagery back to Israel. This imagery worked its way into Hebrew thought, and was also carried forward in Christian notions

---

[13]The remainder of Daniel was written later.

of good and evil, heaven and hell. However, neither Judaism nor Christianity is a dualistic faith. Unlike the Zoroastrian system of duality, the God and Satan of monotheism are not on equal footing.

The late C.S. Lewis, professor of Medieval and Renaissance literature at Cambridge, is perhaps better known as a writer of Christian apologetics and the author of the Christian fantasy, *The Narnia Chronicles*. Lewis had considerable respect for the ancient Zoroastrian faith, which he describes in his book, *Mere Christianity*. He observed that calling one of the dualistic gods "good" and the other "evil" presupposes that they are both measured against some higher, even ultimate, standard. It is at the point of that standard, where good and evil are fully defined, that we meet the monotheistic God of the Judeo-Christian tradition. And, it is because of our individual and collective understanding of that ultimate standard, that we know to call one way "good" and the other way "evil."

C.S. Lewis illustrates this point by treating evil as something that does not have independent vitality; that is parasitic. He argues that most examples of sin are, at heart, distortions of good. The desire to provide comfort and protection to oneself and one's loved ones—a good thing—becomes sinful when money becomes our god. More subtly, it also becomes sinful when we enjoy the benefits of security, but do not strive to extend that security to others outside of our closest kin. The passion and attraction that lead to love, marriage, and procreation—also good things—can be distorted into seduction of the weak by the strong, and into sexual abuse. Likewise, the desire to achieve and do one's best can be turned into puffed-up false pride. Sin takes a good thing and distorts it; it does not spring forth of its own volition. Considered this way, dualism mistakenly treats good and evil as symmetrical. Monotheism, however, calls that which is Godly "good," and that which distorts or attacks God's goodness as "evil." God's way transcends both labels.

To return more closely to the topic of the text, we see that astrologers, possibly practitioners of this dualistic Zoroastrian faith, step onto the scene while following a star. They are moving from their insightful, but limited, dualistic philosophy toward a transcendent conception of the divine. They are drawn to a light, and are "overwhelmed with joy" when they reach their destination (Matt. 2:10). This passage suggests that they have made the spiritual connection to the true God, beyond dualistic ideas of lesser deities, good and evil.

The Sign

Astronomers and scholars through the years have pondered what type of phenomenon might have been seen in the skies near the time of Christ's birth. We have already placed his birth toward the end of Herod the Great's reign in Israel, around 4 B.C., with a less probable date being closer to 6 A.D. Within five to ten years of the estimated range of dates for Christ's birth, a number of unusual celestial signs were seen. These included Halley's Comet's periodic visit to the skies above the Earth; the conjunction of Saturn and Jupiter low in the sky, creating a bright light; and the Mesori Star (meaning "Prince Star" in Egyptian, connoting a royal birth) rising at sunrise and displaying itself in a different fashion than normal. If this story is understood in a literal sense, it may be that the Magi witnessed one or more of these astronomical signs and were drawn toward Jerusalem.

These pagan philosophers observed the signs of nature and walked faithfully in the belief that they were being led toward one born to become the king of the Jews.[14] However, as they did not know the precise place where the child was to be born, they went to Jerusalem, the seat of religious and political authority, seeking that knowledge. Herod called his court priests, who were familiar with Old Testament prophecies concerning the birth of the Messiah. They confirmed that it was expected to occur in Bethlehem. Thus, Jewish tradition and Scripture provided a more substantial content to flesh out the general framework of theistic faith that the Magi already possessed.

The Gifts

The Magi are reported to have brought gifts of gold, frankincense, and myrrh to the Christ child. Each gift was of high value, rare and precious. And each held a certain symbolic significance. Gold was a gift fit for royalty. Beautiful and incorruptible, it was a currency accepted throughout the Mediterranean world. Frankincense was a gift fit for a high priest. It was the pure incense used in temple worship to please God. Myrrh was a gift fit for one who is to die. It was the perfume used in preparing the body for burial. All were extravagant, and none were

---

[14]In an episode of Luke-Acts, Saint Paul affirms an understanding of the divine nature being apparent through such a general revelation. See Paul's speech to the men of Athens in Acts 17.

particularly suited for a child. And so, the gifts the Magi bring in the birth narrative fore-shadow the royal, priestly, and sacrificial identity of the adult Christ.

The Title

When in Herod's court, the wise men ask where is the one born "King of the Jews." These mysterious Gentiles appear in the opening chapters of Matthew and ascribe an exalted title to Jesus at the very beginning of his life. It is a title that will be repeated in Holy Week by another Gentile who appears at the end of Christ's life. Then, Pontius Pilate will nail the words "King of the Jews" on an executioner's cross at Golgotha.

The Future

The Magi also foreshadow the extension of Matthew's church mission. If Gentiles came from the East at the time of the child's birth to pay him homage—while "all of Jerusalem" responded with fear rather than joy—could it be that the Christian message is intended not only for Matthew's predominately Jewish Christian audience, but also for the Gentile world as well? Matthew's birth narrative sows the seeds for justifying an extension of that mission to the Gentiles. The seeds will come to full bloom in the Great Commission, the final verses of the gospel, where the risen Christ sends apostles out to make disciples of all nations.

The biblical story of the Magi ends with them still attuned to the spiritual world. They are warned in a dream to go home by a different route, instead of honoring Herod's request to bring him news of the child's location. Danger looms in Herod's shadow. The conflict of kingdoms begins. Still walking in faith, the wise men follow the counsel of dreams, and evade Herod's trap.

The Traditions

Many traditions have sprung up around the story of the Magi. While their precise number is not mentioned, an early belief was that there were two astrologers. Later, the number went as high as twelve, perhaps representing the twelve disciples or the twelve tribes of the new Israel. The final number settled by church tradition was three, corresponding to the number of gifts given.

Other traditions around the Magi include naming their places of origin. We have already tentatively placed them in Persia (modern-day Iran), or in Arabia, both of which are east of Jerusalem. Another tradition is that they were from different places: Arabia, India, and Persia, all located in the East. Artistic renderings show yet another tradition, with each of the Magi displaying different skin color and other physical traits. This suggests that one is of Asian descent, another of African, and a third of European.

These Magi are among the most mysterious characters who present themselves in the Bible. Whether they are real people, or are symbolic of God in Christ being available to all humanity, we do not know. Yet, whether real, symbolic, or both, their connection to the spiritual world and their willingness to abandon their comfortable surroundings and venture far into the realm of the unknown is a lasting model for our own faith journey. As we, too, venture beyond the known and into the unknown, we can take from this story that God is available to all who seek him.

In "Journey of the Magi," the poet T.S. Eliot speaks with the voice of one of the wise men, who had, years before, gone through this hard and difficult journey—seeing both death and life—and returned home to an "alien people clutching at their foreign gods." He longs for fulfillment of the Epiphany promise that, even in the midst of darkness and suffering, God offers a light to transform a sick, battered and broken world. So let it be with us.

1. The wise men from the East are not practitioners of the Jewish faith. But they accept what the Jewish leadership of Herod's court does not—the place of Jesus in God's saving action. Does that insight tell us something about remaining open to God's revelation and grace outside our own religious institutions?

2. Not only Joseph—a Jew descended from David—but also pagan wise men from the East, respond to dreams. Does God speak to us in dreams? How can we tell?

3. The sign to the unsophisticated shepherds was simple. The sign to the sophisticated wise men was ethereal. Does this mean God meets us where we are? Do you have examples from your own personal experiences?

4. This section speaks of the influence that another religious tradition, Zoroastrianism, might have had on Judaic thought. Does the story imply that Christians should be open to the faith experience of other peoples? Do we lose our particular call when we are? Or, do we gain other insights into the experience of God when peering through a different lense?

5. The pericopes studied in this chapter immerse us in questions of literal versus literary approaches to Scripture. Are there points where we are able to wade in the waters of both? Those with more mystical leanings can thrive in the ambiguity. Others tend to get caught up in historical speculation. We have to remind ourselves to give the left hemisphere of the brain a rest, and let the right one work for a while.

6. The rector at my home church, an exceptionally able clergyman, speaks of a willingness to die in some ditches, but not in others. What he is talking about is differentiating between our core religious and ethical principles and those which hold a lesser claim. But he doesn't give easy solutions, leaving it up to individual conscience to decide which principles are critical to one's own faith life. Can you identify some set points to which you must hold? Are there others where you are more flexible? Can you know whether you have chosen the right ones? Are those choices, once made, still open to change through growth? And, more to the point, in which ditches are you willing to die?

†††

CHAPTER SEVEN

From Bethlehem to Nazareth: A Transitional Journey

Both Luke and Matthew locate the birth of Jesus in Bethlehem, permanently linking his entry into the world to the area where the Messiah was expected to appear. Both evangelists imbued their stories with signs that require their audiences, from the earliest pages, to seriously consider what they represent about the identity and mission of the child.

With these important lines of connection drawn to the Old Order regarding the birth of the Messiah, the evangelists' task now is to continue to tell their stories in a way that not only relocates the child from Bethlehem of Judea to Nazareth of Galilee, but also expands on the themes already begun. Matthew and Luke could have just written a brief summary about Joseph and Mary eventually taking the baby to Nazareth, without providing anything that enlightens or leads us in some worthy direction. Fortunately, though, both authors recorded traditions that impart to us something much richer and deeper.

In Luke's case, the road from Bethlehem to Nazareth will be marked with celebration and solemn reflection. In Matthew's, it will be marked with catastrophe and hope. Each author will depict transitional journeys from birth toward adulthood in ways that leave lasting impressions on us all.

✝ LUKE 2:21–24 **Jesus Is Presented and Circumcised at the Temple**

> **21After eight days had passed, it was time to circumcise the child; and he was called Jesus, the name given by the angel before he was conceived in the womb. 22When the time came for their purification according to the law of Moses, they brought him up to Jerusalem to present him to the Lord 23(as it is written in the law of the Lord, "Every firstborn male shall be designated as holy to the Lord"), 24and they offered a sacrifice according to what is stated in the law of the Lord, "a pair of turtledoves or two young pigeons."**

1. Luke, a Gentile, goes to considerable lengths to describe the Holy Family's observance of Jewish law. What might be his purpose?

The Rites of Circumcision and Purification

Bethlehem was located about six miles from Jerusalem, the site of the temple. Going from one place to the other was not as difficult a journey as the earlier one, from Nazareth to Bethlehem, which Luke has already described. Nonetheless, it required the considerable efforts of Joseph and Mary, who were now charged with the responsibility of caring for a newborn around whom such great expectations hovered that it caused angels to sing. They make this further trip, even though they are already away from what Luke tells us is their home. They live without proper lodging in circumstances that can hardly be described as comfortable, or even normal. That they make the journey from Bethlehem to the Jerusalem Temple proves their devotion to the Judaic law, and their commitment to following the path that they believe they have been called to walk. In this way, we see that Joseph and Mary, like Zechariah and Elizabeth, are "righteous."

Would Luke, our gentile evangelist, have offered this account had he not strongly believed that it was essential to maintain a connection to Judaic tradition? Perhaps this is his way of honoring the ancient people of God, even as he proclaims his story to a new people—previous strangers to Jewish ways.

Luke describes some of the Jewish customs and legal requirements. The circumcision of a boy was to occur at eight-days old, an ancient rite dating back to Genesis. This practice had its roots in the story of God giving Abram a new name, Abraham, and establishing circumcision as marking a male's entry into the covenant community (Gen. 17:9–14). By presenting Jesus at the temple for circumcision, Mary and Joseph honor the old ways and assure the child's place in the community.

The circumcision requirement, and the requirement of a woman's purification after giving birth, were codified at Leviticus 12:1–8:

¹The Lord spoke to Moses, saying:

²Speak to the people of Israel, saying: If a woman conceives and bears a male child, she shall be ceremonially unclean seven days; as at the time of her menstruation, she shall be unclean. ³On the eighth day the flesh of his foreskin shall be circumcised. ⁴Her time of blood purification shall be thirty-three days; she shall not touch any holy thing, or come into the sanctuary, until the days of her purification are completed. ⁵If she bears a female child, she shall be unclean two weeks, as in her menstruation; her time of blood purification shall be sixty-six days.

⁶When the days of her purification are completed, whether for a son or for a daughter, she shall bring to the priest at the entrance of the tent of meeting a lamb in its first year for a burnt offering, and a pigeon or a turtledove for a sin offering. ⁷He shall offer it before the Lord, and make atonement on her behalf; then she shall be clean from her flow of blood. This is the law for her who bears a child, male or female. ⁸If she cannot afford a sheep, she shall take two turtledoves or two pigeons, one for a burnt offering and the other for a sin offering; and the priest shall make atonement on her behalf, and she shall be clean.

†††

Though only the mother was obligated to participate in the post-natal purification ritual, Luke speaks of "their" purification. Luke, a Gentile, may have misunderstood these technical requirements of the Hebrew law as being applicable to more than just the mother. Yet, his report serves as a reminder, inadvertent or otherwise, that the care of a child and participation in religious observance are more complete when the family as a whole participates.

Luke also treats the purification and circumcision dates as occurring simultaneously. Here, as well, he demonstrates a less-than-complete familiarity with the Levitical law. The quoted OT text shows that the new mother's purification ritual was to occur forty days after the birth of a male child. The baby's circumcision was to take place only eight days after his birth. Hence, the two rites were separated by a number of weeks.

There may be one more error to consider before completing what could become a tedious legal analysis. Jesus was presented and dedicated to God, as required of a first-born male. However, the law provided that such a child was to be "redeemed"—or "bought back," as Professor Culpepper says—for five shekels of silver (Num. 18:15–16). There is no mention of the redemption payment in Luke's summary. The failure to mention it, though, does not necessarily mean the payment wasn't made. Since Mary and Joseph are depicted as observant Jews, we may assume they discharged their obligations under the law to the extent of their ability. It is likely that such a payment was made, though the text does not mention it.[1]

And, this notion of doing what they are able also tells us a little more about the Holy Family. Luke reports that the offering made for Mary's purification was a "pair of turtledoves or two young pigeons," tracking the OT edict of the new mother making a burnt offering and a sin offering, and the priest making atonement. Mary's offering is the one allowed the poor, as two additional birds were a considerably less expensive sacrifice than a lamb, the preferred burnt offering for those who could afford it. Again, we see Luke identifying Jesus with the poor, not the rich.

1. We have observed here how Luke, a Gentile, shows an imperfect understanding of the Judaic law. Yet, he honors that tradition to the extent of the knowledge and ability he does possess. Does Luke's approach teach us something about effort rather than perfection? About the limits of knowledge? Does it tell us something about

---

[1]Alternatively, one might argue that the omission is intentional—Jesus is not "bought back" because his consecration to God is complete. This interpretation, though theologically sound, is historically suspect. Since Luke has not shown a thorough knowledge of the details of Judaic law, it is fairly likely that he is unaware of the redemption provision, which is found in another book of the Hebrew Bible.

reaching beyond our own cultural conditioning and seeking common ground with other communities? How can we achieve these goals?

2. Luke's imperfect descriptions of Old Testament law show that the Bible is not completely consistent internally. Does that knowledge tend to weaken the basis of your faith? If so, can that "weakness" be turned into a strength? For instance, does the fact that even an evangelist can make a few mistakes, and still get his book in the Bible, liberate you in your own interpretive efforts? Can it help you to risk being wrong, knowing that God is more concerned with your conscientious commitment than with your unerring knowledge?

†[†]†

✝ LUKE 2:25–40 Jesus Is Blessed and Proclaimed

²⁵Now there was a man in Jerusalem whose name was Simeon; this man was righteous and devout, looking forward to the consolation of Israel, and the Holy Spirit rested on him. ²⁶It had been revealed to him by the Holy Spirit that he would not see death before he had seen the Lord's Messiah. ²⁷Guided by the Spirit, Simeon came into the temple; and when the parents brought in the child Jesus, to do for him what was customary under the law, ²⁸Simeon took him in his arms and praised God, saying,

> ²⁹"Master, now you are dismissing your servant in peace, according to your word;

> ³⁰for my eyes have seen your salvation, ³¹which you have prepared in the presence of all peoples,

> ³²a light for revelation to the Gentiles and for glory to your people Israel."

³³**And the child's father and mother were amazed at what was being said about him.** ³⁴**Then Simeon blessed them and said to his mother Mary,**

> *"This child is destined for the falling and the rising of many in Israel, and to be a sign that will be opposed*
>
> ³⁵*so that the inner thoughts of many will be revealed—and a sword will pierce your own soul too."*

³⁶**There was also a prophet, Anna the daughter of Phanuel, of the tribe of Asher. She was of a great age, having lived with her husband seven years after her marriage,** ³⁷**then as a widow to the age of eighty-four. She never left the temple but worshiped there with fasting and prayer night and day.** ³⁸**At that moment she came, and began to praise God and to speak about the child to all who were looking for the redemption of Jerusalem.**

³⁹**When they had finished everything required by the law of the Lord, they returned to Galilee, to their own town of Nazareth.** ⁴⁰**The child grew and became strong, filled with wisdom; and the favor of God was upon him.**

1. Two aged people, a man and a woman, pronounce great things about the child. What about their statements and actions seem most significant to you?

2. Simeon links the role of the child in fulfilling God's saving action both to Israel and to the Gentiles. What does this suggest about the way the child's life will be lived?

3. And what of Anna? She speaks of the redemption of Israel, but is silent as to the Gentiles. Might Luke be trying to remind his gentile audience of something when reporting this part of the story?

†††

Blessings and Honors Bestowed

The attention that the prophetess Anna and the aged Simeon, infused with the Holy Spirit, lavish upon the baby Jesus is far more remarkable than the Holy Family's compliance with Judaic law. These two venerable characters appear to be among those that the late William Barclay, Scottish scholar, biblical interpreter, and professor at the University of Glasgow, describes as "the Quiet in the Land," a group who waited on God's gentle saving action, instead of expecting a war-like Messiah to restore Israel's fortunes. It is these practitioners of patience, virtue, and prayerfulness who witness God's instrument of salvation entering the world, even while others may look and listen, but not see and hear.

With Simeon's blessing of the child, we turn our attention to the ancient hymn the Church has called the *Nunc Dimittis*, often sung in religious communities at night before retiring.[2] It is both joyful and foreboding. Triumph is found in God's salvation, "prepared in the presence of all people." The hymn also speaks of ushering in profound change, as the child will precipitate the fall and rise of many, and the soul of the mother herself will be cut like a sword.

Yet, even in these words of forewarning, the abiding image is one of peace—for Simeon in particular—and for the salvation of the people, their delivery from danger, and their journey toward restoration. The baby will embody God's salvation. He will be a light to the Gentiles, perhaps also to the Roman oppressor, perhaps even to Luke's audience.

The words of the *Nunc Dimittis* inspired T. S. Eliot to write the poem, *A Song for Simeon*, reflecting the aged man's long faith journey and anticipating what is to come, which Simeon himself will not see. It closes like this:

> According to thy word.
>
> They shall praise Thee and suffer in every generation
>
> With glory and derision,
>
> Light upon light, mounting the saints' stair.
>
> Not for me the martyrdom, the ecstasy of thought and prayer,
>
> Not for me the ultimate vision.
>
> Grant me thy peace.

[2]This is the fourth ancient hymn in Luke's birth narrative. We have looked closely at the fist two, the *Magnificat* and the *Benedictus*. We have also read the third hymn, called the *Gloria*, which the heavenly host sang to the shepherds on the night of the nativity.

(And a sword shall pierce thy heart,

Thine also).

I am tired with my own life and the lives of those after me,

I am dying in my own death and the deaths of those after me.

Let thy servant depart,

Having seen thy salvation.

Simeon has reached his fulfillment, and has seen God's salvation. But it is not without cost. Many will fall and rise, and God's salvation—instead of being uniformly recognized—will be opposed in some quarters.[3] We do not yet see what Mary will suffer; only that she will. We do not yet see how the light will shine on the Gentiles; only that it will. We do not yet see who will be brought high or made low; only that the world will be turned upside down. We love Simeon's images, even though we do not yet understand them fully, and we rejoice with him on the occasion of his peaceful departure.

A Proclamation

Luke also tells us of the prophetess Anna, who appears in the temple at the conclusion of Simeon's blessing. If we look beneath the surface, we see more in this short description than what initially meets the eye.

First, let us make note that Luke pairs Simeon's epiphany with Anna's proclamations about the baby. Luke previously paired Zechariah's and Mary's encounters with Gabriel. He repeats the pattern of introducing male and female characters with similar experiences, validating the prominent place of both in the Jesus movement. Luke is subtly egalitarian, not willing to cling too closely to the patriarchal ideas that prevailed in the first-century world; ideas which are sometimes reflected in New Testament writings outside the Lukan tradition.[4]

---

[3]As we shall see, that opposition will principally take root among the powerful. But all (including us) share a measure of responsibility for our obstinate resistance to the way of the kingdom of God.

[4]See, in particular, the letters to Timothy and Titus. These "pastoral letters," along with passages from other works attributed to Paul (but which most mainline scholars regard as having been written by some later figure) disclose some gender-based hierarchies. Such texts are best understood as reflecting church order in certain early Christian communities. We have no reason to believe that these systems were generally applicable in all churches then, much less that they are normative or mandatory for gender roles among Christians today.

We may also hypothesize about why Luke records Anna's age. She is described as having been married seven years —the number of fullness, as we have already seen in studying Matthew's gospel. Eighty-four years of her life are also noted. This number is the product of seven times twelve. The number seven is found yet again. The number twelve is also filled with symbolic significance. There were twelve tribes of Israel; twelve books of the minor prophets; and twelve disciples specially commissioned and sent out as apostles. By going to pains to report these numbers, Luke may be telling us that Anna is whole and holy, and that we should therefore pay attention to what she has to say. When a number is used in the Bible, especially in a revelatory setting, it is often highly significant.

Finally, let us observe how Anna serves as an archetype. Her name is similar to and has the same root as Hannah, the OT character upon whose life we touched when examining the connections between the birth of her son, Samuel, and the Lukan nativity. Both women's names mean "grace." Both are found in settings where a child is consecrated to the Lord. Both are examples of faithful observance. Our New Testament Anna connects us to Hannah of the Old Order, and also serves as a model for Christian living. She is a prophet, one who proclaims God's word.[5] She is also a model of devotion and commitment, even with the eccentricities or calling that kept her always in the temple "with fasting and prayer night and day."

With Joseph and Mary having satisfied the legal requirements associated with the birth of a child, and Simeon and Anna having proclaimed his identity, their time in Judea is finished. The family returns to Nazareth in Galilee, where "[t]he child grew and became strong, filled with wisdom; and the favor of God was upon him." For Luke, the transitional journey is complete. He will resume his story of Jesus in twelve years.

---

[5]Anna's function as a prophet tells us that, from early Christian traditions, women were prominent both in deed and word. Authentic letters of Paul (as distinguished from those which, in later times, were written in his name) describe women as prophets and apostles. It was only later that the Church limited women's scope of function, citing as its justification legalistic-sounding texts that arose out of some (but not all) strands of the Christian movement. Why, when it comes to defining proper behavior, do some people consider the passages of the Bible that portray the stories of people's lives in a good and holy way as being secondary to those passages that sound like a rule book? One cannot help but think it is grounded in ideas of reward and punishment. "If I follow the rules, all will go well. If I break them, I will suffer."

Poetry and Evangelism

We have twice made reference to the works of T. S. Eliot. In the opinion of many, Eliot was the greatest poet of the twentieth century. He was born an American, but lived as an expatriate in England. Eliot, who was rather fussy, disdained American earthiness and ruggedness. His spiritual journey took him from an agnostic inclination through a religious conversion that led him to become a High Church Anglican. There is no suggestion that either his conversion, or his faith life, bore much resemblance to popular piety. An arch conservative, Eliot is often pictured formally dressed, with patrician appearance and demeanor.

Yet, in his poetry, Eliot speaks to others whose orientation is quite different. For example, I consider myself to be a thoroughly patriotic middle-class American, more low, or broad, church than high, and more sympathetic to inclusive ideas than elitist ones. Yet, when Eliot writes, I find myself enthralled.

Why? Perhaps it is because Eliot's perspective on the Christian story transcends differences, unites what is disparate, draws the reader into a closer connection with the first observers of God's work in Christ. In his own way, T. S. Eliot was an evangelist.

1. The stories of Simeon and Anna connect the Old Order and the New. They unite male and female, young and old, Jew and Gentile, around Jesus. How can we build on this work that they have begun?

2. Simeon and Anna are exemplars of those who have given their lives fully to God. Many of us are bound by familial and other obligations that those Quiet in the Land may not have had. Even so, can we still find ways to emulate them?

3. The temple is featured favorably, in this pericope, as the center of worship. The identity of Jesus is affirmed and confirmed in it. The temple also receives this treatment elsewhere in Luke-Acts. Yet, the other Synoptics and John do not contain favorable depictions. In fact, some scholars interpret Jesus' final conflict with the authorities during Holy Week in Mark as culminating in the "disqualification" of the temple from further service. *See*, particularly, *Mark's Story of Jesus,*

by Professor Werner Kelber of Rice University. What is the reason for this disparate treatment? Is there some conflict for which the temple serves as a lightning rod? Do we experience similar conflict around institutions today? How do we resolve it?

†††

Luke leaves us with a joyful scene at the temple. He tells us that, after the child is eight days old, the family goes back to Nazareth. Matthew, however, takes us to places where we do not want to go.

✝ MATTHEW 2:13–23   The Flight into Egypt, the Slaughter of the Holy Innocents, and the Journey to Nazareth

¹³Now after [the wise men] had left, an angel of the Lord appeared to Joseph in a dream and said,

> *"Get up, take the child and his mother, and flee to Egypt, and remain there until I tell you; for Herod is about to search for the child, to destroy him."*

¹⁴Then Joseph got up, took the child and his mother by night, and went to Egypt, ¹⁵and remained there until the death of Herod. This was to fulfill what had been spoken by the Lord through the prophet, "Out of Egypt I have called my son."

¹⁶When Herod saw that he had been tricked by the wise men, he was infuriated, and he sent and killed all the children in and around Bethlehem who were two years old or under, according to the time that he had learned from the wise men. ¹⁷Then was fulfilled what had been spoken through the prophet Jeremiah:

> *¹⁸"A voice was heard in Ramah,*
>
> *wailing and loud lamentation,*
>
> *Rachel weeping for her children;*
>
> *she refused to be consoled,*
>
> *because they are no more."*

¹⁹When Herod died, an angel of the Lord suddenly appeared in a dream to Joseph in Egypt and said,

²⁰"Get up, take the child and his mother, and go to the land of Israel, for those who were seeking the child's life are dead."

²¹Then Joseph got up, took the child and his mother, and went to the land of Israel. ²²But when he heard that Archelaus was ruling over Judea in place of his father Herod, he was afraid to go there. And after being warned in a dream, he went away to the district of Galilee. ²³There he made his home in a town called Nazareth, so that what had been spoken through the prophets might be fulfilled, "He will be called a Nazorean."

When we were last with Saint Matthew, he told us of wise men from the East having journeyed to see the Christ Child. They followed their astrological arts to the limit of their distance, and, near the end, also needed the guidance of Scripture. Upon completion of their journey, they were warned to go home by another route so that Herod would not know the child's location, and so that the baby would avoid the reprisals Herod intended to inflict on the one who would be king. They followed the counsel of their dreams, and went home without reporting to Herod. Now we will see what is left in the wake of their departure.

1. The wise men have not betrayed the location of the baby to Herod. The Holy Family escapes when Joseph responds to a dream. But those left in Bethlehem reap the whirlwind. What is the meaning of this troubling passage?

2. We have seen how both Joseph and the wise men respond to dreams. Do we take dreams seriously today? Why (not)?

3. The text implies that Joseph had lived in Bethlehem, and only moved to "the district of Galilee," where he "made his home in a town called Nazareth" after being warned. How does this differ from Luke's version? What significance (if any) do those differences hold for our current belief systems?

4. This passage contains three examples of Matthew's prophecy/fulfillment pattern. We will see in the commentary section how these hold together more firmly from a literary rather than a literal perspective. You may wish to keep such an interpretation in mind when reading these texts.

In the World of a Tyrant

Joseph again heeds the message of a dream. He is told to take Mary and Jesus to Egypt in order to avoid the coming violence. The conflict-of-kingdoms theme that Professor Boring describes is brought to a sharp point here, as the powerful persecute the weak in order to maintain their privileges and priorities.

Herod the Great feeds a dark wrath that leads to mass infanticide. If we chalk his behavior up to simply being the result of an evil and depraved heart, we can miss a direct warning to us. Before jumping to simple characterizations, let us first read this segment against the context of his life as a whole. At times, Herod had been a wise and prudent ruler who protected his

The Holy Family's Flight into Egypt
(circa 4 B.C.E.)

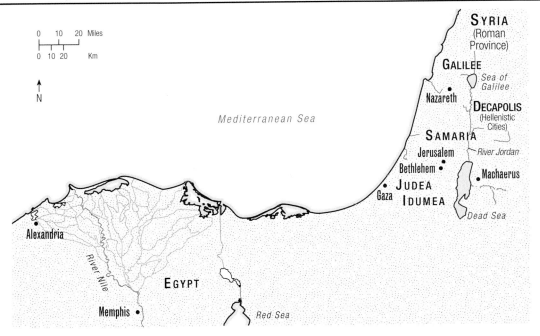

people from economic and other distress, and brought order out of chaos. Herod emerged victorious out of a struggle for the throne, and thereafter maintained the peace. According to various commentators on Matthew, he often ruled wisely, expanding and renovating the temple, remitting taxes when times were difficult, and melting his own gold to fund the growth of his people's crops.

Yet, he was also a case study in the corrosive effects of power. Herod became a paranoid personality who desperately grasped at, and held onto, power by whatever means necessary. On more than one occasion, he caused the deaths of scores of his own people, mostly the Jewish leadership. He ordered the murder of the Sanhedrin—the highest judicial body—and, at the end of his life, killed many of the Jewish leaders in Jerusalem. Herod also killed his wife, and two of his sons, leading Augustus to observe that it was safer to be his pig than a member of his family.[6]

While there is no historical record outside Matthew for Herod having killed all children under the age of two in a particular locale, a gap of this nature in the record is not surprising. Brutes through the ages have inflicted their will on the weak; it has not always been considered "newsworthy." Moreover, the frequency and extent of Herod's vindictive measures and cruelty leave little room to doubt that Herod was ready, willing and able to take this type of action in order to maintain his grip, and the grip of his surviving family members, on the throne. Even those scholars who view the account of Herod slaughtering the Holy Innocents, not as an historical fact, but as a literary composition echoing the story of Pharaoh killing the Hebrew children, do not question his capacity for this sort of atrocity.[7] It was beyond dispute.

A point of the story is that, despite the barriers the wicked may put in the way, God's will perseveres. We see this idea confirmed in Matthew's citations to the Old Testament references, which can be read almost as a commentary on the events Matthew describes. Though much agony is inflicted, Herod's plot does not work. Joseph, who faithfully responds to a dream, takes Mary and the child to Egypt. As in the OT story of Moses, God continues to work his purposes out, even in the face of fierce opposition.

In the 1,200–1,300 years that passed between scholarly estimates of the date of the Hebrews' escape from Pharaoh's kingdom and the birth of Christ, Egypt, that great civilization west of the Red Sea, had become a more hospitable place for Israelites. The city of Alexandria

---

[6]The implication is that, with Jewish prohibitions against eating swine, a pig was safe, but a family member might easily be slaughtered.

[7]A substantial body of scholarly thought views Matthew's story through the OT lens of the story of Moses. Using this approach, Matthew's Jesus is regarded as the new Moses, leading the covenant community toward its destiny in the same way that the original Moses led Israel out of bondage in Egypt. This approach to Matthew's gospel is discussed in more detail in the next chapter.

served as a place of retreat for Jews in distress. It has been estimated that as many as one million Jews lived in Alexandria at around the time of Jesus; they had left other areas to seek refuge there. It is to this haven that Joseph takes his family.

Connections to the Past, According to Matthew

The story of the flight into Egypt, the slaughter of the Holy Innocents, and the return, form part of Matthew's literary pattern. In it, we find a number of citations to the OT that serve better as symbolic references than as a concrete prophecy/fulfillment link. In one case, the citations are actually non-existent. Matthew borrows liberally from Old Testament descriptions of past events, interpreting them as Messianic prophecies that are fulfilled by Jesus. This serves to connect his Jewish Christian community to the old ways.

The first Old Testament reference in this section—that of God calling his son out of Egypt—is chapter 11 of the book Hosea. This passage describes, in the past tense, how God had already delivered Israel from slavery and bondage in Egypt. Yet, she rebelled and followed the pagan god and idol, Baal. In this way, Hosea describes how Israel's emergence from Egypt is followed by the desertion of her own religion—the opposite of what we associate with the coming of the Messiah. This passage of Hosea was not generally considered to be a Messianic prophecy. Matthew has chosen it to employ his favored literary device of the echo effect,[8] an approach in keeping with the Rabbinic practice of *midrash*.

The citation to the OT passage about Rachel weeping over her children is also a connection with past events, and becomes a prophecy of the Messianic era by the memories it evokes. Found in Jeremiah 31, the passage speaks to the Babylonian exile, where the image is given of Rachel, long dead, now weeping over her exiled children. In Jeremiah's context, it is not a prophecy about a future slaughter in Bethlehem, but about the events of his own time. Matthew, like Jeremiah before him, uses Rachel as an image from the past, but now to mourn the murdered children of Bethlehem. There is a little glimmer of hope in Jeremiah, though, as the return of her children to the Holy Land is promised. A return is also found in Matthew's story.

Finally, Matthew makes reference to a prophecy about Joseph taking the family—not back to Bethlehem, where the text implies he had lived—but to Nazareth, a new place, in order to fulfill the promise that the Messiah will be called a "Nazorean." The explanation is that the

---

[8]*See* the section on The Rabbi's Journey, chapter 2, at p. 31, *supra*.

family needed to avoid the Judaic reign of Herod's son, Archelaus.[9] If nothing else, this passage suggests that Joseph had great good sense. Archelaus possessed all his father's brutality, and none of his competence. He killed 3,000 influential Israelites upon his ascent to power. Rome removed him from his position because of that brutality and incompetence, and resumed direct rule over Judea. There is ample historical justification for steering clear of such a powerful, incompetent and vicious man, and for staying away from Judea itself. After the death of Herod the Great, Judea became enmeshed in civil unrest. And, we shall see, when we look more closely at life in what Matthew calls "the district of Galilee," it was as good a place to go as any.

Beyond the historical conditions we have described, we also see Matthew make a specific connection to Nazareth. He fashions a prophecy/fulfillment link to it, just as he has to Bethlehem— but it takes some creative work. The principal reason is that no scholars studying the Bible over the last 1,900 years have found any reference to Nazareth, or to a Nazorean, in the OT. It appears either that Matthew has made a mistake (not having the benefit of the printing press; a bound Bible divided into books, chapters and verses; a concordance; or a CD-ROM); or, perhaps, he has made a play on words. The similar-sounding OT term "Nazarite" refers not to a person from a particular locality, but to one who is set apart, as Samson and Samuel were. We see in the life of Jesus someone set aside, consecrated for a particular mission. This could be what Matthew means. Alternatively, the similar-sounding OT term "Nezer" does not refer to a place, but means "branch." It is sometimes used to pertain to the branch of Jesse, the father of David. If Jesse is the root, then, through his son, David, Jesse has many familial branches, including the one where we find the Messiah. Matthew, who has already declared Jesus to be the Son of David, may very well be using a play on words to identify Jesus with the great OT tradition that included Nazarites and Nezer.

With this knowledge about how Matthew has used the Old Testament, we have several choices. Option A is to fret over the uses Matthew makes of Scripture because he is not as literal-minded and clear as we would like him to be. Option B is to set it all aside and pay no attention to Matthew's ideas of prophecy and fulfillment on the grounds of historical unreliability. Option C is to stick our heads in the sand, pretend that the problems don't exist, and insist on a literal understanding of this segment even though it is not compatible with basic intellectual honesty. Option D is to interpret these particular passages, not in a literal

---

[9]As we saw in the last chapter, a common position among mainline scholars is that the family was originally from Nazareth, and that the Bethlehem nativities were composed to make a connection to Micah's prophecy of the Messianic era. Luke has Mary and Joseph travel from Nazareth to Bethlehem. In Matthew, it seems, they already lived in Bethlehem, and the child was born at home. Having acknowledged that point, we focus here more on the story as told.

way, but rather in a literary way as a connection between the Old Testament and the New Covenant in Jesus. With Option D, the memories of the Old Testament carry forth. Their echo effect can help us to hear the story of Jesus more clearly.

A Theological Problem with Matthew's Story

Some commentators believe that there is a latent problem with the theology of the story of the slaughter of the Holy Innocents. The issue is framed in this way: If Joseph were warned in a dream to leave, but many other families were left behind for their children to be slaughtered, then what does that say about God? Does it make him single-minded, lacking compassion toward the families of Bethlehem? Does it make him powerless to stop the slaying of the others? Or, does it even make him complicit in the murder of the children left behind because he intervened on behalf of one, but not on behalf of the rest, when he had the ability to do so? Does this problem of what appears to be selective beneficence hold true whenever one person receives some form of divine grace, while others similarly situated do not?

Professor Boring addresses this issue articulately and thoroughly in his *New Interpreter's Bible* commentary on Matthew, even telling a story from the perspective of the other families of Bethlehem to force us to confront the problem. In the spirit of that work, let us first eliminate the shallow rationalizations Boring identifies. Some would rationalize that, had all the people of Bethlehem been warned in a dream and fled, Herod would have discerned a mass movement of people and hunted them all down. Another rationalization is that the other people did receive a warning, but only Joseph heeded it. A particularly troubling corollary to this second approach is that the infant children —whose parents may have received a warning, but not heeded it, and who were of such tender years as to have utterly no control over their own destinies—suffered the extreme penalty for their parents' deafness. This notion is completely at odds with the Old Testament tradition, embodied in the latter prophets, particularly Ezekiel 18:1–4:

> The word of the Lord came to me: ²What do you mean by repeating this proverb concerning the land of Israel, "The parents have eaten sour grapes, and the children's teeth are set on edge"? ³As I live, says the Lord God, this proverb shall no more be used by you in Israel. ⁴Know that all lives are mine; the life of the parent as well as the life of the child is mine: it is only the person who sins that shall die.

The idea that innocent babes died due to the deafness of their parents would flout Ezekiel.

Both of these rationalizations are ultimately unsatisfying. They may help us get out of the moment, but they do not resolve the problem. As to the first, there is no indication that Herod would have been able to track every family down and have his orders executed to the same degree as could occur with all of them remaining present in Bethlehem. Moreover, this rationalization would take us entirely into the field of imagination, speculating about the breadth and length of Herod's reach as he chased down families in flight.[10]

The implications of the second rationalization are downright alarming. It assumes that all people received a similar warning and that the faithless failed to respond to it. Therefore, we blame the victims and make them responsible for their own suffering, all the while letting the world know that God did his doggone best. Is this the sort of piety we wish to cultivate? And what does it suggest about God's own competence?

If we look closely, we see how Matthew himself struggles with the issue. The prophecy/ fulfillment patterns in the other parts of the pericope involve events occurring either to fulfill the word of the Lord, or what the prophets have said. The idea seems to be that these events come to pass as part of a divine plan. However, the slaughter of the Holy Innocents reads a little differently. The explanatory language says, "Then was fulfilled what had been spoken through the prophet Jeremiah." It is passive; it does not make God, or his word, the initiator.

Having identified the problems, let us now look at a few alternatives to answer these difficult theological questions. One is that this story is not based on historical fact, but is an example of the echo effect. Over 1,200 years earlier, Pharaoh had slaughtered children to avoid a challenge to his reign, which was embodied in Moses. Now, Herod does the same. Therefore, the connection is literary, not literal. This interpretation gains considerable weight in our estimation if we closely examine the idea of Jesus as the new Moses, a theme developed more fully in the next chapter.

Another possibility (again, relying on Professor Boring), is that the story uses confessional language, not an objective report of what has actually occurred. God acted through Joseph to preserve Jesus for his future work, which was fundamental to the restoration of Israel and the redemption of humanity. The point of the story is not to ponder a report of events as if given by a detached and objective observer. The point is for the Matthean community to embrace

---

[10]The point of this statement is not to restrict our theological ponderings to the literal words of the Bible, unaided by history, tradition, reason, or imagination. Imagination plays a powerful role in faith life. After all, what was Jesus doing when telling parables, if not appealing to the imagination? The point is that when we conjure up inadequate rationalizations for a difficult text, we create a straw man to accept our burdens and carry them away so we don't have to deal with them, instead of trying to address the deeper theological questions that the text raises.

an authentic faith in God's redemptive purposes, which are inevitably going forward despite the most desperate and depraved opposition.

And a third possibility for responsible interpretation may be to gain a sense of grace out of tragedy. Divine signs had led the wise men to Bethlehem, unwittingly putting Herod on notice of a "rival." Herod, willful and wicked, upon learning of that "rival," would never begin to understand the nature of the kingdom he was to establish. Herod retained a God-given freedom to respond in whatever way he chose—and his response was unspeakably evil.

Joseph, too, was free. He could respond to the threats around him by fight, flight, or freezing in denial. Perhaps lying down to sleep with a sense of impending danger, he had a premonition, a foreboding embodied in a dream. He had no way of "knowing" that this was a message from God; he could have written it off as the nightmare of an anxious new father. But, acting on faith, he paid attention to the language that God was speaking to him, and led his family to safety.

One family is plucked out of the death march of human evil; others are not. But the family that escapes for now will be subjected to evil again later, as another generation of the powerful attempts to crush the hope of the weak. And, at the heart of the gospel story, that final confrontation will be transformed into true liberty.

On the Place of Dreams in Scripture

In Matthew, God communicates with Joseph and the wise men through a dream state. This form of communication is more difficult for us to internalize and accept than it was for people of antiquity. In ancient times, it was widely believed that God spoke to people through dreams. Joseph, the son of the great Old Testament figure Jacob, was reviled by his brothers but highly valued by the incumbent Pharaoh for his ability to experience and interpret prophetic dreams. The prophet Daniel earned the trust of the Babylonian ruler for his ability to interpret dreams; he also experienced his own dreams as God's revelation. The power of dreams was assumed; the ability to interpret them was honored. It is a tradition repeated in the New Testament, not only in Matthew, but also in Acts and Revelation.

Then, sadly, within a few hundred years after the birth of Christ, St. Jerome changed all of this.[11] While he made the Scriptures themselves more accessible to Roman citizens by translating

---

[11]For the following information about dreams generally, and the actions of St. Jerome particularly, I am indebted to Steve Davis, PhD., of Asheville, who shared this information with my adult Christian Education class.

them from Greek into Latin, the "vulgar" tongue (his translation became known as *The Vulgate*), St. Jerome also erected barriers that prevented the faithful from completely participating in the life of the church and the experience of the holy. He effectively eliminated dreams as a theologically acceptable means of communion with God by declaring that they were the result of evil influences. Jerome thereby strengthened the Pope's hand as the mediator between God and humankind, and as the authoritative interpreter of the will of God.

In later years, the Ecclesiastical authorities took their exclusive powers as intermediaries a step further by still using *The Vulgate* long after Latin was no longer the spoken tongue. Speaking Latin in the liturgy, while the laity spoke only the colloquial language, became a control system, eventually abandoned by Pope John XXIII in the Second Vatican Council of 1962–1965. It is difficult, if not impossible, to calculate the spiritual cost the world has incurred as a result of certain domineering clerics telling their flocks what are the "right" and "wrong" ways to experience God. Rather than trusting in the good and true emerging out of the free marketplace of ideas, the Church has often assumed the role of censor, establishing hierarchies to protect the positions of the powerful, and to perpetuate their own centrality to the experience of the Divine.

Some professionals with expertise in depth psychology urge a reconsideration of dreams as a means of communication with God. It is even argued that all dreams are messages from God, or at least reveal something of that aspect of the Divine that dwells deep within us and moves us toward the true selves we are called to be. Whether we accept this proposition or not is a function of our own knowledge and understanding, and, like Joseph, of our own free will.

If we are willing to live with the possibility that our dreams can somehow move us in the direction of the Spirit, we can look to Joseph and the wise men as role models. We also have the balance of the biblical witness, there being no better example than Joel 2:28–29:

[28]Then afterward
I will pour out my spirit on all flesh;
your sons and your daughters shall prophesy,
your old men shall dream dreams,
and your young men shall see visions.
[29]Even on the male and female slaves,
in those days, I will pour out my spirit.

Let us be open to the places where God might speak to us. Joseph, for example, was attuned to the world of dreams as a place where he might hear, deep within himself, the call of God. That call took him to great lengths, returning even to the land of ancestral bondage, but this time for the protection of those in his care.

1. We have seen how Herod the Great took his promise and ability and turned them toward unfathomable evil. Do we do better to attribute this solely to his bad character, or to consider its implications for our lives? Can our gifts be brought to bear, either in service to the kingdom of God or against it? Where in your life do you experience these challenges?

2. According to Matthew, the wise men innocently created the circumstances leading to destruction. Even in much less dramatic circumstances, how do we cope with those times when our well-intentioned actions lead to ill results?

3. Matthew's interpretation of Scripture, largely using the echo effect embodied in *midrash*, does not fit neatly into the cause-effect mentality of a scientific age. Does this difference affect our appreciation of what Matthew is trying to say? If so, how can we change to benefit from the message it contains?

4. This section argues against shallow rationalizations, and for a literary—rather than a literal—interpretation of many passages of Scripture. Is that approach itself a rationalization? Is it a byproduct of bringing modern mental disciplines to bear when considering ancient works? Or, is it likely that Matthew himself intended a literary, rather than a literal, understanding of his words? Lest we assume our forebears were too "unsophisticated" for this type of composition, let us remember that not only the Bible, but also such works as *The Iliad*, *The Odyssey*, the Greek comedies and tragedies, and *The Aeneid*, came out of this and earlier periods.

✝✝✝

✝✝✝

CHAPTER EIGHT

From Nazareth to the Jerusalem Temple: A Journey to Adulthood

Joseph, Mary and Jesus have successfully arrived in Nazareth of Galilee, where the Gospels tell us Jesus grew to manhood. We will read little of his journey to adulthood directly--one episode is all. But we can examine the influences that life in Nazareth may have had on Jesus. The information scholars can provide about life in first-century Galilee, and the world not far beyond it, will assist our looking at the adult Jesus from the perspective of his contemporaries. Then, we can better understand their reactions to a Mediterranean Jewish peasant proclaiming the kingdom of God with authority.

But for now, let us return to The Gospel According to Saint Luke for a childhood story. We will then explore some other traditions about Jesus, particularly as a child, and see how they relate to our present-day concerns. Finally, we will reconsider our two infancy narratives as a whole, offering a fresh perspective and interpretation of each.

✝ LUKE 2:41–52 Jesus Visits the Temple at Twelve Years

[41]Now every year his parents went to Jerusalem for the festival of the Passover. [42]And when he was twelve years old, they went up as usual for the festival. [43]When the festival was ended and they started to return, the boy Jesus stayed behind in Jerusalem, but his parents did not know it. [44]Assuming that he was in the group of travelers, they went a day's journey. Then they started to look for him among their relatives and friends.

[45]When they did not find him, they returned to Jerusalem to search for him. [46]After three days they found him in the temple, sitting among the teachers, listening to them and asking them questions. [47]And all who heard him were amazed at his understanding and his answers.

[48]When his parents saw him they were astonished; and his mother said to him,

"Child, why have you treated us like this? Look, your father and I have been searching for you in great anxiety."

[49]He said to them,

"Why were you searching for me? Did you not know that I must be in my Father's house?"

[50]But they did not understand what he said to them.

[51]Then he went down with them and came to Nazareth, and was obedient to them. His mother treasured all these things in her heart. [52]And Jesus increased in wisdom and in years, and in divine and human favor.

1. Nothing is mentioned about the time passing between the family's trip to Nazareth in the birth narrative and Jesus returning to the Jerusalem Temple at the age of twelve. How does it strike you that we know nothing of these years?

2. If you were reading this story for the first time, would it come as a shock that neither parent knew where the child was throughout the course of a day-long journey?

3. Is there any significance behind Luke reporting that it took Mary and Joseph three days to find their child? How about his description of the child's age?

4. What do you make of the interaction between Jesus and the teachers?

A Pilgrimage with a Twist

This passage reports that Jesus and his family were in the habit of going to Passover in Jerusalem each year. Passover was a major feast; those who could travel to Jerusalem were expected to participate there. Jerusalem's distance from Nazareth would have required the family to walk the better part of a week. As with a recent episode in Luke—the infant Jesus' presentation at the temple and the rites of purification and circumcision—the Holy Family's Passover observance in Jerusalem says something about them. Luke the Gentile uses it to show how Jesus' family was thoroughly Jewish, honoring the traditions of their people and observing religious festivals in the most proper way.[1]

And, we can safely assume that Jesus' age on this particular trip is critical to the meaning of the story. When the Bible uses a number, we need to look closely to see whether the story

---

[1] Some prominent scholars argue that Jesus' socio-economic status would have prevented him from coming to Jerusalem regularly, and that, as an historical matter, Holy Week may well have been the first time he was there. Obviously, this approach would exclude the trip to the temple at age twelve from the historical data bank. This sort of reliance upon information from the culture at large, which often casts considerable insight on the story of Jesus, can occasionally go too far. This hypothesis may be one such case.

Just because Jesus was probably poor, and may have even approached the destitute (a topic considered elsewhere in this series), does not mean that he (or others similarly situated) didn't make the pilgrimage to Jerusalem, at least occasionally. To exclude the possibility of him making this trip is to insist too strongly on corroborative evidence

is telling us more than first meets the eye. When we explore it in that light, we see that this is the story of Jesus' journey to adulthood, condensed into twelve verses.

Jewish boys celebrate entry into manhood upon completion of their thirteenth year, with the observance of their bar mitzvah. In the normal course leading toward that rite, twelve-year-old boys spend more time in the company of men, including their fathers, and study more seriously. It is a natural progression; and, it is precisely what Jesus is doing here. However, in his case we can observe a few twists. Jesus is not portrayed spending time with Joseph, but in the Jerusalem Temple, a place understood to be the home of his heavenly father rather than his earthly one. We also see his remarkable astuteness, as the teachers are "amazed" by his knowledge. Both developments signify something unique in Jesus' development.

When we see Jesus at age twelve, we are seeing him near the close of childhood proper, during a transitional period that will lead to him becoming a man. But he is not yet there; he is still a child, still grappling with a shift in identity. And so, he goes to Jerusalem to celebrate the foundational event of Israel's history: the Passover. It is the time each year that the Jews remember God's favor resting upon them and Moses having led them to liberation from bondage, breaking free of Pharaoh and the oppression of Egypt. While other festivals may have been more solemn—Yom Kippur, for instance, the Day of Atonement, when the High Priest made expiation for the sins of the people—Passover may well have been the favorite.[2]

After celebrating Passover, Luke tells us, Mary and Joseph departed Jerusalem with the homeward-bound Nazareth clan. At the end of the day, they are stricken with anxiety to learn that Jesus is not among them, and return to Jerusalem to search for him. After three days,[3] they finally find the child and express their understandable displeasure to him. Jesus, however, is

---

before taking an event as true. It is an overly rigorous method, transforming something altogether reasonable on its face—such as that even a poor Jewish family would occasionally go to Jerusalem—into the historically suspect.

However, there is a considerable distance between saying that Jesus probably did go visit Jerusalem from time to time with his family, and treating this particular story as a detailed report of what happened on one such visit. As we shall shortly see, the dialogue in the story, and particularly the words of Jesus (the first reported in the canonical Gospels), are the focal points of the whole episode. Much of the remainder provides a setting that aids our interpretation of the dialogue itself. Hence, it may have come from the oral tradition, or been composed by Luke, more for illustrative purposes than historical ones.

[2]A semi-retired priest at my church (meaning, we pay him part-time compensation, but get full-time work out of him) calls Passover a combination of the Fourth of July and Christmas: a great political and religious celebration. If you think about these American holidays, both are festive. We tend to bury their serious sides under that festivity in a way that we do not do, for instance, with Memorial Day and Easter. These latter holidays, also political and religious, respectively, hover too closely around the memory of suffering and death for us to approach them without circumspection. They remind us that both freedoms were purchased at momentous cost.

[3]Does this time period foreshadow the three days of darkness that will occur twenty years later? Some commentators suggest not. And, even though they identify the issue as one worth raising, they don't offer much information to explain their reservations.

imperturbable. He has been astonishing the people in the temple—possibly including the Sanhedrin, the highest judicial body of the Israelites, which met there during Passover—with his intelligence in asking questions and giving answers. When confronted, Jesus reminds his mother that he must be about his "father's business." The whole episode points toward this statement, which we must address if we are to gain the most from the intended message.

In this statement, we glimpse Jesus' rite of passage from his mother's primary care to the world of his father as he stands on the threshold of adulthood. Since we have seen in Luke's birth narrative how the boy will be called "Son of the Most High," his statement about his "father's business" can be understood as a moment of unveiling. Jesus is coming to understand his unique relationship to God as Father. Though the story itself gives us little more to consider about that topic, it is a powerful foretaste of the rest of the gospel.

With Jesus having made that connection, we can linger in this revelatory moment a little longer to consider the mystery of the Trinity. When looking uncritically at trinitarian statements, some people might think that Jesus' identity as God the Son conferred complete knowledge, even omniscience, upon him. This line of thought would render the three persona of the Trinity indistinguishable, attributing to the Son characteristics of the Father. It approaches Docetism, an ancient heresy that so minimized the humanity of Christ as to make it virtually disappear. And, with that sort of disappearance, we would lose our human connection to Jesus. So, let's consider another approach.

We can still acknowledge the depth of Jesus' insight, profound to the point of knowing others' thoughts; yet, the synoptic Gospels do not depict Jesus as an "all knowing" presence. He is sometimes surprised or amazed (*See, e.g.,* Mark 6:6, where Jesus is amazed at the lack of faith in his home region; and Matt. 8:10, where Jesus is amazed at the Roman Centurion's faith). He confesses a lack of knowledge on at least one occasion (*See* Matt. 24:36, concerning the end of time).[4]

The same sort of problem, an omniscient Jesus, would persist if we argued that he did not have to acquire knowledge through the process of education. He is depicted as gaining that knowledge with particular deftness in the temple. This occasion demonstrates something of his fully human nature meshing with his fully divine nature. The passage shows the boy Jesus as a precocious student who learns much, and, in the process, inspires the teachers to learn as

---

[4]To the extent he shows divine insight, it is more within the scope of acquired wisdom and matters of the spirit than, say, within the scope of scientific knowledge about molecular biology or quantum physics. For this reason, it would be difficult to conceive of Jesus as fully human if the Bethlehem infant knew at his birth, or the child knew at age twelve, that the world was round and the Sun was 93 million miles away from Earth.

well.[5] In this way, he "increased in wisdom and in years, and in divine and human favor." Jesus was engaged in a fully human maturation process.

That process included him continuing under his parents' care and authority. He is reported as returning to Nazareth in their company, and being obedient to them.[6] This obedience shows not only that he is still a child, even though on the threshold of adulthood, but also that he respects the Jewish law of honoring his father and mother.

This story, like others we have studied, has an otherworldly feel to it. Does it sound realistic that the parents would walk all day and only realize at the end that Jesus is not there?[7] Do three days of searching before looking in the temple (which they had come to visit in the first place) sound realistic? Or, does it work better to treat this passage as one intended to impart knowledge through a story rather than a factual report? Might it be an adaptation of a time-honored oral method—something in the nature of folk wisdom, perhaps—put down in writing? In the folk genre, meaning can be found in tools such as repetition and overstatement. The extent of the parents' neglect, the amount of time it took them to return and find the child, the business in which he was engaged, and the obvious reasons for his choice of staying in the temple (once he explains to the unwitting supporting cast) tell us much more as a story than a literal understanding of the event ever could.

Our interpretive process continues as we consider Mary's reaction. Even though she has: been visited by Gabriel; had the child's destiny confirmed by Elizabeth; experienced the visitation of shepherds and angels; and heard the proclamations of Simeon and Anna, she still does not seem to be any the wiser. Indeed, she and Joseph are reported as not understanding what Jesus says to them about his reasons for being in the temple.

But, do Mary's and Joseph's cognitive limitations disqualify them from serving as credible witnesses to the unfolding story? Far from it. They participate faithfully even when they do not fully understand, and so model how we can live even though we often lack understanding

---

[5]The rabbis did their most authoritative teaching from a seated position. Reflecting on this practice, some speculate that Jesus' "sitting among the teachers" is a way for Luke to place him at their level of knowledge even before he became an adult. This approach seems to bend the text a little, making Jesus almost unrecognizable as a child. Again, taken too far, it opens the way to a Doscetic understanding that we want to avoid.

[6]Given the reaction his parents had to Jesus being AWOL, that sort of obedience may have been necessary for his very survival! It brings to mind the quip that we don't see anything of Jesus from age twelve to age thirty because Mary had grounded him that long.

[7]Some superficially plausible explanations have been offered about what might have occurred. One is that the men and women were traveling in different parties, and Mary and Joseph each thought Jesus was with the other. But that effort is not completely satisfactory, as it seems that at least one of them should have known where Jesus was at the start of the day and raised a concern if he were not present. Given these shortcomings, other interpretations are needed.

about many things in life. That Mary treasures those things in her heart which she does not understand with her head may be the author's way of telling us that these events fall outside the normal range of human experience. They are something to be treasured more than understood, accepted more than analyzed.

If we, like Mary, can be surprised, and still treasure what we do not understand, we are better able to grapple with the mystery of what God has put before us. Sometimes, a story tells us much more than a room full of theologians and philosophers can.

The Nicene Council, that great fourth-century gathering convened by Emperor Constantine, consisting of bishops, scholars and clerics, formulated a difficult doctrine such as the Trinity in a way that continues to be proclaimed over 1,600 years later. But it cannot make us treasure things in our hearts. That ability comes from another source.

1. How do we distinguish between reporting and storytelling, specific facts and greater truths, prose and poetry? How important is it to our faith lives to know when we are operating in one sphere and when we are operating in another?

2. Why do you think Jesus' parents were described as "astonished" when they finally found him? The word "astonish" means to strike with overpowering wonder; to surprise greatly; or to amaze. Does this word describe how you would feel if you had lost your child three days ago? Why not use "relieved," or "upset," or "overjoyed" as a descriptive word?

3. Does the story tell us something about the way Jesus grew into his identity? Does it connect with the way you have grown, or seen others grow, on journeys to adulthood?

4. How do the persona of the Trinity—Father, Son and Holy Spirit—fit together? Is it a matter of function? Are they different faces of God? Where do they blend? Do you find yourself talking, or praying, differently with each aspect of God?

A Different Tradition

Luke's childhood episode depicts Jesus acquiring and sharing knowledge as critical steps toward gaining maturity. He is growing into his identity as the Son of God. The discovery process he goes through, both spiritually and personally, opens doors from mundane knowledge to the sublime awareness of wisdom.

But wisdom and knowledge, essential as they are to growth, are insufficient by themselves for someone to reach full stature. There is no better testimony, both to the importance of these qualities *and* to their limitations, than chapter 13 of Paul's First Letter to the Corinthians:

> [1]If I speak in the tongues of mortals and of angels, but do not have love, I am a noisy gong or a clanging cymbal. [2]And if I have prophetic powers, and understand all mysteries and all knowledge, and if I have all faith, so as to remove mountains, but do not have love, I am nothing. [3]If I give away all my possessions, and if I hand over my body so that I may boast, but do not have love, I gain nothing.
>
> [4]Love is patient; love is kind; love is not envious or boastful or arrogant [5]or rude. It does not insist on its own way; it is not irritable or resentful; [6]it does not rejoice in wrongdoing, but rejoices in the truth. [7]It bears all things, believes all things, hopes all things, endures all things.
>
> [8]Love never ends. But as for prophecies, they will come to an end; as for tongues, they will cease; as for knowledge, it will come to an end. [9]For we know only in part, and we prophesy only in part; [10]but when the complete comes, the partial will come to an end. [11]When I was a child, I spoke like a child, I thought like a child, I reasoned like a child; when I became an adult, I put an end to childish ways. [12]For now we see in a mirror, dimly, but then we will see face to face. Now I know only in part; then I will know fully, even as I have been fully known. [13]And now faith, hope, and love abide, these three; and the greatest of these is love.

Even while affirming the importance of knowledge and mystery, Paul subordinates them to faith, hope, and, above all, love. This passage in its wholeness leads us to understand how to live in Love itself. Not from a shallow place, but a deep one.

Gnosticism

We as Christians sometimes forget the truths of 1 Cor 13, as we overly concentrate on doctrine. Gnosticism, an early Christian movement, was especially focused on the acquisition of knowledge. The word "gnostic" is derived from the Greek term *"gnosis,"* which means "knowledge." While Gnosticism was a major movement within early Christianity, there have been significant barriers to understanding it for most of the last 1,600 to 1,800 years. Between the time that Gnosticism died out as a major movement in the early centuries of the Church, and the 1940s, what was known about it was based more on the writings of its opponents than on the writings of the Gnostics themselves. The opponents were leaders of a group that called itself the Orthodox movement—meaning, "right thinking" movement. The Orthodox, ancient ancestors of our modern Church, considered the Gnostics to be heretics, and left a body of work criticizing and denouncing Gnosticism.[8]

With the post-World War II discovery of Gnostic Gospels and other works at Nag Hammadi in Egypt, a new assessment of that movement became possible.[9] Gnosticism appears to have been a much more diverse movement than the surviving writings of its Orthodox opponents had suggested. In fact, given the diversity among and within Orthodoxy, Gnosticism, and other movements of the early Church, our modern divisions are minor by comparison.

While a comprehensive discussion of Gnosticism is far beyond the scope of this book, some knowledge of it may help us interpret this section of Luke's gospel and better understand the broader relationship between knowledge and other components of Christian life. Luke considered it important to tell his audience something about Jesus being involved in the discipline of learning at an early age. Paul has told us how important knowledge is, but has subordinated it to the cardinal theological virtues of faith, hope and love. Luke and Paul are proper intersection points to see where Orthodoxy and Gnosticism meet. For instance, Marcion, the Gnostic heretic, included revisions of letters of Paul and parts of the Gospel According to Saint Luke in his canon, the first Christian compilation of a body of work. If Gnosticism and Orthodoxy converge in these works, it is a good place to examine their relationship.

---

[8]While the Orthodox are the forebears of the modern Eastern Orthodox Church, the term is really broader, and includes the Roman Catholic and Protestant traditions, as well.

[9]These gnostic writings were not discovered by archaeologists or scholars, but by a renegade involved in a blood feud. They were found in an earthen jar and brought home. The discoverer's mother actually burned many of the pages as fuel for a fire before leaving the rest intact. The subsequent history of academics and fortune seekers jockeying over possession and ownership of the works, and an accessible study of the contents themselves, are found in the book, *The Gnostic Gospels,* written by Professor Elaine Pagels of Princeton University.

The Infancy Gospel of Thomas

Among the Nag Hammadi books that originated with, or were used by, the Gnostic Christians is the Infancy Gospel of Thomas.[10] It tells some rather unusual tales of Jesus using miraculous powers as early as age five and speaking in a mystifying way. Some of the miracles seem to be only for effect or to intimidate. There are other episodes where he even imposes curses on those he considers to be his adversaries. The curses are lifted when people begin to show knowledge, or *gnosis*, of Jesus' relationship to God.

The Infancy Gospel of Thomas goes on to show the development of the child Jesus' character as he matures from one who engages in arbitrary and petulant uses of power toward one who performs miracles to alleviate human suffering. The gospel ends with Jesus entering the temple at age twelve, where an incident quite similar to Luke's recent account takes place. In fact, the two stories often use nearly identical wording. At the end of the boy's time in the temple, the Pharisees in the Thomas gospel praise him to his mother, and the family returns home.

The message of the Infancy Gospel of Thomas seems to be that, as Jesus gained knowledge and maturity, he turned his power away from petulant use and toward responsible use. The reactions of the people to him also changed as he grew into this better way of living. The reader is given the chance to focus on his increased knowledge and maturity as an example to follow, and to affirm the importance of knowledge in spiritual discernment. The Gnostic idea was that gaining knowledge, particularly of a mysterious and secretive variety, was the road to wisdom and goodness. To the Gnostics, it was at the heart of Christian life.

While there is some benefit to be gained from reading books such as the Infancy Gospel of Thomas, we should remain aware of their limitations. Gnostics believed that a special knowledge, or *gnosis*, was the means for entering into a higher relationship with God; the canonical texts, they argued, were for wider distribution among the more simple-minded or less gifted folk.[11] To the Gnostics, the process of becoming qualified to receive secret teaching distinguished the spiritually mature from the immature.

In its more extreme forms, Gnosticism considered "spirit" to be good and "matter" to be evil. The real God, argued some, was not the creator of the world. Rather, emanations came

---

[10]This work is not to be confused with the Gospel of Thomas, a collection of sayings made by or attributed to Jesus. Fragments of the sayings gospel were found prior to the Nag Hammadi discovery. A more complete version was present there, among the gnostic texts. Some contemporary scholars trace many of the Thomas sayings back to early oral tradition, as old as Mark and Q. Other scholars date Thomas much later.

[11]It appears many Gnostics accepted the writings that eventually formed our NT canon as authoritative to the broader church membership. They used their special sacred traditions as additional material for initiates deemed ready to learn the higher mysteries.

from the real God. As the emanations became further and further removed, they eventually became hostile to that God. The Demiurge —the being that they claimed created the Earth— was one such hostile emanation; he declared himself to be the only God, driven by jealousy of the reality birthing him. While Gnosticism was often an allegorical, rather than literal, mode of thinking, it was nonetheless antagonistic to OT depictions of God.

And, we must remember, the pictures of God in the Old Testament and in the New Testament are sometimes vastly different; but that is more image than concrete fact. The God of the OT, even with the wrathful imagery that often surrounds him, is still depicted as ultimately loving his people and desiring their reconciliation to him. Beyond that, and according to what some of the latter prophets proclaim, this same God of the Israelites is willing to extend his love to the rest of the world. It is an image consistent with the one we see in the NT.

This evolving picture presents a further development in our human understanding of God. It is a process many modern believers seek as they grapple, for instance, with texts that describe God as directing the mass killing of dumb animals and all Canaanites, including children, in the Holy Land. To someone on a redemptive path, understanding this sort of biblical text literalistically is too limited; the Spirit leads toward a higher truth about God. We see biblical evidence of our need to open ourselves to a more complete understanding of God in 1 Cor. 13:8–13, *supra*. We now understand only partially, Paul argues. Later, we will understand fully. Openness to God's continuing revelation allows the Church, like its founder, to grow "in wisdom and in years."

Perhaps that is part of the resiliency of Orthodoxy. It accepted developing and diverse ideas of the biblical God. Some Gnostics took a different route; they disassociated the creator of the world from the ultimate reality called "God." The Gnostic route, which has not survived the test of time, held that to get back to the real God, who is above and beyond the creator, special knowledge needed to be obtained.

By following esoteric paths, such as special genealogies and liturgies, the Gnostics set out to acquire the knowledge which would eventually lead one back through the process of spiritual enlightenment toward the true God. Jesus was guide. But their views, even of Jesus, were different. Teachers passed his wisdom, as recorded in their traditions, onto their own disciples. The process required serious study, initiation into mysteries, and more. As the creator was associated with matter, and hostility to the true God and the ways of the Spirit, some Gnostics viewed Jesus as a purely spiritual being. They even believed that he didn't leave footprints or have physical form, but gave only the illusion of form. And some Gnostics believed it was not Jesus himself who died on the cross, but some representation of him. This was a particularly sore point for many of the Orthodox, who braved and suffered persecution and death precisely because that was what Jesus modeled. The sort of Gnosticism that proclaimed a never-killed Messiah was unacceptable to the Orthodox.

Contrary to the Gnostic movement's emphasis on esoteric knowledge, the canonical books of the New Testament hold that one enters into a right relationship with God through his mercy and grace, and reaches maturity through the Great Commandment, rather than through acquisition of secret knowledge.[12] But Orthodoxy, while offering a more inclusive approach, was not without its limitations. For instance, the Orthodox tended to concentrate authority in the person of the bishop while the Gnostics were more attuned to individual encounters with the Divine. The Orthodox used authoritarian means to destroy Gnostic works and to establish Orthodox preeminence. In doing this, they displayed patterns that were repeated in later years, often with worse consequences, after the Church had become more powerful. By then, heretics were not only opposed in mind—in the marketplace of ideas—but also in body: with weapons of torture and murder.[13] Somewhere in their desire to stamp out "bad" knowledge, the Orthodox forgot Paul's ultimate call to love (*See* 1 Corinthians 13, *supra*).[14]

A Broader Orthodoxy

While Gnosticism eventually fell by the wayside, it was a slice of the wide array of understandings of the life and role of Jesus that were present in the early Church. However, to avoid conferring too much reliability on these and other texts that were excluded from our canon, we should remember why they are not part of the NT. The wide use of Matthew, Mark, Luke and John among early Church communities reflected the greater degree of reliability that these

---

[12]The Great Commandment, of loving God and one's neighbor, is studied later in this series.

[13]An outline of a particular branch of my ancestral history that was at the receiving end of Roman Catholic arms is described in the Preface of this book.

[14]The most rigid Orthodox of old, and authoritarians of all eras, might argue that they were serving the higher good in keeping heresy and, in their eyes, damnation at bay. Their ends, they would claim, justified their means. At least in 1 Cor. 13, Paul serves as a witness against them when he describes love: "It does not insist on its own way; it is not irritable or resentful; it does not rejoice in wrongdoing, but rejoices in the truth. It bears all things, believes all things, hopes all things, endures all things. . . ." Paul's understanding of love, to which knowledge and even faith (misunderstood sometimes as primarily meaning adherence to doctrine) are subordinate, does not recommend vociferous attacks, even against "heretics." Of course, the great Apostle himself could be vociferous from time to time. But, in 1 Cor. 13, we see Paul at his highest and best. In his own introductory words, "I will show you a still more excellent way."

communities believed such works possessed. Their inclusion in the canon was based on their wide-spread acceptance as authoritative.[15]

Yet, the New Testament is far from a narrow scope of faith writings. It contains everything from the mysticism of the Johanine works; to the social gospel of Luke-Acts; to the role of Christ breaking down the barriers between Jews and Gentiles and becoming the new Adam in the works of Paul; to the revolutionary force of Mark; to the heavy ethical content of Matthew. Within this array, the Church recognized a broad—not a narrow—Orthodoxy.

The Church has long been comfortable with a canon that contains divergent thoughts, sometimes conflicting stories and factual discrepancies, and differing theologies. As we will see throughout our studies of the synoptic Gospels, not all accounts are the same, and sometimes the differences are material. Our 21st century understanding of events and ideas that fit neatly into trial transcripts, films, audio tapes, and other "just the facts, ma'am" processes were not the ways of the NT writers. As we will see repeatedly, Matthew and Luke respect Mark enough to incorporate huge chunks of it in their gospels, but still take liberties with its order, narrative, and the way it tells of the life of Christ so that they can offer their own stories to their own people.

Modern theologian, Luke Timothy Johnson, a critic of an overly historical approach to the Gospels, points out that it is not absolute consistency of views and stories, but rather the broad themes and patterns of the life of Christ found in the Gospels, including his obedience, suffering, death and resurrection, that are the heart of the New Testament (*See* Johnson's *The Real Jesus*, at chapter 6). One size does not fit all, or God would have made us all alike.

1. The Gnostics developed their own traditions and authored their own works in a time before the canon was settled. The Orthodox criticized them, sometimes savagely. Yet, is there something Gnosticism still has to teach us? When treating the child Jesus in the Infancy Gospel of Thomas as a literary figure, rather than as the real thing, does it have something to say about wisdom and the proper use of power? Are there other religious writings you can think of that are not authoritative, but nonetheless can open your eyes to a new way of thinking?

---

[15]"Authoritative" means trustworthy and credible; it should not be confused with "absolute." When Scripture is viewed as an absolute, and our interpretation of it is overly literalistic and legalistic, unaided by tradition, reason, and experience, we transform God's gift of Scripture through his human vessels into an idol. Scripture is to be studied, not worshiped.

2. Take, for example, the way that the Infancy Gospel of Thomas portrays the development of its picture of Jesus. As story rather than Scripture, can we learn something from it about the importance of wisdom, knowledge, and restraint? Its teachings could have offered something valuable to members of the royal classes who needed to teach their children not to abuse power. Younger generations of rulers often acted wickedly beyond measure compared with their ancestors—who had gained the power in the first place. This brutality was frequently unaccompanied by the ancestors' competence. We have already seen a Judean devolution from Herod the Great to Archelaus. For Roman examples dating to the NT era, we see how the reign of Augustus was followed in later generations by such vicious and mad incompetents as Caligula and Nero. Might their subjects have benefitted from the rulers having received the sort of teaching that the Infancy Gospel of Thomas had to offer?

3. Old Testament images of God include his giving the Israelites directions to kill every living thing (children and animals included) in their conquest of the Holy Land. Many people, who have studied these passages, have suggested ways of interpreting them that do not involve God as the author and finisher of mass, indiscriminate destruction. Instead, they argue, the passages reflect developing understandings of God, and suggest how these texts can be used for various purposes—for example, exploring themes of obedience to the will of God. Could it be that the Gnostics were seeking a resolution to the problems presented by a narrow early understanding of Yahweh as a "warrior god," but gave up too quickly on gaining a fuller image of him that they might still have met in the Hebrew Bible? A developing understanding of God can be witnessed in considering the OT story as a whole, rather than just isolated episodes. Remember the Book of Jonah; God directed extraordinary efforts to save the wicked Gentiles of Nineveh and their animals.

4. Do we see abandonment of the whole idea of God in our times because there is something to which people object, or that they do not understand? Have you ever struggled with issues such as these? What resolutions—tentative or otherwise—have you reached? Does 1 Cor. 13 help your process?

5. Many splinter movements arise because the dominant forces are not meeting the needs of all the people. This may have been the appeal of Gnosticism to some early

Christians. It may have been, for instance, that some members of the Orthodox leadership were intolerant of other ideas that tended to put their authority into question. Could their power, not fully infused with the love that Saint Paul described, have driven others away? Is there a risk of that today? Doctrinal issues can be very important to some people; yet when they cut against the grain of love, it may be that they have become too important. If faith, hope and love still abide, and outlast all other virtues, does this principle help form your measuring stick for testing even firmly held convictions? How?

Jesus and Moses; Jesus and Augustus

Some scholars believe that Matthew's and Luke's birth narratives were placed at the beginnings of their respective gospels some time after the principal texts[16] were written. One basis for this theory is that the principal texts make no direct reference back to the birth narratives, whereas the birth narratives foreshadow the themes of the principal texts. The relationship between the two strands suggests that the birth narratives were written with knowledge of what followed in the organizational scheme, while the principal texts show no knowledge of the birth narratives that precede them.[17] Take Mary, for example. In Luke, she receives revelations during the birth narrative, but does not reflect on them in the principal text.

If this theory is sound, then the birth narratives were written after the principal texts as overtures. We might expect to see a certain thoughtful complexity and subtlety in works of that nature. We might see them, not only as introductory pieces—or even as simply foreshadowing later events in the life of Jesus—but also as establishing his role as the pivot point of history. If these are our expectations, we will not be disappointed.

We have already seen Luke make a clear connection between the ministries of John the Baptist and of Jesus (*See* chapter 4, *supra*). However, there is another facet to Luke's approach: He makes a more ambitious connection, one between Jesus and Augustus, the great Roman figure highly regarded by a first-century gentile audience. Making such a connection is critical

---

[16]The term "principal texts" is used in this section to distinguish the remainder of the gospels from the birth narratives.

[17]The passage previously studied in this chapter, involving the boy Jesus appearing in the temple at age twelve, is also believed to have been added later for some of the same reasons.

to Luke's purpose, whether the audience is one man named Theophilus, or a community called by that name, which means "lover of God" (*See* chapter 2 at p. 36).

Also, we have seen how Matthew makes connections between the Old Testament and Jesus. There is a more specific OT connection between Jesus and Moses, the lawgiver, and perhaps the greatest figure of the Old Order. But, we have not yet defined precisely how that connection between Moses and Jesus is made.

Just as Augustus is a critical figure to a predominantly Gentile Christian audience, Moses is a critical figure to a predominantly Jewish Christian audience. Yet, the comparisons are not equal between Jesus and Augustus, or between Jesus and Moses. Both comparisons reason from the past to the future, from the lesser to the greater. What God is doing in Jesus exceeds in importance both the story of Augustus, and the story of Moses.[18]

Matthew will be our starting point for reexamining the two birth narratives as overtures connecting Jesus with the great movements of the past. Much of Matthew's story to date tells of Jesus as the fulfillment of Old Testament prophecy and as the culmination of Israel's history in his role as Messiah. He is a deliverer, one who in his own way repeats the works of Moses from more than 1,000 years earlier. The Bible tells stories of the births of each of them. Both stories disclose (1) a ruler's plot, followed by (2) a father's courageous and difficult decision, and then by (3) the child's escape from the plot. Let us consider the following:

(1) In the Old Testament book of Exodus, Pharaoh was determined to kill the male Hebrew children for fear of the growing population of that enslaved people. Later traditions, reported by the Jewish historian, Josephus, and other people who wrote during the first-century A.D. (some anonymously), held that Pharaoh's purpose was actually to kill *one* child, foretold by the scribes as being destined to overthrow Pharaoh's rule of the Hebrews. The child was Moses. Matthew's Jewish Christian audience would have been aware of this interpretation of the Exodus story, even though it was not found in the Hebrew Bible itself.

Similarly, in Matthew's gospel, Herod's plot is to eliminate the coming king by killing the children of Bethlehem. It is a step he undertakes only after consulting with his own scribes. Both stories involve reflective decisions made by powerful rulers to eliminate threats to their reigns that are embodied in a child whose greatness has been foretold.

(2) The second phase of each story is the father's decision. In order to avoid having their newborn sons slaughtered, the Hebrew slaves underwent a "general divorce" during which

---

[18]The primary sources used in this analysis are *Jesus: A Revolutionary Biography* by John Dominic Crossan and *The Meaning of Jesus: Two Visions* by Marcus Borg and N.T. Wright.

husbands and wives agreed to abstain from sexual relations, and so prevent the procreation that would lead to any sons being massacred pursuant to Pharaoh's edict. The general divorce involved living under one roof, but not as husband and wife. According to the *Book of Biblical Antiquities*, written after the destruction of the temple in 70 A.D., a Hebrew belief was that Amram, the father of Moses, and his wife defied the prevailing practice, and refused to honor the general divorce. As a result, Moses was born.

Like Amram, Joseph swims against the tide of reproductive convention and rejects what was understood to be the legal requirement of divorcing Mary, his betrothed[19]—or worse, as stoning her would have presumably been within the bounds of Jewish law. Instead, Mary becomes his wife. Joseph thus exposes himself to humiliation by taking a pregnant woman for his wife, and the family as a whole is at risk, legally and socially.

(3) Finally, there is the child's escape. Moses was hid in the bulrushes and eventually adopted. He grew to "save his people from Egypt," leading them on their journey out of bondage and into the promised land.

Matthew has his own story of escape. With the flight into Egypt, Joseph brings the family to temporary refuge. Ironically, Jesus' own escape was to go to pagan Egypt, and later to come out of it, as Moses did, but this time to "save his people from their sins."

By this technique, Matthew connects Moses and Jesus; the Old and the New. A critical point to both stories is the presence of grace in tragedy, as God brings light and hope out of deepest darkness and despair. But the connections between the two do not cease there. Scholars see parallels to Moses throughout the balance of Matthew's gospel. Jesus gives five major speeches, corresponding to the five books of the Torah. There are Twelve Apostles, corresponding to the twelve tribes of Israel. Jesus gives his authoritative teaching on "the mount," just as Moses gave his authoritative declamation of the law on Mount Sinai.

Luke also must make connections, but ones that resonate more with a Gentile audience than a Jewish one. The more important comparison for Luke's church was not the one between John and Jesus (which he has already made), or the one between Moses and Jesus (as occurs in Matthew), but between Caesar Augustus and Jesus. Crossan shows how these two men, from the Western and Eastern Mediterranean, respectively, within the span of a century, left colossal footsteps on their respective worlds, which are still present today. They have these events in common:

---

[19]As we have seen, betrothal was a more serious legal commitment than engagement of our day, and could only be dissolved by divorce.

1. *a.* The Roman Senate deified Augustus' father, Julius Caesar, in 42 B.C. By virtue of familial ties, Augustus thereby became a son of god during his own lifetime.

   b. Almost three quarters of a century later, Jesus was acclaimed as the Son of God during his lifetime by some of those who witnessed his words and deeds.[20] He is called the Son of the Most High in the birth narrative itself.

2. *a.* Augustus was proclaimed to be a god by the Roman Senate in 14 C.E., which occurred only a month after his death.

   b. As the Christian Church grappled with its understanding of the resurrection, its affirmation of faith became that Jesus was God incarnate. This title was developed more by process than by any single event, with his identity as the second person of the Trinity eventually being formulated as God the Son during the Nicene Conference of the fourth century.

3. *a.* Roman poetry (particularly, Virgil) spoke of an age of peace and justice attributed to Augustus.

   b. Jewish prophecy foretold of an age of peace and justice under the Messiah, and Luke proclaimed its fulfillment in Jesus, beginning in the birth narrative.

4. *a.* Augustus' birth was described (including by inscription at a pagan temple dating to 9 C.E.) as good news; his role, being a savior who brought a peaceful order to Rome (the *Pax Romana*). And, his reign was legitimized by his descent from the great ruler, Julius Caesar.

   b. Jesus' birth is described as good news in Luke's birth narrative, and his role and identity are as Savior. He ushers in the era of peace and goodwill, and is descended from the great ruler, David.

---

[20]The title "Son of God" during Jesus' life was not yet as unique a designation as it soon became. Angels and kings were called sons of God in the Old Testament. For Christians, Jesus changed the qualitative meaning of this term.

In an era when the gospel was being spread from Jews to Gentiles, and when people in both worlds had become accustomed to looking at the circumstances of a leader's birth to interpret the later events in his life, Matthew and Luke tell their birth stories. These narratives, written after the destruction of the temple and at a time when Christians had already been subjected to persecution, served as lights in the darkness. They were poignant even unto death for those looking toward the faces of their own accusers, or even down the throats of lions, and whose faith told them that the claims of God through Christ were greater than those of the Herodians or the Caesars.

1. We have probed some of the historical holes in the birth narratives and suggested that, at times, a literary interpretation is better than a literal one. Do the connections drawn above between Jesus and Moses, and Jesus and Augustus, help that process by offering a new perspective? Do they hinder it in some ways? Are there aspects to each of these stories that speak to you deeply?

2. Do we interpret our world better by looking at the patterns of history, just as Matthew and Luke have done? For instance, in chronological order, Socrates, Jesus, Saint Steven, Abraham Lincoln, Mahatma Gandhi, and Martin Luther King were all killed by people whom they came to serve, or even save. Yet, they all left the world better off for their lives, and even in ways by the events and manners of their deaths. Are you anxious about whether you can answer such a call, if given?

3. The birth narratives reflect on earlier events involving other people. Do these comparisons make the stories of the birth of Jesus more powerful? Or, do they understate the significance of his own particular story? Can you relate your own story to the stories of others in a way that offers spiritual truths?

†††

CHAPTER NINE

Out of the Old Order and into the New: John Proclaims the Ultimate Return from Exile

So far in our synoptic journeys, we have not studied any true parallels—similar episodes reported in more than one gospel account. In this chapter, for the first time, we will begin to study the earliest of these parallels, and to experience their sense of theme and variation. We will look at how the wording and meaning of some segments are virtually identical. In other segments, we will see divergence. This nuance will tell us something about what was critical to each of our evangelists and their early Christian communities.

Where parallel texts appear in the same sequence in the synoptic Gospels, we will usually begin by studying Mark, the oldest gospel. Then, we can see how Matthew and Luke follow or modify this source as they tell their own stories of Jesus. By the time we get to the end of this chapter, we will be prepared to meet the adult Jesus.

John the Baptist Appears

☦ MARK 1:1–6 The Coming of John the Baptist, According to Mark

¹The beginning of the good news of Jesus Christ, the Son of God. ²As it is written in the prophet Isaiah,

"See, I am sending my messenger ahead of you, who will prepare your way; ³the voice of one crying out in the wilderness: 'Prepare the way of the Lord, make his paths straight,'"

⁴John the baptizer appeared in the wilderness, proclaiming a baptism of repentance for the forgiveness of sins. ⁵And people from the whole Judean countryside and all the people of Jerusalem were going out to him, and were baptized by him in the river Jordan, confessing their sins. ⁶Now John was clothed with camel's hair, with a leather belt around his waist, and he ate locusts and wild honey.

1. Mark's suddenness confronts us. Its introduction is direct; there is no scholarly prologue, no studious genealogy. In fact, the story seems to start in the middle, and to assume an audience already knowledgeable about Jesus' and John's identities. How do you react to Mark's style? How do you compare it to Luke's and Matthew's styles?

2. Given Mark's assumptions about his audience, do you believe it was written primarily for the faithful? Luke is more explicitly a persuasive work composed to show Theophilus "the truth concerning the things about which you have been instructed" (*See* Luke 1:4). Do these differences affect the way you read each gospel?

Mark's opening goes straight to the point. He identifies what he is doing in four ways: (1) He is telling good news (2) about Jesus; (3) who is the Christ—the Greek version of the Hebrew word "Messiah," meaning "anointed"; (4) and who is also the Son of God. Each one packs a wallop. Let's look at them, using these four numbered points for ease of reference.

1. Mark is the first Christian book that uses the term "good news"—"gospel"—to describe itself.[1] Mark's book proclaims the good news in the form of a story, pointing the reader to the defining moments in Jesus' earthly life and moving quickly along the paths Jesus walked.

2. The book is about Jesus. It is *his* story.

3. Jesus is the Anointed—one set aside by God for some particular purpose.

4. Jesus is the Son of God. This title is not found in verse one of some ancient manuscripts of Mark, and may have been inserted in later manuscripts, as the book circulated, to reflect a developing understanding of Jesus' identity. In the Markan context—which arose quite early in the Christian tradition—the phrase "Son of God" does not necessarily suggest a specific set of ideas about Jesus' divine nature, such as the ones used in the Nicene Creed. Rather, Mark likely uses "Son of God" to describe Jesus' special relationship with, and close connection to, the Father. As we have already seen, the phrase "son of God" was used in the Old Testament to describe angels, kings of Israel, righteous people, and even Israel itself. Only later was that connection made to Jesus in an especially unique way.

After the introductory verse, Mark abruptly shifts to Old Testament prophecy. There, as we often see in our studies of the Gospels, we find more than first meets the eye. His specific reference is to Isaiah 40:3, an OT passage which the NRSV translates this way:[2]

> **A voice cries out:**
> **"In the wilderness prepare the way of the Lord,**
> **make straight in the desert a highway for our God."**

---

[1]Letters of Paul, all of which were likely written earlier than Mark, make reference to Paul's gospel. However, the connotations are different. Paul has already *spoken* words of good news about Jesus (See, e.g., Gal. 1 and Rom. 1). His letters serve as reenforcements of that oral gospel. And, of course, there is no book we possess called, *The Gospel According to Saint Paul.*

[2]Mark's "quotation" of Isaiah is actually a paraphrase which combines an Isaiah passage with Malachi 3:1, a prophetic verse showing Elijah as the forerunner of God.

There is a subtle difference between the text of Isaiah itself and how Mark paraphrases it. By looking at both, we can open ourselves to new interpretive possibilities.

In the NRSV, Mark's arrangement of key words suggests that the *voice* is to be found in the wilderness. Isaiah itself, however, has a different emphasis. The word "wilderness" does not so much describe the location of the voice as it does *the place where the highway is to be built*. To Jews living in first-century Judea—and understanding the prophetic tradition—Isaiah's road through the wilderness is none other than the route their ancestors took when returning home from the Babylonian exile 500 years before.

And yet, the post-exile restoration of Israel had proven incomplete. Some Israelites had stayed behind and been assimilated into Babylonian culture. Those who did return carved out a new life, but the Davidic glory was not restored. When John proclaims anew the way in the wilderness, it means that a complete return from exile is close at hand. Judea is on the threshold of receiving the full fruit of restoration, far beyond what was earlier realized. When understood this way, John is indeed delivering good news. To a people under occupation, who had lost their way even in their own homeland, the promise of complete renewal was an especially welcome proclamation.

And the wilderness through which the road goes—where Mark tells us the voice is crying—is not just any wilderness. It is not the Black Forest of Germany, or Pisgah Forest of North Carolina, or the Cascade Mountains of Oregon and Washington. Nor is it just any arid desert, such as the Gobi or the Sahara or the Sonora. It is a desert route that begins in Babylon and ends in Judea, the predominately dry wilderness where the Jordan River runs. Biblical scholars, including Professor Crossan and Professor Pheme Perkins of Boston College, who is affiliated with the Roman Catholic Church, show how the wilderness site is filled with powerful associations. It is a place of refuge, where Moses, Elijah, and David all fled in times of trial. It is the place where one goes to regroup, and then to return and reassert.

This wilderness was also the place from which deliverance came. Moses led the people out of Egypt, through the desert, and toward the Promised Land. Then, under Joshua's leadership, they gained entry into Canaan from the desert. If a human tendency is to attempt to replicate the successful patterns of the past, we should not be surprised that first-century Judaism displayed a powerful connection to the wilderness near the Jordan. It was a place charged with expectations.

More than once during the decades around the life of Jesus, Jewish gatherings in the wilderness were associated, fairly or otherwise, with nationalistic or rebellious intentions. At least two movement founders had the specific goal of gathering the people in the wilderness and reenacting Joshua's conquest of the Holy Land—now under Roman arms—by crossing the

Jordan and marching toward Jerusalem. Rome crushed every such venture. On at least one occasion, the decimated marchers were unarmed.

A gathering of Jewish people in the desert, at the Jordan River, east of Jerusalem, was not to be taken lightly. It signaled an extraordinary occurrence. And, in his opening verses, Mark uses one such occurrence during the days of John the Baptist to put us on notice that we are witnessing the extraordinary. But, it is not taking place in the way conventional wisdom dictated. We see no evidence of a rebellious plot. What we see is a different sort of revolution: one of the spirit. By repenting (a word which means turning away from one direction and heading in another), the people were physically acting out changes of heart, word and deed. Repentance is not about tucking our tails between our legs in response to finger-wagging lectures; it is about a liberation from sad and sick patterns and a return to a healthier way of living. Baptism in the Jordan was an outward and visible sign of this inward and spiritual grace. We are witnessing a transformative and sacramental experience.

No doubt, the people participating in the ritual and practicing the repentance that John preached were hoping to experience God's favor as a result of their actions. The fact that they were carrying out this rite in the waters of the Jordan at the eastern wilderness suggests they were not merely seeking forgiveness, but restoration. As Crossan states, "[w]hen people came to [John], he kept sending them back *from* the wilderness, *through* the Jordan, which washed away their sins, and, purified and ready, into the Promised Land, there to await the imminent coming of the redeeming and avenging God."[3] This was powerful business.

The person who is baptizing them also powerfully captures our attention. John the Baptist, wild man of the desert, was a sight to behold. He had the sparse and bizarre diet of an ascetic. He was "clothed with camel's hair, with a leather belt around his waist, and he ate locusts and wild honey" (Mark 1:6). The camel's hair would have been itchy and uncomfortable. The locusts—like our grasshoppers—would have been protein-rich, but hardly of good flavor. The picture Mark paints is an earthy, real, and palpable one.

To describe John is to make a clear connection to the return of Elijah, the forerunner of the Lord proclaimed in Mal. 3:1.[4] Elijah was a powerful OT prophet. Living in the northern kingdom of Israel, after its rift with Judea in the south, Elijah had single-handedly defeated the priests of the pagan idol, Baal. We are told that, at the end of his days, Elijah did not die, but was taken bodily into heaven in a fiery chariot. This Elijah was "a hairy man, with a leather belt around his waist" (*See* 2 Kgs. 1:8).

---

[3]Crossan, *Jesus: A Revolutionary Biography*, at 43.
[4]*See* footnote 2, *supra*.

In a later volume of this series, we will see an image of Elijah in the company of Jesus and Moses at the Mount of the Transfiguration. Right now, though, there is a different image of the spirit of Elijah. It is found in the time of John the Baptist, with all his rugged glory, who makes his first appearance in the first verses of Mark. We will see that he is the forerunner of the One who is to come. And, he is baptizing the people in, of all places, the river Jordan!

1. How do we relate to a character like John? From our comfortable surroundings, we might look upon this wild man of the dessert as mad if we had not been taught that he was holy. After all, would we live like that? Could we give up our creature comforts, such as hot and cold running water, indoor plumbing, soft furniture, and microwave ovens, in order to respond to God's call? Could it be that John, who chooses this ascetic lifestyle, was compelled by a divine madness? Keep this thought in mind as we continue to study his appearance.

2. In *Meeting Jesus Again for the First Time*, Marcus Borg argues that there are three macro-stories, or overriding epics, in the Bible. The first is the Exodus. It is about escape from bondage. The second is the Babylonian exile. It is about return from exile and estrangement. The third is the Priestly story. More of a theme than a story proper, it is about repentance and forgiveness of sins. We find strands of all three macro-stories in this passage:

   a. Mark commemorates the Israelites' escape from bondage as the Judean people under Roman occupation reenact the ancient crossing of the Jordan.

   b. Mark commemorates the return from the Babylonian exile with the voice crying, "in the wilderness, prepare the way of the Lord."

   c. Mark commemorates the Priestly story with baptism for the forgiveness of sins.

   If Borg is correct about the three macro-stories, do they all converge right here in what Mark calls "the beginning of the good news of Jesus Christ?" And, what might that say about the passages we are now interpreting?

✝ MATTHEW 3:1-6 The Coming of John the Baptist,
According to Matthew

¹**In those days John the Baptist appeared in the wilderness of Judea, proclaiming,**
²**"Repent, for the kingdom of heaven has come near." ³This is the one of whom
the prophet Isaiah spoke when he said,**

> *"The voice of one crying out in the wilderness:*
> *'Prepare the way of the Lord,*
> *make his paths straight.'"*

⁴**Now John wore clothing of camel's hair with a leather belt around his waist,
and his food was locusts and wild honey. ⁵Then the people of Jerusalem and
all Judea were going out to him, and all the region along the Jordan, ⁶and they
were baptized by him in the river Jordan, confessing their sins.**

1. Do you notice any differences between Mark's version and Matthew's?

2. If the weight of scholarship is correct, and Matthew relies on Mark, what do you
   think might underlie the changes Matthew makes?

The connections Mark draws between Elijah and John the Baptist would have been clear
to a large portion of his audience, which consisted of both Jewish and Gentile Christians.
These connections would have been even clearer to Matthew's predominately Jewish-Christian
audience, whose members were well-versed in the Old Testament tradition.[5] This latter group,
heavily grounded in Judaism, was painfully aware that the authentic voice of prophecy had
been silent in Israel for hundreds of years before John's arrival. The last major prophet, Daniel,
had spoken in the days of exile during the sixth century B.C.E.

---

[5]It is likely that Matthew's church used Mark as an authoritative text, at least before Matthew was written. The
author of Matthew incorporated as much as ninety percent of Mark into his gospel, modifying it and adding additional
material from Q and M to meet the emerging needs of his own community. While The Gospel According to Saint
Matthew may have then become their most authoritative work, Mark was still known within the community.

The Ultimate Return from Exile
(circa 30 C.E.)

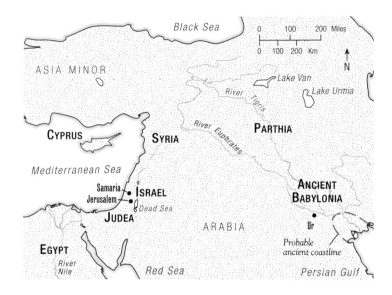

After such a long silence, John's commanding presence ushered in dynamic change. It was strong enough to draw many people of Jerusalem, and other parts of Judea, away from the comforts of home and into the desert to be baptized. They were a people in need of spiritual renewal, ready to embrace even the stern message of John that we will soon hear.

While relying heavily on Mark's version of the appearance of John, Matthew describes his baptismal practices in a different way. To Matthew, John's is *not* a baptism "for the forgiveness of sins" (*see* Mark 1:4). Forgiveness is a function left for Jesus. But, John's baptism *is* about repentance and confession (*see* Mat. 3:6). It is about a change of heart and of life itself. It is a reorientation toward the prophetic traditions of the past. These traditions were about living in a right relationship with God and with one's neighbors. They are embodied in what Micah is said to have proclaimed to the Israelites during other troubled days three quarters of a millennium earlier:[6]

> **8He has told you, O mortal, what is good;**
> **and what does the Lord require of you**
> **but to do justice, and to love kindness,**
> **and to walk humbly with your God?**

---

[6]*See* Mic. 6:8. Most scholars date the historical Micah, and the early parts of the book bearing his name, to the time of the Assyrian conquest that resulted in the northern kingdom of Israel falling in about 722 B.C. The possible circumstances of authorship of the remainder of the book, including chapter 6, are the subject of greater scholarly debate. They may date to as late as the Babylonian exile.

Religious people through the years have often forgotten this simple ethos as they focused on matters of doctrine and ritual and polity.[7] Ignoring it too long almost begs for a John the Baptist to come forth and proclaim the tradition anew. Matthew's John speaks out about the "kingdom of heaven"—what Mark and Luke call the "kingdom of God."[8] Because the kingdom is the core message of the synoptic Gospels, it is represented in the title of this series. Throughout our journeys, we will continue to explore what this proclamation of the kingdom means, and witness it in Jesus' simple presence, his power to heal, teach, preach, and to tell stories that to this day impart depth, direction and purpose for our journey.

1. Mark identifies Jesus as the Messiah, the Son of God, in the verse before introducing John the Baptist. Matthew does not. Why might this be?

2. How do you react to the sort of prophecy that John embodied? Does it make sense to you? Or, is there too great a cultural disconnection?

3. What do the prophetic messengers of our culture look like?

†††

✝ LUKE 3:1–6 The Coming of John the Baptist, According to Luke

[1]In the fifteenth year of the reign of Emperor Tiberius, when Pontius Pilate was governor of Judea, and Herod was ruler of Galilee, and his brother Philip ruler of the region of Ituraea and Trachonitis, and Lysanias ruler of Abilene, [2]during the high priesthood of Annas and Caiaphas, the word of God came to John son of Zechariah in the wilderness. [3]He went into all the region around the Jordan, proclaiming a baptism of repentance for the forgiveness of sins, [4]as it is written in the book of the words of the prophet Isaiah,

---

[7]Micah's prophecy is arguably the heart of life itself. It is displayed in my rector's study where he reads it every day. My father considers it to be the standard of true religion. As much as I enjoy a good debate, I have had trouble finding a principled way to disagree with the emphasis that either of them places on this powerful verse.

[8]We will more closely consider the likely reasons for the evangelists' different wording later in this series.

"The voice of one crying out in the wilderness: 'Prepare the way of the Lord, make his paths straight. ⁵Every valley shall be filled, and every mountain and hill shall be made low, and the crooked shall be made straight, and the rough ways made smooth; ⁶and all flesh shall see the salvation of God.'"

1. Does Luke take a different approach to introducing John the Baptist than Mark and Matthew do?

2. How do you respond to Luke's introduction of the adult John?

Luke, the careful historian, uses a common method of antiquity to identify the time frame when John appeared. He makes references to multiple events that were known or important to his audience, an approach necessary before the days of uniform calendars. To put the reader in the proper time frame, Luke begins with the Roman political situation and ends with the Judaic religious one—not a surprising approach for a Gentile author to take when framing a story grounded in Judaic history.

When they approximate the date of John's appearance, modern scholars look to where Luke's points of reference intersect.[9] According to Professor O.C. Edwards, Jr., formerly of Seabury-Western Theological Seminary (which is affiliated with the Episcopal Church in the United States of America), the intersections occur in the years 27–29 A.D. These, then, are the most likely dates for the adult John to have made his first public appearance.

This part of the passage serves not only to provide points of reference, but also to provide a broader context. It names some who will be Jesus' or the early Church's opponents or antagonists: Pontius Pilate, Herod, and the High Priestly family. It identifies some who are aligned with Jesus: John and Zechariah, with John also connected to the prophet Isaiah. Luke does not describe John's prophetic appearance and diet, because it is not necessary for him to do so. He already alluded to his identity as a prophet when Gabriel told Zechariah in the temple that John would have the "spirit and power of Elijah" (Luke 1:17).

As with Matthew, Luke reworks some of Mark's ideas around John's baptismal practice. Here, John is not described as actually baptizing people, but simply "proclaiming a baptism of

---

[9]*See, e.g.,* Professor Culpepper's commentary on Luke in *The New Interpreter's Bible* series, at 80.

repentance for the forgiveness of sins." The fact that both Matthew and Luke revise John's baptismal tradition suggests that the early Church was grappling with its significance for some reason— a point we will revisit in the last chapter.

One compelling facet of Luke's version is how he uses the prophecy of Isaiah. Luke is not satisfied simply to describe the voice in the wilderness. Instead, he cites a longer portion of Isaiah, and describes a transformation of the Cosmos itself. The filling of valleys and leveling of mountains is a powerful metaphor of conversion, particularly when proclaiming a baptism.

Nor are there limits to that baptism. Luke's gospel declares that "all flesh shall see the salvation of God." It is a universalistic theme, expanding the people of God beyond the lands around the cleansing waters of the river Jordan. If John were once associated with the Essenes, as some scholars argue (See chapter 5, supra, regarding the Benedictus), he may have begun to identify baptism with the forgiveness of sins while a part of that movement. The Essenes practiced ritual washing, which, like John's baptism, required repentance.

But John transcended the Essenes. They were restrictive and exclusive, expecting God's wrath to be poured out on the sinful masses. By proclaiming a gospel that includes "all flesh [seeing] the salvation of God," Luke shows that John has made a marked departure from the Essene tradition. The grace-filled inclusion of the Christian way overcomes law-filled divisions of some first-century Judaic factions.

Luke uses the term "salvation" here and several other times (See Luke 1:77, 2:29, 19:9). Some people understand it to describe a conversion event—when a person accepts Jesus Christ as Lord and Savior, and is, therefore, "saved." This view can become overly formulaic, as it does not always ask what one is saved from, or saved for, or even what it all means. By returning to the biblical text, we can see a more holistic way to explore the topic. The Hebrew root of the word translated as "salvation" in the Old Testament is one that suggests a broadening or enlarging. The implication is that God rescues and delivers his people from adversity and restores them to prosperity and fullness. The New Testament understands God as saving or delivering his people from present and future bondage.

Viewed this way, Luke's idea of all flesh seeing the salvation of God is more closely akin to entering and maintaining a liberating relationship with God, than merely to being plucked out of a fallen state. It not only conserves, but builds. Salvation becomes more a process than an isolated event.[10]

---

[10]This point is true even though a conversion experience might be an important step along the way, and understood as an essential one in some faith traditions. One's conversion may be experienced as a close connection to God and to the Christian community. It can, and should, lead more deeply into the Christian journey.

1. What do you make of Luke's changes to how Mark describes John's baptism? Are the changes significant to your understanding of John's mission?

2. What does Luke mean when he says, "all flesh shall see the salvation of God"? Does seeing it equate with experiencing it? How do you understand "salvation"?

3. Have you ever been to a large baptismal celebration? What was it like?

Having studied our first parallel that crosses three Gospels, we now move to another kind of synoptic parallel: one involving Q. As we saw earlier in this volume, Q is a "lost gospel," originally a collection of Jesus' sayings now preserved in another form.[11] Matthew and Luke each incorporated the Q sayings into their narrative Gospels, which then became the vehicles for Q's continuing vitality.

Most scholars believe that Luke: (a) more closely resembles the original order and contents of Q; and/or (b) is based on an earlier version of the Q text than Matthew possessed. Their reasons include that Luke's Q sayings are often pithier and shorter than Matthew's, making them easier to remember and more likely traceable back to the oral period before the Gospels were written. Where parallel Q texts appear in the same sequence in Matthew and Luke, we will often begin by studying Luke's version, as it is usually the closer approximation of the Q source. Then, we can see how Matthew modifies Q to tell his story.

†T†

[11]*See, generally,* chapter 2, p. 26 *supra*, The Galilean Journey of the Q Community.

John the Baptist Speaks

✝ LUKE 3:7–9 John Preaches Wrath and Repentance, According to Luke

⁷John said to the crowds that came out to be baptized by him,

"You brood of vipers! Who warned you to flee from the wrath to come? ⁸Bear fruits worthy of repentance. Do not begin to say to yourselves, 'We have Abraham as our ancestor'; for I tell you, God is able from these stones to raise up children to Abraham. ⁹Even now the ax is lying at the root of the trees; every tree therefore that does not bear good fruit is cut down and thrown into the fire."

1. Wow!! Wrath? Axes cutting trees at the root? Being thrown into the fire? What is going on here?

2. On the other hand: Bearing worthy fruit? Repentance? Turning stones into people? What is going on *here?*

I heard a preacher once describe John as "our country cousin," the one we don't really want to talk about, who we want to shuttle off into the closet so he doesn't embarrass us. After all, aren't we sophisticated, modern people? People of good taste and breeding? Educated and decorous?

But John comes back, time and again, gets in our face, and says "Deal with it!!!" And so we shall—for self-preservation, if for no other reason. After all, do you remember anything good that ever happened to the kings of Israel and Judah who ignored the prophetic wild men of their own eras?

So, with our resolve stiffened, let us venture back into the text. We have seen the Israelites as a spiritually hungry people, in need of new direction. Many of them went into the wilderness to see John. Their pilgrimage shows an awakening; but, once they are out there, a decision still awaits about responding to John's call. How, ultimately, will they react?

John's word pictures provide a starting point against which to measure the crowd's possible reactions. The initial name given to the "crowds"[12] is "brood of vipers!" Among the many dangers found in the wilderness east of Jerusalem were poisonous snakes. And these were not new dangers. In the most ancient Judaic traditions, we see the serpent in Eden teasing along the Fall as he appeals to pride, vanity and ambition. The serpent symbolizes the ancient adversary, hostile to God's purposes. He is a threat to the people. By using these images, John questions the authenticity of the crowd that comes out to see him. Are they there to repent, with true change of heart and behavior? Or, are they there only to flee the coming wrath?[13]

The word metaphors continue. John speaks of trees. To bear fruit is to be a good tree. To bear fruit worthy of repentance is to show a change of direction that signifies an authentic desire for baptism, not a convenient purchase of insurance against God's wrath.

We also have the image of stones. A prevalent belief in some first-century Jewish groups was that God had chosen their people out of all humanity for privilege. To be a child of Abraham was to be aligned with God's favor. To be a child of someone else . . . well, you can figure out the rest. This selective view of what it meant to be God's chosen people had distorted ideas of covenant. To some lines of thinking, God's election did not carry with it the responsibility of bringing his redemptive work to the rest of the world. Such ideas ignored the latter prophets, and the higher requirements of the law, both of which pointed to responsibility toward the world at large, and to a sense of God's inclusive nature.

By claiming that God can turn stones into children of Abraham, John the Baptist is rejecting this particularly misguided notion of what election means. John's concept seems to arise out of Isaiah 51:1–3 (emphasis added), as follows:

---

[12]In Luke, we sometimes see different words used to describe different groups. The "people" are often found in large numbers, and are favorably disposed to Jesus. The "crowds" are also large, but are not necessarily favorably disposed to him; they are more ambivalent.

[13]Even with a negative image of the slithery reptiles, we still do not tend to think of snakes as traveling in broods, and fleeing a threat in large numbers. Instead, we often envision them slithering along in their solitary designs, acting with swift certainty when an opportunity arises to satisfy their appetites or to defend their domains. When they are grouped together, as in a nest of copperheads or in the gang of snakes that Indiana Jones met in *Raiders of the Lost Ark,* they are seen not as endangered, but as dangerous.

Of course, there are exceptions to that rule. In wild fires of the deserts, snakes and other creatures would come out of their burrows and dens, moving rapidly away from the approaching threat. When they did, they were fleeing for their lives. This may have been the image John had in mind when speaking out against the vipers' brood.

Listen to me, you that pursue righteousness,
   you that seek the Lord.
Look to the *rock* from which you were hewn,
   and to the *quarry* from which you were dug.
²Look to *Abraham* your father
   and to *Sarah* who bore you;
 for he was but one when I called him,
   but I blessed him and made him many.
³For the Lord will comfort Zion;
   he will comfort all her *waste places*,
 and will make her *wilderness* like Eden,
   her desert like the garden of the Lord;
 joy and gladness will be found in her,
thanksgiving and the voice of song.

John is out in the desert, the waste places, the wilderness. He is crying out for righteousness. He is proclaiming the transformation of stones into children of Abraham, as God had once hewn the chosen people from rock. It is an affirmation of God's saving power; the Lord will accomplish his work by whatever means necessary.

Where will John's audience align itself in this developing saga? The message about them remains mixed. God is prepared to take the ax to the very root of the trees, a place that—if destroyed—will allow the trees no recovery. The image is one of immediacy; it is an eschatological, or end-times, image. The trees' choices are to bear the fruit of repentance, or to be cut down and burned. The time for a decision is now.

And the cutting will be followed by feeding the fire. In the Bible, images of fire can have different meanings. Fire can be destructive, and represent judgment. Or, it can be refining, and represent purification. In John's case, the words he speaks here more strongly connote a threat of judgment and destruction. When we hear them, we should prepare for a firestorm.

1. John's images are powerful and his words are harsh. How do you react to them? How do you compare the forerunner's message to what you know of the Messiah's message?

2. John is challenging a crowd that has come a long way just to see him. What is your response to that? How do you compare his behavior to modern ideas about the ways we communicate with those we are trying to persuade?

3. Have you ever listened to a street preacher? Or maybe one that frequents college campuses? How do you react to them? How do you think others react? Can you compare these evangelists to John the Baptist?

4. Is John trying to appeal to fear? To hope? How does he balance the two? Which way speaks more clearly to you now? Has it always been that way?

✝✝✝

✝ **MATTHEW 3:7–10 John Preaches Wrath and Repentance, According to Matthew**

7But when he saw many Pharisees and Sadducees coming for baptism, he said to them,

"You brood of vipers! Who warned you to flee from the wrath to come? 8Bear fruit worthy of repentance. 9Do not presume to say to yourselves, 'We have Abraham as our ancestor'; for I tell you, God is able from these stones to raise up children to Abraham.

10Even now the ax is lying at the root of the trees; every tree therefore that does not bear good fruit is cut down and thrown into the fire."

1. How does Matthew's version differ from Luke's? How is it the same?

2. What do you believe are the reasons for the differences between Luke's and Matthew's versions?

Matthew's gospel follows the Q source closely, though with one major variation. The recipients of John's invective are not the generic "crowds" of Luke (and, presumably, Q), but are two quite specific groups, the Pharisees and the Sadducees. We often lump these two groups together because they are considered opponents of Jesus. But that quick association is only marginally helpful; a more thorough understanding is better for our interpretive process.

Rather than being monolithic, the Pharisees and the Sadducees were actually often at odds with each other. The word "pharisees" means "separated ones." The Pharisees, who were part of a reform movement, founded a rabbinic tradition. They made the Judaic law applicable to all aspects of life and practiced a strict, ritualistic faith. Their zeal for the law—both as written in the Old Testament and as practiced through their oral traditions—caused them to set themselves apart from the rest of the community. They accepted the entire Hebrew Bible as authoritative, and believed in resurrection. Pharisees were relatively popular with the common people. Their movement was essential to the survival of Judaism after the destruction of the temple in 70 A.D. at the close of the Jewish-Roman war.

The Sadducees did not leave a rabbinic record. Most of what we know about them comes from their opponents. The Sadducees were aristocratic and wealthy, and controlled the Jerusalem Temple apparatus. They accepted only the first five books of the OT—sometimes called the Pentateuch or the Torah—as authoritative. They preserved their power partially through collaboration with Rome, something the "separated ones" would not have dreamed of doing, as Gentile contact would have defiled their ritual purity. The Sadducees did not believe in the resurrection. They were harsher on issues of crime and punishment than the Pharisees, and were less popular with the people.

The two parties also differed on the question of human freedom. Sadducees believed in free will. Pharisees had a more complex view: not exactly free will, nor quite yet the determinism that another group we have met, the Essenes, embraced. The distinctions among these groups, and the practices that defined them, will be important to us throughout our synoptic journeys, as we seek to understand the world in which Jesus walked.

It is remarkable that the Pharisees and Sadducees are depicted as coming to hear John, someone who may have once been associated with the Essenes. If so, he was an adversary to both movements. The context of John's speech suggests that the Pharisees and Sadducees had not come to the river Jordan for purposes of demonstrating religious commitment. As both groups will be opponents of the Jesus movement in Matthew's gospel, we can deduce that they are present—at best—as observers or opponents, and—at worst—as spies or agent provocateurs.

Given how the characters of this pericope are cast, we can see a concern of Matthew's church. The Sadducees were among Jesus' most powerful opponents during Holy Week.

Between that point in time (around 30 A.D.) and when Matthew was written, much had changed. The Church had been founded and the Jewish rebellion had occurred, leading to the destruction of the Jerusalem Temple in 70 A.D. By Matthew's day, some five-to-fifteen years later, the temple-based Sadducees had begun to dissipate into a memory. Even so, a substantial recollection of their power would have remained.

On the other hand, the Pharisees were a group that was actually strengthened in the post-temple era. In all probability, they were fierce opponents of Matthew's church. The Pharisees of Antioch, in the late first century, may well have precipitated the excommunication of the Christians from Matthew's hypothetical "synagogue across the street."[14] In this light, we should view a convergence of Pharisees and Sadducees at the river Jordan, just prior to the appearance of the adult Jesus, as a dark shadow. It is much like Herod's presence at the time of the nativity.

Yet, it would be a mistake to view Matthew's purpose in drawing attention to these groups as simply being a way to separate "us" from "them," "good" trees from "bad." These groups also represent improper directions in religious life. The Sadducees were powerful collaborationists, steeped in liturgy, worldly, and supercilious. The Pharisees were legalistic and literalistic, more wedded to the written word than its underlying meaning. Both represent faith gone awry. They stand as examples not to be followed, as warnings to Matthew's own church. By extension, they are warnings to us as well.

1. Had you thought of Pharisees and Sadducees as being alike? Allies? Do they bring to mind the Eastern maxim, "the enemy of my enemy is my friend?" Are we, too, guilty of drawing such divisions?

2. Does it feel better to see John's ire directed specifically at Jesus' eventual opponents, rather than broadly at "the crowd"? Why (not)? Do we lose the possibility of hearing a call to us when we view his denunciation that way?

3. The Pharisees and Sadducees may have been aligned only in their opposition to the Jesus movement. It is not a holy alliance. Conversely, are there holy alternatives for us today? Have you participated in any constructive ecumenical and interfaith

---

[14]*See* chapter 2, The Rabbi's Journey.

alliances? Have you been able to reach common ground while maintaining your own identity? Examples might include service projects, such as Habitat for Humanity or urban ministries.

✝✝✝

✝ LUKE 3:10–14 John Proclaims his Message to Special Groups

¹⁰And the crowds asked him,

> *"What then should we do?"*

¹¹In reply he said to them,

> *"Whoever has two coats must share with anyone who has none; and whoever has food must do likewise."*

¹²Even tax collectors came to be baptized, and they asked him,

> *"Teacher, what should we do?"*

¹³He said to them,

> *"Collect no more than the amount prescribed for you."*

¹⁴Soldiers also asked him,

> *"And we, what should we do?"*

He said to them,

> *"Do not extort money from anyone by threats or false accusation, and be satisfied with your wages."*

1. Why does John single out these groups for special attention?

2. Are there any unifying themes in the instructions that John gives?

Returning to Luke, we again hear John addressing "the crowds." His words are not specifically directed to the eventual opponents of the Jesus movement. By speaking to the greater gathering, John clarifies the meaning of his message. Then, by responding to specific questions, he breaks that message down into smaller pieces.

Before we explore what John says, let us first address *what he does not say*. John is *not* calling the crowd to ritual purity. Nor is he calling it to believe a certain set of propositions about the nature of God. He is not calling the people to gather at the Jordan in order to march on occupied Jerusalem. And he is not calling them to participate in sacrificial rites at the Jerusalem Temple.

Rather, John is calling the crowd to justice and mercy. Just as Micah did centuries ago, a point upon which we reflected earlier in this chapter. The heart of John's message is grounded in ethics; in love; and in individual compassion. The audience is to respond to human need by giving sacrificially, so that no one will be wealthy while others are hungry, cold, and poor.

Then, John addresses two smaller groups. Luke says that "even" tax collectors came to be baptized, as if the idea were unthinkable. Why this choice of words?

The tax collectors (the term "toll collectors" may be the better translation, as this group collected money from travelers) were Jews who collaborated with Rome to gather tribute from the occupied Israelites. They were despised for such a perceived betrayal of their own people. They were ceremonially unclean due to their regular contact with Gentiles—a necessity of carrying out their trade. They were profiteers functioning in a corrupt system. By hook or by crook, they aspired to collect as much money as the law prescribed, plus whatever they could get away with. The tax gatherers were the worst of the worst.[15]

The soldiers were not much better. These men were not highly trained and motivated Roman legionnaires. Rather, they were likely to be local mercenaries, aiding and abetting the empire in its control system. They would have been more closely aligned with the latest Herod than with the latest Caesar. Poorly paid, they often sought to augment their income by the power of intimidation.[16]

---

[15]A description of the precise mechanics by which toll collectors carried out their work is saved for a later volume in this series.

[16]Professor Culpepper writes that this was a common problem in Palestine. He cites writings by contemporary figures, such as the Jewish historian, Josephus, to show how widespread the military practice of extortion was. He even suggests that this sort of pocket-lining was almost expected, given the way that the soldiers' compensation system was structured (*See The New Interpreter's Bible* commentary on Luke, at 85).

One is left to wonder why both so little and so much has changed. For instance, families of enlisted American service personnel are sometimes on food stamps because of the poor compensation. Yet, they do not bully people to try to get more money. If the soldiers have learned so much, why can't the governments?

And yet, the toll collectors and the soldiers went out to the Jordan to be baptized, and to seek John's direction. Unlike the Pharisees and Sadducees of Matthew—the "good" people of the day—Luke does not report John singling out these unsavory characters for a harangue. Instead, he takes their questions seriously and offers a curious, life-giving response. They are not to be defined by what they acquire, but by what they give.

The call to them is to be just. Tax collectors should take no more than what is due; soldiers should not bully; all the people who have plenty should share with those who do not. The requirement is to live out God's call on a day-to-day basis. What matters most is not ritual, or creed, or military conquest of the Holy Land. What matters, above all else, is justice and mercy and humility.

1. How do you react to John's "remedy" for the crowd? Does his content, which has more to do with individual and social justice than with belief systems, challenge your view of what lies at the heart of Christianity?

2. How are we called to live out John's message? Do we respond properly? Can we know for sure?

3. Are you surprised that, to Luke, John's harsh call is fundamentally about kindness?

4. By specifically mentioning the tax collectors and soldiers here, does Luke signal something about the company Jesus will keep?

✝✝✝

CHAPTER TEN

From Nazareth to the River Jordan: "You Are My Son, the Beloved; with You I Am Well Pleased"

We have arrived at the last chapter of the first volume in this series. While we have not yet met the adult Jesus, we have received many clues about what he will look like. The foreshadowing events of Matthew's and Luke's birth narratives set the stage for what we can expect. Luke's story of the how the boy Jesus began to live into his identity further develops who he will become as a man. Then Mark, in all his bluntness, comes forth with a specific declaration about who, exactly, Jesus is. Using this technique, Mark compels us to dive into the heart of the good news, where Matthew and Luke have joined him after completing their extended introductions.

Here, we see our synoptic Gospels converge, like so many roads, upon the desert lands and flowing river where John the Baptist is preaching. What will John tell us about this Jesus? How will John be his forerunner? How will we react to John's interpretation of what is occurring?

By the time we get to the end of this chapter, the Gospels' introductory work will be complete. We will encounter the adult Jesus. And, as we come to the end, we will hear the voice of his Heavenly Father, echoing the words of the Psalmist from the distant past, proclaiming the time of God's favor resting on his people, and resonating through the ages, even to our own time.

✝ MARK 1:7–8 John Preaches about the Coming One, According to Mark

⁷[John] proclaimed,

> *"The one who is more powerful than I is coming after me; I am not worthy to stoop down and untie the thong of his sandals. ⁸I have baptized you with water; but he will baptize you with the Holy Spirit."*

1. Much attention has been focused on John. Now, John himself points elsewhere. How do you think his redirection of attention is important to the story Mark is telling?

2. John distinguishes baptism by water from baptism by the Holy Spirit. What do you think this distinction means?

We have heard John's mighty proclamation calling his pilgrim audience toward repentance. Now, he shifts direction. John intentionally deflects attention away from himself, and points instead toward the higher purpose God intends for his ministry.

Fortunately, though, with this shift, John does not back down from his potent use of imagery and metaphor to make his points. The descriptions of himself and the "more powerful [one] coming after me" prepare us for a message, and a man, that are above and beyond John. And, given what we know of John already—committed, strong-willed, plain-spoken—his self-effacing words serve to catalyze the change all the more.

To illustrate just how much ground John is conceding to the coming one, Professor Barclay tells how slaves of antiquity had a duty to remove their masters' sandals. The heat and dust of Palestine made this task unpleasant, something John's and Mark's ancient audiences would have known well. By using the image of stooping and untying sandals, John the Baptist—the first prophetic Jewish voice to appear in centuries[1]—offers a surprisingly stark comparison between himself and the one who is to follow. Despite the unique role John is playing, he considers himself to be so far beneath the dignity of the "more powerful one" that he shies away even from the role of slave, citing his own unfitness for service.

John's contrasts continue. The baptism he offers pales by comparison to the baptism the coming one offers. John "only" gives water—precious, cleansing, and valuable, but still a natural product widely available in the world. The coming one will baptize with the Holy Spirit.[2]

To Jews, the Holy Spirit was the wind, breath, and power of God. It brought Truth to God's people and enabled them to understand it. While the concept was not yet as fully developed as it became with the formulations of the Trinity in later centuries, the theological core was present. The power of the Holy Spirit is boundless.

The Old Testament prophet Joel, at chapter 2, verse 28 of his book, assured the people of God's promise:

> I will pour out my spirit on all flesh;
> your sons and your daughters shall prophesy

The power of the Spirit will infuse the world and become universally accessible. And the "coming one," who will baptize with that power, will bring the presence of God directly to the people, abundantly and gratuitously, without limit.

1. How do you respond to John's announcements about the coming one? How do you respond to the comparisons he makes between the baptisms each of them offers?

---

[1] It is not only Christians who have held John the Baptist in high regard. Josephus, the worldly and wary first-century Jewish historian who wrote extensively of his people's struggles (particularly with Rome), speaks of John in laudatory terms, if not always candid ones (See, e.g., Crossan, *Jesus: A Revolutionary Biography*, at chapter 2).

[2] John's use of images like water and Spirit may reflect experience in the Qumran community (see *The New Interpreter's Bible* commentary on Mark, at 532–33). They are further evidence of a connection between John and the Essenes.

2. The Holy Spirit might well be considered the most elusive face of God. Yet, it remains our constant companion. Do these characteristics lead you to a sense of contradiction? Of paradox? Do they transcend definition and description for you?

3. How do you experience the presence of the Spirit in your life? In the lives of those around you, such as your family, neighbors, co-workers, friends, or church community?

✝✝✝

✝ MATTHEW 3:11–12 John Preaches about the Coming One, According to Matthew

¹¹[John said]

"I baptize you with water for repentance, but one who is more powerful than I is coming after me; I am not worthy to carry his sandals. He will baptize you with the Holy Spirit and fire. ¹²His winnowing fork is in his hand, and he will clear his threshing floor and will gather his wheat into the granary; but the chaff he will burn with unquenchable fire."

1. What do you notice about the similarities and differences between Mark's version and Matthew's? What might these signify?

2. Mark did not use the fire metaphor in his parallel. Do you think Matthew's use of it makes a difference to the meaning of his text?

3. Matthew's John speaks of being unworthy to "carry," rather than "untie," the sandals of the coming one. Is there a reason for this difference? What might it be?

In both Matthew and Luke, we see John the Baptist use fire as a metaphor for judgment. Fire awaits the trees not bearing fruit worthy of repentance (Matt. 3:10; Luke 3:10). Here, when coupled with the Holy Spirit and connected to baptism rather than to destruction, fire carries a different implication. It is, first and foremost, a force that illuminates and purifies.

Yet John, having just made such a positive use of the fire metaphor, immediately swerves back to a destructive and judgment-oriented use of fire. His vacillation can leave us unsettled. We can appreciate our need for the refining fire, even if we don't enjoy it; the consuming fire is another matter. Moreover, its "unquenchable" nature exceeds mere consumption and destruction. It carries a supernatural threat that is everlasting.

Let us consider, though, whether there might be more congruity than incongruity between these paired images of fire. The threshing floor represents the end of the harvest, when wheat and chaff are separated. The time for reckoning has come. To Professor Boring, it carries a twin purpose: the fire destroys the unholy, and purifies the holy (See *The New Interpreter's Bible* commentary on Matthew, at 157–58). Judgment and purification are two sides of the same coin.

Moreover, the text connects the power of fire to the power of the Holy Spirit. The Spirit is often symbolized by wind; it is God's power to move and to change. Elusive as the Spirit may be, we are guided by its symbols—not only the wind, but also the breath and power of God bearing truth and understanding. It is a redemptive and refreshing force. When combined with the refining and judging character of fire, it bears us mightily along in a positive direction— the direction of the coming one.

The baptism Jesus offers is qualitatively different from John's. It is not simply performed in water, for repentance. It is not even limited to the destroying and refining power of fire. This baptism exceeds all; it is found in the transforming power of Joel's vision, where men and women become nothing less than spirit-filled prophets.

1. Are you tossed about by John's imagery, unable to get a consistent picture? Does John leave us more with image, or with substance?

2. How do you compare John's imagery to the imagery Jesus used, for instance, in his parables?

3. Elijah, the harsh OT prophet, was succeeded by Elisha, a gentler figure. Is this a pattern we see repeated in John and Jesus? Do shifts in temperament from one generation of leaders to another pose problems to our human desire for predictability? How do we overcome these challenges?

✟ LUKE 3:15–18 John Preaches about the Coming One, According to Luke

¹⁵As the people were filled with expectation, and all were questioning in their hearts concerning John, whether he might be the Messiah, ¹⁶John answered all of them by saying,

"I baptize you with water; but one who is more powerful than I is coming; I am not worthy to untie the thong of his sandals. He will baptize you with the Holy Spirit and fire. ¹⁷His winnowing fork is in his hand, to clear his threshing floor and to gather the wheat into his granary; but the chaff he will burn with unquenchable fire."

¹⁸So, with many other exhortations, he proclaimed the good news to the people.

1. What do you notice about the similarities and differences between Luke's version and the other two? What might they signify?

2. Why do you think Luke connects John's baptism to questions about the Messiah?

The people, upon hearing the most credible prophetic voice of their time, are in a state of heightened awareness. They are living under Roman occupation, but hoping for deliverance. How might things get better? Who will deliver them? Does this voice, crying in the wilderness, belong to the Messiah, the obvious vehicle of that deliverance?

John himself will provide a two-part answer. One part is a denial of the title (albeit an indirect one). The other part points to the "more powerful" one who is to come. John's self-effacing words are another installment in Luke's pattern of comparing John and Jesus. Beginning in his birth narrative, Luke recognizes John's greatness, but consistently makes him subordinate to Jesus. For example, the circumcision of John occurred in the hill country. But the circumcision of Jesus occurred in the greater dignity of the Jerusalem Temple. Likewise, thirty-some years later, John's baptism with water is of less value than Jesus' baptism with the Holy Spirit and fire.

Luke's emphasis on the contrasts between John and Jesus may reflect an historical concern of his community. Early Christian missionaries in Acts of the Apostles—the second part of

Luke's two-volume work—encountered John's disciples during their travels. Some years after John's death, these people were still members of his movement. Their presence, and the continuing vitality of that movement, created a problem for Christians. The reason: the Christian claim that John was a forerunner of Jesus. Because of that status, John's movement should have merged into the Christian community, rather than continuing on its own.

This integration had not completely occurred. Therefore, Christians felt the need to establish John's credentials firmly as the forerunner, without letting those credentials bleed over into, or intrude upon, Jesus' role as Messiah. For Luke to convey this story is to establish the proper relationship between John and Jesus by using the words of John the Baptist himself. John denies being the Messiah, and points to someone else, implying that the "coming one" will fulfill that role. This episode clarifies relationships, relieves the tension between the John and Jesus movements, quiets competing ideas among their followers as to who is rightly called the Messiah, and offers a consistent message that the Luke-Acts community can use in its mission.

As with Matthew, Luke connects baptismal ideas of fire and the Spirit. But Luke offers more tools to help us understand that connection, including a dramatic one still commemorated in a major Christian feast. Chapter 2 of Acts contains this story:

> [1]When the day of Pentecost had come, they were all together in one place. [2]And suddenly from heaven there came a sound like the rush of a violent wind, and it filled the entire house where they were sitting. [3]Divided tongues, as of fire, appeared among them, and a tongue rested on each of them. [4]All of them were filled with the Holy Spirit and began to speak in other languages, as the Spirit gave them ability.

Luke's second book shows us the power of the Spirit connected to the symbol of fire. What John proclaimed before the outset of Jesus' ministry comes into maturity after Jesus' resurrection. It is a gift from God that can be seen, heard, and felt.

The people of the world, once fragmented by the differences in their language, speak in others' tongues. Also, they hear their own languages on the lips of those present. The ancient divide of the peoples, dating to the Tower of Babel, is bridged.[3] Those who were formerly separated by the perils of human ambition are now united in the kingdom of God. The purifying and illuminating power of the Holy Spirit is at work.

---

[3]See Gen. 11.

1. By looking at the connections between Luke and Acts, how are your interpretive efforts affected? Are there other connections you could explore as well?

2. How do you respond to the images of water, fire, and spirit? Would this image change if you defined "spirit" in the Jewish way, and called it "wind"?

3. The biblical understanding is that God created us out of dust (*See* Gen 2:7), and that we shall return to dust (*See* Gen. 3:19). If we, both as creatures of dust and objects of baptism, are added to the mix of images, then "earth" would be present, along with wind, fire, and water. These are the four substances the ancients understood to be elemental. Viewing the world through their eyes, we can conclude that *everything* converges in the baptismal imagery. Does this approach allow us to look at the biblical story of baptism from a new vantage point? Does it say something about completeness?

†††

♱ LUKE 3:19–20 The Herodians Terminate John's Ministry

¹⁹But Herod the ruler, who had been rebuked by [John] because of Herodias, his brother's wife, and because of all the evil things that Herod had done, ²⁰added to them all by shutting up John in prison.

1. What is Luke telling us? What evil things might Herod have done to cause him to shut John up? Was prison his personal tool for avoiding accountability?

2. Didn't John baptize Jesus? How could he have done that, if he was in prison?

Here we reach a deviation in Luke's story—a detour from the route we typically take when following Jesus' life. We are aware from other traditions that John baptized Jesus in the river Jordan before the start of Jesus' ministry. We are also aware that the baptism was followed in short order by the testing of Jesus in the desert—sometimes called "the temptation." But the baptism is not presented here, the place where we would expect to find it.

Why are our expectations not met? Throughout Christian history, believers have mentally combined various aspects of the gospel stories, harmonizing them to form as unified a whole as possible. It is a necessary step when reflecting on experiences and formulating a cohesive belief system. For example, a person reading a mystery follows story lines and develops theories. In a collective setting, when a jury hears different evidence from different witnesses, it harmonizes the accounts it considers credible and reconstructs what is most likely to have occurred when it searches out where the truth lies. The process is altogether natural and essential for memory, problem solving, and building a foundation to support our beliefs.

One purpose of this series on the synoptic Gospels is to take us away from mental harmonization in order to meet each text on its own terms. We explore the points each evangelist is trying to make, and learn something more as we study both the areas where they agree and those where they disagree. This process engages us in the responsible interpretation of Scripture. By grappling with the stories of Jesus, and of the early Church, we can learn what matters most and why.

Luke has taken a different route than the other two synoptic evangelists. According to his script, John the Baptist now exits stage right. Luke uses John's departure to prepare for the appearance of Jesus in a different way than does Mark, his primary source.

Luke tells us that John the Baptist was imprisoned because he spoke against the Herodians' evil deeds. Elsewhere in the gospel accounts, we will see that these deeds include Herod Antipas—"Herod the Ruler" of this pericope, and a son of Herod the Great—stealing the wife of his brother, Philip.[4] Herod has no desire to be confronted about it. When he is, the solution is to deprive John of his freedom and put him, and his meddlesome words, as far away from public attention as possible.

Sources outside the Gospels also tell of John running into conflict with the Herodian power structure. Josephus' explanation is that John was imprisoned, not because he was a moral or social critic, but because he was a political risk.[5]

---

[4]See Mark 6:17–29 and Matt. 14:3–12.
[5]See Crossan's *Jesus: A Revolutionary Biography*, chapter 2.

Of course, imprisonment could have been imposed on John for both reasons. John's practice of baptizing in the river Jordan, in the desert east of Jerusalem, could have given the impression of a mass movement gathering and leading toward revolt.[6] The risks of a popular uprising were increased by John's eschatological, or end-times, preaching about the "threshing floor." These themes of repentance, deliverance and judgment could easily have aroused the crowds. If he threw in a few choice words about the Herodians—poster children for corruption and worldliness, whose behavior was entirely antithetical to John's movement—then his position in their realm would have been all the more tenuous.

What John has done is speak the truth to power. He has seen betrayals of brother by brother, of husband by wife, and called them by name. There are also betrayals of the trust placed in the ruling powers, conduct particularly unsettling for Jews, whose prophetic tradition often associated the people's suffering with the evils perpetrated by their rulers.[7] John cannot witness this and keep silent; it is not in his nature. Because he speaks the truth, he pays the price: imprisonment now, and death later. His integrity and courage are to be honored, and the Herodians' abuse of power is to be condemned.

Luke knows this story of John and alludes to it. He uses an historical event for literary, theological, and community-building purposes. By placing it here, Luke takes John the Baptist out of the picture and accomplishes a literary end, as Jesus is ready to assume center stage. It also meets Luke's need to subordinate John and his movement to Jesus and his movement for his community. We will soon read about his theological purpose in telling of John's arrest.

1. How do you respond to the detour Luke takes: telling about John being shut up in prison rather than about him baptizing Jesus?

2. Are there other examples you can think of where the gospel stories are different, but where you may have mentally superimposed one story upon another, or harmonized them in some fashion? Is it helpful in your faith journey to try to unwind that process and consider each segment in its own right?

3. Do the tools of responsible interpretation of Scripture: historical context, theological meaning, literary quality, and response to community concerns or crises, help you interpret divergent texts?

---

[6]See chapter 9, *supra*, at 175.
[7]In point of fact, Josephus attributed a later military defeat of Herod Antipas to his maltreatment of John.

4. How do you respond to the example John sets? Have you experienced times to speak, and times to remain silent? Did John make the right choice about when to speak, and against whom? Why (not)?

†[†]†

✝ MARK 1:9–11 The Baptism of Jesus, According to Mark

⁹In those days Jesus came from Nazareth of Galilee and was baptized by John in the Jordan. ¹⁰And just as he was coming up out of the water, he saw the heavens torn apart and the Spirit descending like a dove on him. ¹¹And a voice came from heaven,

"You are my Son, the Beloved; with you I am well pleased."

1. Here we return to the main storyline that most of us remember: John baptized Jesus. What led to that baptism?

2. Why was Jesus' baptism by John necessary?

3. First-century Jews invested the river Jordan with meaning and expectation. What should our expectations be?

4. At the segment's close, we hear a voice from heaven declaring Jesus' identity. What function does the voice serve?

In this passage and its parallels, we reach the climax of our volume. The introductory words of the pericope, "in those days," draw the reader's attention toward what follows. It is Jesus' first appearance in Mark.

Jesus has come out of Nazareth to the river Jordan. He has not taken a short walk into the wilderness, but has made a purposeful trip. Nazareth in Galilee is quite some distance from where the Jordan flowed through Judea, the place of John's baptismal activity.

Jesus' first public appearance is tied to the work of John the Baptist. John is leading a movement that begins in the desert and courses through the Jordan River. There, his followers are immersed in the water, and they undergo a symbolic death to the old ways. They emerge, cleansed and transformed, before returning to the populated places of Judea. John is leading a movement away from emptiness and exile, and toward God. Away from death, and toward new life.

When the two meet, John baptizes Jesus. This was probably not their first encounter. John may have been living in the Qumran community near the Dead Sea, and came out from it to practice a public ministry different from the separationist ways of the Essene movement. But

Nazareth and the Jordan
(30 C.E.?)

how Jesus got from Nazareth to the river Jordan is of less importance to us than what happened when he arrived at the Jordan. It is here, the place of retreat and renewal, where a voice from Heaven is heard. It punctuates Mark's narrative and affirms Jesus' identity as the Son of God.

This is a powerful scene that we will better understand as we explore not only its specific words and phrases, but also its broader context. As we do this, we face a problem that the early Church also had to address. Why is Jesus being baptized?

To Mark, John's baptism is one "of repentance for the forgiveness of sins" (Mark 1:4). For Jesus to submit himself to this rite raises a perplexing question. Early Christianity had already embraced the notion that Jesus was sinless. For Paul, whose writings predated Mark's gospel, this principle was a basic one (*See* 2 Cor. 5:21).[8] When we take this into account, it seems unnecessary for John to baptize Jesus because: (a) there was nothing to forgive in a sinless man; and (b) no repentance was needed. Therefore, we might conclude, no baptism was required. So, why was Jesus baptized?

The problems do not stop with the question of sinlessness. By baptizing him, John appears to be bringing Jesus into his fold. This development would seem contrary to John's earlier proclamation: The one who is to follow is the greater one. If he is greater, why is he being initiated into a movement where John is the principal leader? How do we resolve this baptismal problem?

---

[8]*But see* Mark 10:18, where Jesus deflects a description of himself as "good."

We will consider these questions more thoroughly when we explore Mark's parallels, along with some non-canonical Christian writings and the Gospel According to St. John. For now, we will set them aside as we consider other aspects of Mark's text. We will then return to the problematic questions about baptism when we see what Matthew and Luke do with the story.

John's baptism of Jesus is a mighty event. We read in Mark that the heavens were torn apart. It is an image showing God's direct intervention in the world. The same type of image is reflected at the end of Mark's gospel, when the crucifixion is accompanied by a rending of the curtain in the Jerusalem Temple from top to bottom. These beginning and ending images frame Mark's story as a whole. Just as the hand of God rips the heavens open to proclaim Jesus' identity in the baptismal beginning, it also rips the Jerusalem Temple curtain from heaven earthward to proclaim what that identity means at the end of the story: No man-made curtain can separate us from God's sacrificial love.

Out of the sky's rupture, the Holy Spirit descends, borne on the wings of a dove. A voice from Heaven speaks. It says nothing to the crowds, nor even to John the Baptist. The words are directed to Jesus, in the second person. "You are my Son, the Beloved; with you I am well pleased." Jesus, and Jesus alone, receives the message of God's favor.

1. Mark's baptismal scene develops as quickly as the introduction to the gospel itself. Did you feel prepared for such a scene? What interpretive challenges does it create for you?

2. Images of torn heavens, rending of a curtain in the temple, doves, and voices from above create a sense of the holy. Where might these images lead us?

✝✝✝

✝ **MATTHEW 3:13–17 The Baptism of Jesus, According to Matthew**

¹³Then Jesus came from Galilee to John at the Jordan, to be baptized by him.
¹⁴John would have prevented him, saying,

> *"I need to be baptized by you, and do you come to me?"*

¹⁵But Jesus answered him,

> *"Let it be so now; for it is proper for us in this way to fulfill all righteousness."*

Then he consented. ¹⁶And when Jesus had been baptized, just as he came up from the water, suddenly the heavens were opened to him and he saw the Spirit of God descending like a dove and alighting on him. ¹⁷And a voice from heaven said,

"This is my Son, the Beloved, with whom I am well pleased."

1. We ask two questions again here that we will ask repeatedly in this series: What do you notice about the similarities and differences between Mark's version and Matthew's? What might they signify?

2. Does Matthew have a different understanding of the practice of baptism than Mark?

3. What does "righteousness" refer to in this passage?

The last time that we were with Jesus in The Gospel According to St. Matthew, he was a baby. Joseph had moved the Holy Family to Nazareth when their days in Egypt ended. While the dangers of Judea were less acute than at the time of the slaughter of the Holy Innocents, it was far from a safe place. Judea was under the rule of the brutal and incompetent Archelaus. An angel had warned Joseph to take the family to Galilee, where they settled.

Now, thirty-some years have passed. Jesus is an adult. Matthew's story resumes with Jesus traveling from Galilee to see John at the Jordan. Jesus has come to be baptized by John.

When studying Mark's version, we questioned why, exactly, Jesus was to be baptized. We found no easy answers. Our still-challenging task may be a little more approachable in Matthew's gospel, as he has already taken a few steps to help us along the way.

Matthew eliminates one problem. He does not describe John's baptism as being for the forgiveness of sins.[9]

Matthew helps us solve a second problem by describing the baptism in a slightly different way. The same question we raised in Mark—why does John baptize the "more powerful one," instead of the other way around?—is resolved by the verbal exchange between John and Jesus.

---

[9]John's baptismal candidates do, of course, confess their sins in Matthew (*See* Matt. 3:6). Even so, the baptismal rite itself is not specifically connected to forgiveness of sins, as in Mark.

John argues that Jesus should be the one baptizing him. His idea is compatible with the description of the coming one as "more powerful." However, Jesus shows John to be operating under a misconception. Righteousness itself requires the baptism Jesus seeks.

Why? There is some thought that Jesus is simply affirming the relationship between the two of them. John's description of one "coming after me" speaks not to the timing of their public appearances, but to Jesus having been John's disciple.[10] This linkage would properly place John in the role of Jesus' baptizer. From this perspective, Jesus' decision to have John baptize him makes perfect sense.

The use of the word "righteousness" to explain the baptismal decision also aids the reader. According to Professor Long (*See* footnote 10, *supra*), there are two main lines of thought about what righteousness means in this context. One is that the term refers to human righteousness, or the possibility of human beings entering into a right relationship with God, and each other, through Jesus' "total involvement in the human condition, his sharing in the fullness of human experience, in order that humanity may be forgiven, saved, and made righteous."[11] The second idea is that the phrase denotes a cry to God for his righteous deliverance in order to "set things right."[12]

Either interpretation leads to the same outcome. By stepping into the baptismal waters of the Jordan, a place frequented by sinners who came to hear John preach, Jesus is identified with humanity itself. It is a sacramental expression of what the opening verses of Matthew foretell. Jesus is called "'Emmanuel,' which means 'God with us'" (Matt. 1:23).

Matthew also follows a different course than Mark in describing the heavenly voice. Here, the heavens are opened up—not torn—and Jesus sees the Spirit of God descending like a dove to alight on him. A voice from Heaven then says "This is my Son, the Beloved, with whom I am well pleased." The baptismal experience Matthew describes is not a private communication, as in Mark; it is a third person declaration to those present that Jesus is the Son of God.

What might be Matthew's purpose in having the heavenly voice publicly validate Jesus? As is often the case, we can look to the Old Testament for clues. Chapter 42 of Isaiah begins this way:

---

[10]A disciple is one who learns. Calling Jesus a disciple of John does not subordinate either his character or his power to John's. As used here, the word describes the process through which Jesus gained the knowledge and discipline that his human nature needed in order to carry out his mission. For more on this and related topics, *see* Professor Boring's commentary on Matthew in *The New Interpreter's Bible* series, at 159–160. *See also* Thomas G. Long's commentary on Matthew in the *Westminster Bible Companion* series, at 32–34. Professor Long is an ordained minister of the Presbyterian Church in the United States of America. He has been affiliated both with Columbia Theological Seminary and Princeton Theological Seminary.

[11]*See* Long, *supra*, at 33.

[12]*Id.*

> [1]Here is my servant, whom I uphold,
> my chosen, in whom my soul delights;
> I have put my spirit upon him;
> he will bring forth justice to the nations.
> [2]He will not cry or lift up his voice,
> or make it heard in the street;
> [3]a bruised reed he will not break,
> and a dimly burning wick he will not quench;
> he will faithfully bring forth justice.
> [4]He will not grow faint or be crushed
> until he has established justice in the earth;
> and the coastlands wait for his teaching.

By invoking Isaiah's prophecy, Matthew connects the Old Order to the New. Jesus is identified as God's servant upon whom his Spirit rests. His mission is to establish justice, practice mercy, and walk humbly with God. The prophetic tradition of Micah 6:8 continues.

1. Mark's version of the baptism holds more mystery than Matthew's. Does one speak to you more than the other? Why?

2. In Mark, we see a tendency to conceal information about Jesus' identity. In Matthew, we see a tendency to disclose it. Mark's technique is sometimes called the "Messianic secret," a concept to which we will be more formally introduced later in this series. Why might Mark use this technique? Why might Matthew take a different approach?

✝ LUKE 3:21–22 The Baptism of Jesus, According to Luke

[21]Now when all the people were baptized, and when Jesus also had been baptized and was praying, the heaven was opened, [22]and the Holy Spirit descended upon him in bodily form like a dove. And a voice came from heaven,

"You are my Son, the Beloved; with you I am well pleased."

1. What do you notice about the similarities and differences between Mark's version and Luke's? What might they signify?

As with Matthew, Luke has already taken Jesus to Nazareth. Our most recent episode presented him as an adolescent, returning home an obedient child after first taking leave of his parents. The reason for his absence: Jesus was about his "father's business" in the Jerusalem Temple.

The parallel paths of John and Jesus, brought forth from the beginning of Luke's gospel, are moving toward this moment—but they do not quite intersect. Luke does something with John that our other two synoptic evangelists do not. He has already reached a point in his narrative when John has been shut up in prison. Even so, the current segment is still (at least partially) about Jesus' baptism. With John in prison, how does the baptism occur?

Luke's Jesus has participated in a large, general baptism. There is no mention of him seeking out John, or of John having baptized Jesus. Nor do we witness the baptism itself. It is described in the past tense. It is not clear from the text itself whether it is the immediate past, or a lengthier period has intervened.

Luke also subtly shifts away from baptismal images and leaves us with another one: Jesus praying. For Luke, prayer is the time when God's revelation occurs. He frequently connects important episodes in his story with Jesus praying.

Jesus' prayer is answered by a remarkable communication with God. As in Mark, the voice is in the second person, telling Jesus, "You are my Son, the Beloved; with you I am well pleased." God's words of favor are directed at Jesus, with no indication that others can hear them.

In Luke, then, we have another gospel story, containing another version of the baptism and description of the Spirit moving toward Jesus. Yet, even Luke does not exhaust all possibilities. The early Church had many different accounts of the baptism.[13] The Gospel According to St. John even goes so far as to omit any reference at all to Jesus being baptized. John the Baptist is simply described as witnessing the Spirit in the form of a dove coming from heaven and resting on Jesus (See John 1:19–34).[14]

---

[13]See generally Gospel Parallels, at §6, and sources cited therein. Some of these ancient witnesses contain: (a) detailed discussions about whether and why Jesus was to be baptized (See The Gospel According to the Hebrews, a text used in Greek-speaking Jewish Christian circles around Egypt); (b) more expansive words from the Heavenly voice (See The Gospel of the Ebionites, a text used by Jewish Christian groups who denied the virgin birth and believed Jesus' sonship to God was dependent upon the work of the Holy Spirit at baptism); and (c) additional signs being given at the baptism (See again, The Gospel According to the Hebrews).

[14]In the fourth gospel, John the Baptist's description of Jesus is mystically theological. He denies having known Jesus, except as divinely revealed.

Why do we see all this contradiction and controversy around the baptism of Jesus? In addition to the theological reasons we have explored, there may be issues rooted in cultural history. Baptismal practices first arose in Eastern mystery religions that involved images of a god's and his followers' death and resurrection.[15] By contrast, Jewish rites that involved administration of water were, at first, limited to issues of ritual cleanliness. Only later did Judaism adopt baptism. Even then, Jewish baptismal practices were reserved for Gentile converts. Because they viewed themselves as children of Abraham, Jews did not practice baptism of their own people. That tradition changed with John.

Ironically, these discrepancies in the various baptismal traditions do not lead scholars to doubt the historical probability of the event. Quite the opposite, as both mainline and cutting-edge scholars consider the baptism to be among the most probable events in Jesus' life. There are so many signs that point to John having baptized Jesus that *the question is not whether it took place, but how we understand it.*

Even with all the theological and cultural challenges that the traditions of John baptizing Jesus create, it remains the defining moment of Jesus' first public appearance. If we do not try to sidestep the baptism, or explain its difficulties away, we can see different approaches to understanding it. We have already compared Mark, Matthew, and Luke. But differing traditions exist within the Lukan corpus itself. There are textual variations among the ancient Luke manuscripts. In some, the heavenly voice says: "You are my son; *today I have begotten you.*" (Emphasis added; *See Gospel Parallels*, §6, and sources cited therein). Because the emphasized words do not appear in all manuscripts, the discrepancies within the Lukan tradition may be quite intentional. For instance, they may reveal a tension in the early Church between groups who understood the virgin birth as an historical event, and those who questioned or disputed it. The latter group believed God adopted Jesus as his Son at baptism, rather than miraculously conceiving him thirty years earlier by the power of the Holy Spirit.

What may really lie at the bottom of all these diverse texts is the faith story of different people struggling mightily to find proper words and images that describe the reality of Jesus' relationship with God. The controversy around his baptism served as a lightning rod to bring that relationship into focus.

Some New Testament writers portray how Jesus' identity as the Son of God is revealed a little differently. The earliest NT writings are those of Paul. In his Letter to the Romans—one of Paul's later works, though written before any of the canonical Gospels—Paul describes the

---

[15]C.S. Lewis saw the hand of God in these mystery religions, foreshadowing the coming of Christ and preparing the world for God's definitive revelation. *See Mere Christianity* at 39.

"gospel concerning [God's] Son, who was descended from David according to the flesh and was declared to be Son of God with power according to the spirit of holiness by resurrection from the dead" (Rom. 1:3–4). To Paul, the resurrection is the defining event of Jesus' Sonship. We have seen that Mark, who begins his gospel at around the time of the baptism, suggests that the baptism is the critical moment for declaring Jesus' identity. Luke and Matthew go back to Jesus' birth to establish his Sonship. Finally, The Gospel According to St. John—"The Mystic's Story" of *The Four Witnesses*[16]—reaches far beyond, into eternity, and proclaims the preexistence of the divine *logos*, or word of God, that was made flesh in Jesus Christ (*See* John 1:1–18).

Seeing the difficulty the early Church experienced in coming to grips with the precise meaning of both baptism and sonship, it might be helpful for us to refocus on core truths rather than going too much further when considering important, but potentially speculative, questions about "what really happened." The connections among sin, repentance, forgiveness, and baptism are complex. We cannot reproduce with absolute certainty either the verbal interchange between John and Jesus, or the precise way in which Jesus (and perhaps others) experienced the heavenly voice. What we can do, though, is remember that the adult Jesus went to the desert as a preliminary step in a journey toward his ultimate destiny. That there he met John, a man living out the prophetic tradition. That Jesus waded into the river Jordan to be baptized. That, in doing so, he voluntarily aligned himself not only with John's movement in the desert with all it entailed, but also with a humanity in need of cleansing. And that he submitted to the baptismal rite as an outward and visible sign of an inward and spiritual grace. We will see, in the next volume of this series, that he emerged empowered to be with and among his people, and us as well, during our own journeys into the kingdom, the destiny toward which God calls us all.

1. This section discusses the idea that the diverging baptismal traditions nonetheless have a unifying force. Do you agree? Or, does that notion gloss over material differences among the stories?

2. What core values or meanings do you find among the different versions of the baptismal story?

---

[16]*See* chapter 2, *supra*, regarding the book *The Four Witnesses*.

3. We have now met the adult Jesus, who has identified himself with a Judaic movement back toward God. Where will he take us?

✝✝✝

In the baptism of Jesus, we encounter the manifest presence of the Trinity. The voice of the Father; the decisive and participatory action of the Son; and the physical embodiment of the Spirit converge in the river Jordan. It is a critical moment in our history; one difficult to encapsulate fully. Even as we search for our own words, we can still hear the heavenly voice of the baptism echo the ancient biblical words of Psalm 2:

> [7]I will tell of the decree of the Lord:
> He said to me, "You are my son;
> today I have begotten you.
> [8]Ask of me, and I will make the nations your heritage,
> and the ends of the earth your possession."

Amen.

✝✝✝

Looking Ahead

This first volume of *The Synoptic Gospels: A Journey into the Kingdom* has taken us from a Bethlehem manger to the river Jordan. It concludes in waters running through the desert, haunted by memories of lost greatness, but flowing on with the hope of redemption. It is here that the voice of the Father proclaims the character of his Son, as the Holy Spirit descends to consecrate him.

We are now ready to witness the remarkable ministry of Jesus the Anointed, Son of God. The foundation has been laid. What will be built on it? We will begin to see answers to this question in our next volume.

There, we will see how Jesus must first be tested in the wilderness, where he rejects the ways of the world and chooses the path toward the kingdom of Heaven. It will not be the path that his culture expected. For that matter, it will not be the path that our culture expects.

Jesus will preach the good news of the kingdom of Heaven. He will heal the sick. He will call and build disciples. He will tell us about the paradox of what it means to be, rather than merely to seem, "blessed." He will begin to show us the hard and glorious road that leads to life.

I hope you join us for the journey.

†††

Acknowledgments

Writing this book has been a labor of love. As the Preface shows, its roots reach deep into the history of an ancient people. Its trunk grew out of that history, fed and fertilized by personal experience. And branches have grown out of that trunk, marking the routes I have followed in my quest to lay claim to the highest and best traditions of Christianity, particularly as they are grounded in its foundational document, the Holy Bible.

What I have found is that reading and interpreting the Word calls not only for personal inquiry, but also for openness to the experience of others. We discern more of the Spirit of God where personal contemplation and community experience meet than we do when either stands alone. And this book has arisen out of both personal and community experience.

The personal course I charted in the Preface dates first to my ancestry, and then to experiences of the mid-1980s. Since then, my path has been illuminated by years of study, worship, reflection, fellowship, and just plain living. It has led my family and me to Asheville, North Carolina. Here, I am a member of Trinity Parish, part of the Episcopal Diocese of Western North Carolina.

My experience at Trinity Parish in the adult Christian Education class that I co-teach finally prompted me to write this series. I would like to thank the clergy and staff of Trinity, who have been tremendously supportive of the trail our class has been blazing in studying the synoptic Gospels. We have attempted to be bold, fearless, honest, compassionate, faithful, traditional, innovative, and a lot of other things as well. Inevitably, in the course of human striving, we have fallen short of the marks we set. But at least we have tried. Isn't the effort, and the odd mix of success and failure, the place where Divine grace and human commitment most often meet?

Our Trinity clergy members have assisted in the production phase of this volume. Rector Bill Whisenhunt graciously agreed not only to review a draft of this book, but also to seek similar participation by our other clergy, Tom Hughes and Richard Grimball. All are highly educated and committed people, at different stages in career and life, and with different perspectives that they brought to this process. I thank them for their assistance, especially as input and comments by ordained clergy about a theologically oriented book are invaluable to a lay author.

I also extend particular thanks to Katie Chappell and Terri Roberts, who have taught the synoptic Gospels class with me. As with our clergy, each of us as a lay teacher brings a perspective that differs from the others'. Consistent with the synoptic Gospels themselves, we have found that differences of interpretation and understanding offer insight that an unexamined text or life could never offer. I thank Katie and Terri for reviewing this book, and for their words of encouragement and constructive criticism.

Along with the teachers, I am grateful to the class participants. Ours is a study and discussion group. What each person says about a particular passage of the Bible adds to the interpretive data base. From this community approach, we find ourselves digging for truth at a deep level. I hope we can bring something from our shared experience back to our families, the broader church, and our communities. If we do that, we will become better citizens in the kingdom of God.

Other people have also been kind enough to review drafts of this first volume of *The Synoptic Gospels: A Journey into the Kingdom*. They include the Rev. Jim Petty, who has brought a lively engagement of the biblical text to his comments. Jim frequently takes an approach to the Bible and to faith life that challenges conventional wisdom and calls us to approach the text more broadly; to see what it is really about, not just what we thought it was about. The Rev. Judith Whelchel, godmother of Luke Bleynat, Anne's and my youngest child, also reviewed much of the text. She provided not only encouragement, but also some informal marketing assistance, as she has made others aware of its pending publication and encouraged them to read it.

The Rev. O.C. Edwards, Jr., Professor Emeritus at Seabury-Western Theological Seminary, an Episcopal Church institution of higher learning, provided a more academic evaluation of the work. I was a little nervous about what his reaction might be, given his credentials and my lack of same. Instead of finding my work being raked over the coals, I received much positive input, and appreciate how he took the time to review it even while traveling and working on another book of his own.

Thanks also to Tom Whittington, D.C., whose close reading led to clarification and prevented more than one error. Tom actually seemed to enjoy this task, even though his wife, Robbin Brent Whittington—my publisher—has something of a vested interest in this project. If nothing else, she would want to avoid me causing her to suffer professional embarrassment. With Tom there to help, I think we have at least met that goal.

And, to Robbin, I offer particular appreciation. Her gifts and graces as a publisher of spiritually oriented works, and her ability to persuade me to express some of my stronger opinions in a kinder way, have kept this book somewhere in the fairway. She has been a good restraining hand against my occasional tendency to want to knock a ball as far as I can, sometimes ending up in the rough. Even though I enjoy a good fuss, Robbin reminded me more than once that fussing was not a primary purpose of this series.

I would also like to thank the attorneys and staff of Ferikes & Bleynat, PLLC—the place where I work for my day job. It is not always easy to make a law office run smoothly. When someone is moonlighting as an amateur writer, things can sometimes get even more stressful. My office was able to coordinate my schedule, offer needed help, and otherwise temper the climate of my practice to allow me to complete this book without either my legal work, or the writing of this volume, collapsing of their own weight.

And finally, I want to thank the one indispensable person in all of this. Anne Elizabeth Freels and I met as law school classmates. She ended up getting stuck with me for life, and now goes by Anne E. F. Bleynat. When we were married in St. Paul's Episcopal Church, Chattanooga, Tennessee, the officiant commented on the intensity of our vows. This turned out to be uncannily perceptive; our lives have since involved much intensity. We have weathered demanding career paths, started a family, added to it (more than once), and made our way to Asheville, North Carolina, where we now find ourselves in the most beautiful and delightful place on Earth. We try not to miss anything of what this place, and its people, have to offer. Booking and overbooking, our and the children's schedules, have more than once pushed our capacity to the limit.

And then, I added writing a book into the mix. This led to Anne picking up the remaining slack, freeing me to clatter away on a laptop computer at night, sometimes even falling asleep over it. But Anne kept the home fires burning, the children's lives orderly, and me from overloading. She also occasionally—and unequivocally—reminded me that there were other priorities in my life, too.

Our shared tasks were daunting enough that the Rt. Rev. Robert H. Johnson, Bishop of our Diocese and author of the Foreword to this volume, expressed a pastoral concern about the time and potential stress associated with this endeavor. Bishop Johnson was able to see broadly and deeply, to provide both encouragement and support for what he knew was a demanding process. For that, for writing the Foreword, and most especially, for leading this Diocese grandly, I thank him.

As Bishop Johnson hoped and prayed with me, our family has emerged from composition of this volume healthy and happy, if a little tired at times. I think we have lived up to our informal family motto: "We muddle through."

I hope that you not only muddle through this book, but find something of lasting value in it. And, if nothing else, I hope you can see that it is a labor of love.

†††

Reading List

Commentaries

1. William Barclay, *The Daily Study Bible Series, The Gospel of Matthew:* Volume One, Revised Edition, ISBN 0-664-24100-X.
2. William Barclay, *The Daily Study Bible Series, The Gospel of Matthew:* Volume Two, Revised Edition, ISBN 0-664-24101-8.
3. William Barclay, *The Daily Study Bible Series, The Gospel of Mark,* Revised Edition, ISBN 0-664-24102-6.
4. William Barclay, *The Daily Study Bible Series, The Gospel of Luke,* ISBN 0-664-24103-4.
5. *The New Interpreter's Bible,* Volume Eight, New Testament Articles, Matthew and Mark, ISBN 0-687-27821-X.
6. *The New Interpreter's Bible,* Volume Nine, Luke and John, ISBN 0-687-27822-8.
7. Richard A. Edwards, *Matthew's Story of Jesus,* ISBN 0-8006-1619-7.
8. Werner H. Kelber, *Mark's Story of Jesus,* ISBN 0-8006-1355-4.
9. O.C. Edwards, Jr., *Luke's Story of Jesus,* ISBN 0-8006-1611-1.
10. Alyce M. McKenzie, *Interpretation Bible Studies, Matthew,* ISBN 0-664-50022-6.
11. Richard I. Deibert, *Interpretation Bible Studies, Mark,* ISBN 0-664-50078-1.
12. Thomas W. Walker, *Interpretation Bible Studies, Luke,* ISBN 0-664-50075-7.
13. Richard Rohr, *The Good News According to Luke,* ISBN 0-8245-1490-4.
14. Thomas G. Long, *Westminster Bible Companion, Matthew,* ISBN 0-664-25257-5.
15. James L. Mays, *General Editor, Harper's Bible Commentary,* ISBN 0-06-065542-9.
16. David Hester, *Interpretation Bible Studies, First and Second Samuel,* ISBN 0-664-50073-0.

Waldenses

1. Giorgio Tourn, *The Waldensians: The First 800 Years.*
2. Maxine McCall and Kays Gary, *What Mean These Stones.*
3. Prescot Stephens, *The Waldensian Story, A Study in Faith, Intolerance and Survival,* ISBN 1-85776-280-0.

Studies Relating to the Historical Jesus

1. Luke Timothy Johnson, *The Real Jesus: The Misguided Quest for the Historical Jesus and The Truth of the Traditional Gospels*, ISBN 0-06-064166-5.
2. Luke Timothy Johnson, *Living Jesus: Learning the Heart of the Gospel*, ISBN 0-06-064282-3.
3. Marcus J. Borg and N.T. Wright, *The Meaning of Jesus: Two Visions*, ISBN 0-06-060875-7.
4. Marcus J. Borg, *Meeting Jesus Again for the First Time*, ISBN 0-06-060917-6.
5. John Dominic Crossan, Luke Timothy Johnson, and Werner H. Kelber, *The Jesus Controversy: Perspectives in Conflict*, ISBN 1-56338-289-X.
6. John Dominic Crossan, *The Historical Jesus: The Life of a Mediterranean Jewish Peasant*, ISBN 0-06-061629-6.
7. John Dominic Crossan, *Jesus: A Revolutionary Biography*, ISBN 0-06-061661-X.

Christian Apologetics

1. C.S. Lewis, *Mere Christianity*, ISBN 0-02-570610-1.
2. C.S. Lewis, *The Screwtape Letters*, Revised Edition, ISBN 0-02-086740-9.
3. John Polkinghorne, *Belief in God in an Age of Science*, ISBN 0-300-07294-5.
4. J. B. Phillips, *Your God is Too Small*, ISBN 0-02-088540-7.

Biblical Surveys and Criticism

1. John Shelby Spong, *Rescuing the Bible from Fundamentalism*, ISBN 0-06-067518-7.
2. John Shelby Spong, *A New Christianity for a New World*, ISBN 0-06-067084-3.
3. Robert W. Funk and Roy W. Hoover, *The Five Gospels: What Did Jesus Really Say?*, ISBN 0-06-063040-X.
4. Robert J. Miller, Editor, *The Complete Gospels*, ISBN 0-06-065587-9.
5. William Loader, *Jesus and the Fundamentalism of His Day*, ISBN 0-8028-4796-X.
6. Peter J. Gomes, *The Good Book: Reading the Bible with Mind and Heart*, ISBN 0-380-72323-9.
7. Burton L. Mack, *The Lost Gospel: The Book of Q and Christian Origins*, ISBN 0-06-065375-2.
8. Marcus J. Borg, *Reading the Bible Again for the First Time: Taking the Bible Seriously but not Literally*, ISBN 0-06-060918-4.
9. Robin Griffith Jones, *The Four Witnesses: The Rebel, The Rabbi, The Chronicler and the Mystic*, ISBN 0-06-251647-7.

Other Resources

1. T.S. Eliot, *Selected Poems*, ISBN 0-15-680647-9.
2. T.S. Eliot, *Four Quartets*, ISBN 0-15-633225-6.
3. J.R. Porter, *The Illustrated Guide to the Bible*, ISBN 0-19-521462-5.

Early Christian Writings and Christian History

1. Translated by Maxwell Staniforth, *Early Christian Writings*, ISBN 0-14-044475-0.
2. Paul Tillich, *A History of Christian Thought*, ISBN 0-671-21426-8.
3. Marcus Borg, Consulting Editor, *The Lost Gospel Q, The Original Sayings of Jesus*, ISBN 1-56975-100-5.
4. Richard E. Rubenstein, *When Jesus Became God*, ISBN 0-15-601315-0.
5. Karen Armstrong, *A History of God: The 4,000 Year Quest of Judaism, Christianity and Islam*, ISBN 0-345-38456-3.
6. Elaine Pagels, *The Gnostic Gospels*, ISBN 0-679-72453-2.

Contemporary Christian Thought

1. Bruce Bawer, *Stealing Jesus: How Fundamentalism Betrays Christianity*, ISBN 0-609-80222-4.
2. Robert Boston, *Close Encounters with the Religious Right: Journeys into the Twilight Zone of Religion and Politics*, ISBN 1-57392-797-X.
3. Russell Shorto, *Gospel Truth: The New Image of Jesus Emerging from Science and History, and Why It Matters*, ISBN 1-57322-659-9.
4. Paul Tillich, *The Courage To Be*, ISBN 0-300-08471-4.
5. Paul Tillich, *Systematic Theology: Volume One*, ISBN 0-226-80337-6.
6. Paul Tillich, *Systematic Theology: Volume Two*, ISBN 0-226-80338-4.
7. Paul Tillich, *Systematic Theology: Volume Three*, ISBN 0-226-80339-2.
8. Jim Hill and Rand Cheadle, *The Bible Tells Me So: Uses and Abuses of Holy Scripture*, ISBN 0-385-47695-7.
9. William Sloane Coffin, *The Heart Is A Little To The Left: Essays on Public Morality*, ISBN 0-87451-958-6.

Reference Material

1. Paul J. Achtemeier, *General Editor, Harper's Bible Dictionary*, ISBN 0-06-069862-4.

2. James A. Gould, *Classic Philosophical Questions*—Fifth Edition, ISBN 0-675-20264-7.

3. *The Holy Bible*, New Revised Standard Version with Apocrypha, ISBN 0-19-528330-9.

4. Linda L. Grenz, *Doubleday Pocket Bible Guide*, Revised Edition, ISBN 0-385-48568-9.

5. Burton H. Throckmorton, Jr., *Gospel Parallels: A Comparison of the Synoptic Gospels*, ISBN 0-8407-7484-2.

6. Ken Anderson, *Where to Find It in the Bible*, ISBN 0-7852-1157-8.

Synoptic Gospels
Scripture Excerpts

Matthew

MATTHEW 1:1–17 *The Genealogy of Jesus*   48

MATTHEW 1:18–25 *The Birth of Jesus, from Joseph's Perspective*   90

MATTHEW 2:1–12 *The Visit of the Wise Men*   116

MATTHEW 2:13–23 *The Flight into Egypt, the Slaughter of the
                     Holy Innocents, and the Journey to Nazareth*   139

MATTHEW 3:1–6 *The Coming of John the Baptist, According to Matthew*   177

MATTHEW 3:7–10 *John Preaches Wrath and Repentance, According to Matthew*   186

MATTHEW 3:11–12 *John Preaches about the Coming One, According to Matthew*   196

MATTHEW 3:13–17 *The Baptism of Jesus, According to Matthew*   205

Mark

MARK 1:1–6 *The Coming of John the Baptist, According to Mark*   172

MARK 1:7–8 *John Preaches about the Coming One, According to Mark*   194

MARK 1:9–11 *The Baptism of Jesus, According to Mark*   203

Luke

LUKE 1:1–4 *The Prologue*   42

LUKE 1:5–25 *The Expected Birth of John the Baptist*   61

LUKE 1:26–38 *The Annunciation*   67

LUKE 1:39–56 *Mary Visits Elizabeth*   75

LUKE 1:57–66 *The Birth of John the Baptist*   82

LUKE 1:67–80 *Zechariah's Song: the Benedictus*   85

LUKE 2:1–7 *The Census and the Journey*   106

LUKE 2:5–20 *The Birth of Jesus*   111

Luke *(continued)*

LUKE 2:21–24 *Jesus Is Presented and Circumcised at the Temple*   130

LUKE 2:25–40 *Jesus Is Blessed and Proclaimed*   133

LUKE 2:41–52 *Jesus Visits the Temple at Twelve Years*   152

LUKE 3:1–6 *The Coming of John the Baptist, According to Luke*   179

LUKE 3:7–9 *John Preaches Wrath and Repentance, According to Luke*   183

LUKE 3:10–14 *John Proclaims his Message to Special Groups*   189

LUKE 3:15–18 *John Preaches about the Coming One, According to Luke*   198

LUKE 3:19–20 *The Herodians Terminate John's Ministry*   200

LUKE 3:21–22 *The Baptism of Jesus, According to Luke*   208

General Bible Index

OLD TESTAMENT

Genesis, 51, 54, 101, 131
Genesis 2:7, 200
Genesis 3:19, 200
Genesis 11, 199n. 3
Genesis 17:9–14, 131
Genesis 19, 56
Genesis 29–30, 54n. 13
Genesis 34, 83n. 1
Genesis 35:10, 40
Genesis 38, 54
Leviticus 12:1–8, 131
Numbers 18:15–16, 132
Deuteronomy 22:13–29, 93
Joshua 2, 55
Joshua 6, 55
Ruth 1:16–18, 56
1 Samuel 2:1–10, 77
1 Samuel 16, 112n. 5
2 Samuel 11–12, 56
2 Samuel 12:24–25, 56
2 Kings 1:8, 175
1 Chronicles 3, 53n. 12
Psalm 19, 52
Psalm 137, 52
Isaiah 7:14, 99–101
Isaiah 40:3, 173
Isaiah 42, 207
Isaiah 51:1–3, 184
Ezekiel 18:1–4, 145
Daniel, 122
Daniel 8, 65
Joel 2:28–29, 148, 195
Jonah, 164
Micah 6:8, 178, 208
Malachi 3:1, 173n. 2, 175

NEW TESTAMENT

Matthew 1, 48, 90
Matthew 1:23, 207
Matthew 3:6, 178, 206n. 9
Matthew 3:10, 196
Matthew 8:10, 155
Matthew 14:3–12, 201n. 4
Matthew 24:36, 155
Mark 1:4, 178, 204
Mark 1:6, 175
Mark 6:6, 155, 175, 201, 219
Mark 6:17–29, 201n. 4
Mark 10:18, 204n. 8
Mark 13, 31
Luke 1:1–4, 16, 42
Luke 1:4, 16, 42, 172
Luke 1:17, 180
Luke 1:77, 181
Luke 2:29, 181
Luke 3:10, 196
Luke 3:23–38, 50
Luke 19:9, 181
John, 3, 5, 17, 21–23, 118, 138, 162, 209–211
John 1:1–18, 211
John 1:19–34, 209
John 1:46, 118
Acts of the Apostles, 3, 34, 36–37, 147, 198
Acts 2, 199
Acts 17, 124n. 14
Acts 18–19, 73
Acts 25, 47n. 5
Romans 1, 173n. 1, 211
Romans 1:3–4, 211
Romans 2, 83n. 1
Romans 13, 47
1 Corinthians 13, 158, 162
1 Corinthians 13:8–13, 161
2 Corinthians 5:21, 204
Galatians 1, 173n. 1
Timothy, 136n. 3
Titus, 136
1 John 4:1, 46
Revelation, 6, 31, 147

General Index

A

Aaron, 61, 65
Abraham, xx, 30, 36, 40–41, 48–53, 57–58, 76, 86, 88, 99, 103, 131, 169, 183–186, 210
  children of, 52, 184–185, 210
Abram, xx, 39–40, 60, 65, 131
Adam, 36, 51, 57, 101–102, 163. *See also* New Adam
advent, 52, 73
Aeneid, The, 149
African, 126
Agnosticism, xv
Ahaz, king, 49, 99–100
Alabama, 74
Albert, Charles, Duke of Savoy, xiii
Alexander the Great of Macedonia, xx
Alexandria, 47, 142–143
almah, 100
Amalekites, 45n. 4
American, 79, 113, 138, 154, 190
Amon, 53n. 12
Amos, 49, 53n. 12
Amram, 167
angels:
  angelic messengers, 61
  appeared to Joseph, 90–91, 96, 139–140, 206
  appeared to shepherds in the field, 111–112, 114–115, 156
  Gabriel appeared to Mary, 67–68, 71–72, 156
  Gabriel appeared to Zechariah, 61–62, 71–72, 84
  modern, 74–75
  revelation and, 31
Anna, 72, 134–138, 156
Anno Domini, 60n. 1
Annunciation, 67–69

Anointed One, 30, 50, 173
Anointed, 30, 42, 50, 66, 100, 112, 117, 173, 213
Antichrist, 32
Antioch of Syria, 28, 33, 47, 188
Antiochus IV Epiphanes, xx
anti-Semitic, 30
apocalyptic literature, 31–32
apocalyptic works, 31
Apostles, 56, 167
  The Twelve, 51, 167
apostolic authority, 23, 25, 33–34, 37
Apostolic era, xii
Aquinas, Thomas, Saint, xi
  Summa Theologiae, xi
Arabia, 122, 126
Aramaic, 3, 16, 26
Archaeologists, 5, 27, 159
Archelaus, xxiii, 140, 144, 164, 206
Arian controversy, 39n. 1
Aristotle, xi
Aristotelean, 60
Armstrong, Karen, 39n. 1, 221
Asheville, North Carolina, xvii, 57, 215, 217
Asia Minor, 35–37
Asian, 126
Assyrian conquest, 178
Assyrian Empire, xx
Assyrians, 41
astrologer, 122. *See also* wise men
astronomers, 124. *See also* wise men
Athanasius, Saint, 3
Athens, 64n. 2, 124
atonement, 131–132, 154
attributed, 25–26, 28, 33, 37, 136, 160, 168, 202
Augustus, Roman emperor, xxi, 97–98, 106, 108–109, 142, 164–169

authoritarian religious systems, 8
authoritarians, 95, 162

B

Baal, 143, 175
Babylon, 41, 49, 52–53, 174
Babylonian Empire, xx. *See also* empire
Babylonian exile, xx, 31, 52–53, 58, 88, 122, 143, 174, 176, 178. *See also* exile
Babylonians, 41
baptism of Jesus, 211
baptism with the Holy Spirit and fire, 198
Baptist, xv, 107
Baptist, John the. *See* John the Baptist
bar mitzvah, 154
Barclay, William, xvi, 83, 135, 195, 219
  Daily Study Bible Series, The, 219
Barrabas, 29
Bathsheba, 52, 54, 56
Beatitudes, 26
begat, 48
beloved physician, 34
Benedictus, the, 36, 85–89, 106, 135n. 2, 181
Bethlehem of Judea, 108–109, 112, 116, 120, 129
Bethlehem, 105–113, 115–121, 123–125, 127, 129–131, 133, 135, 137, 139–141, 143–147, 149, 155, 166, 213
betrothal, 93, 167
Bible, Christian, 7
Bible, Hebrew, xx, 7, 31, 99–100, 122, 132, 164, 166, 187
Bible Belt, xiv
Bill of Rights, xiv
biography, 36, 99, 120, 166, 175, 195, 201, 220

birth narrative, 24n. 4, 36, 71, 85, 91, 97, 106, 108–110, 118, 120, 124–125, 135, 153, 155, 165, 168, 198
birth of Jesus, 48, 62, 90, 105, 107–111, 120, 129, 169
bishop, x, xvii, 162, 217
Black Forest of Germany, 174
Bleynat, Anne Elizabeth Freels, iii, xvii, 217
Boaz, 49, 56
Bonhoeffer, Dietrich, 47n. 5
Book of Biblical Antiquities, 167
Book of Common Prayer, xvii, 45–46
Borg, Marcus, 41, 120, 166n. 18, 120nn. 11, 12, 176, 221
    Meaning of Jesus, The: Two Visions, 120nn. 11, 12, 166n. 18
Boring, M. Eugene, 10, 53, 145–146, 197, 207n. 10
    The New Interpreter's Bible, Volume 8 (on Matthew and Mark), 10, 53, 145–146, 195n. 2, 197, 207n. 10, 219
branch of Jesse, 144
branch, 144, 162
Brown, Raymond, 102
burnt offering, 131–132

C

Caligula, Roman emperor, xxi, 164
Calvinists, xiii
camel, 172, 175, 177
Canaan, 39–41, 55, 83, 174
Canaanites, 161
Candler School of Theology at Emory University, 102
canonical ending of Mark, 24
canonical Gospels, 18
cardinal theological virtues of faith, hope and love, 159
Cascade Mountains of Oregon and Washington, 174
catechism, 45, 9
Catholic, 6, 102, 159, 162, 174
celestial signs, 61, 98, 124
Celsus, 101
census, 106–107, 109–110
chaff, 196–198
Chaldees, 39–41, 43, 45, 47, 49, 51, 53, 55, 57–58
Chappel, Katie, xvii, 216

Chicago, University of, 14, 99
chief priests, 116–117
childlessness, 66, 83
children of Abraham, 52, 184–185, 210
Christ Child, 140
Christ, *passim*
Christian age, 3
Christian Bible, 7
Christian calendar, traditional, xxi
Christian Education resource, ix
Christian Crusades, 7
Christian era, 64n. 2
Christian faith journey, 19
Christian faith, xvi, 19, 96–97
Christian liberty, 4
Christian life, 79, 159–160
Christmas, 102, 112, 116, 121, 154n. 2
Chronicler, 34, 36, 44. *See also* Luke
Church, *passim*
Church of the Advocate, 114
circumcision, 5, 72, 83–84, 130–132, 153, 198
classical world, 98
Claudius, Roman emperor, xxi
clerics, 148, 157
codex form, 23, 27
collaboration, 187
coming kingdom, 65, 73
Common Era, 59–60, 59n. 1
community, *passim*
consecration, 77, 132
conservative, 29, 77, 79, 138
Constantine the Great, xxi
Constitution, xiv
Coptic canon, 3
Corbin, Pastor Buddy, xvi
Cottian Alps, xiii
Council of Nicaea, xxi
covenant people, 51–53
covenant, 31, 39–41, 46, 51–53, 58, 62, 78, 86, 88, 90, 95, 131, 142, 145, 184
creed, 173, 191, 7
Crossan, John Dominic, 14, 99, 120nn. 11, 12, 166, 195n. 1, 201n. 5, 220
    Jesus: A Revolutionary Biography, 99n. 7, 120nn. 11, 12, 166n. 18, 195n. 1, 201n. 2, 202n. 6
crowds, 118, 202, 205, 184n. 12
crucified, 29
crucifixion, 4, 14, 23, 27, 29, 205

Culpepper, R. Alan, 107n.1, 180n.9, 190n. 16, 219
    The New Interpreter's Bible, Volume 9 (on Luke and John), 107n.1, 180n. 9, 190n. 16, 219
Cyrus of Media, xx

D

Daily Study Bible Series, The (Barclay), 219
Daniel, the prophet, 65, 147, 177
David, xx, 30, 41–42, 44, 48–53, 56–58, 66–71, 85, 88, 90, 99, 106, 111–113, 118–119, 126, 144, 168, 174, 211, 219
    house of, 67, 88, 99
    household of, 71
Davidic and Solomonic eras, 41
Davidic, 41, 52, 88, 113, 119, 174
Davis, Steve, 147n. 11
dawn from on high, 86, 88–89
Day of Atonement, 154
Dead Sea Scrolls, 86
Dead Sea, 86, 204
death, 2, 27, 31, 52, 55–56, 86, 89, 94–95, 98, 107–108, 126, 133, 136, 139, 144, 147, 154, 162–163, 168–169, 199, 202, 204, 210
Deism, xv
Deists, xiv
Deity, 60
deity, petty, 2
demi-gods, 98
Demiurge, 161
demonic, 23
depth psychology, 148
desert, 36, 51, 86–87, 90, 173–175, 178, 185, 194, 201–202, 204, 211, 213
destiny, 156
destruction of the Jerusalem Temple in 70 A.D., 22, 167, 187
determinism, 187
Dinah, 83n. 1
divided kingdom, 52
divided monarchy, xx
divine inspiration, 45
Docetism, 155
Doctrinal issues, 165
dogma, 7
Domitian, Roman emperor, xxi
dragon, 31
dream state, 147

dreams, 61, 70, 96, 105, 125–126, 140, 147–149
Duke of Savoy, xiii

E

early Church, 5, 17–18, 22, 24, 27–28, 34, 57, 70, 73n. 6, 77, 85–86, 118, 120, 159, 162, 180–181, 201, 204, 209–211
Easter, 3, 154n. 2
Easter Letter of St. Athanasius, xxi
Eastern magi, 36. *See also* wise men
Eastern Orthodox Church, 6, 159n .8
echo effect, 31, 100, 119, 121, 143, 145–146, 149
ecumenically, 6
Eden, 184–185
Edict of Nantes, xiii
Edwards , Jonathan, xv
Edwards, Rev. O.C. Jr., 180, 217
Egypt, xx-xxi, 27, 35–37, 40–41, 139–143, 154, 159, 167, 174, 206, 209
  northern, 35–37
election, 184
Eli, 66
Elijah, 61, 65, 173–177, 173n. 2, 180, 197
Elisha, 51, 54, 197
Elizabeth, 61–62, 65–68, 70, 75–78, 82–85, 89, 108, 130, 156
Elkenah, 99
Eliot, T.S., xvi, 126, 135, 138
  Journey of the Magi, 126
  Four Quartets, xvi
  Little Gidding , xvi
  Song for Simeon, A, 135
Emancipation Proclamation, xiii
Emmanuel, 90, 207
empire, 2, 21–22, 28, 31, 35, 46–47, 58, 60, 64, 97, 107–109, 111, 115, 190
end of the age, 23, 58, 65
Epiphany, 116, 121–122, 126, 136
Episcopal Church, xvii, 45, 180, 216–217
Episcopal Diocese of Western North Carolina, x, 215
Episcopal priest, xviii
Episcopal, 9, 45, 180, 215–217
Episcopalians, 114
Esau, 40, 83, 99
eschatological, 87, 185, 202

eschatology, 4
Essenes, 86–89, 181, 187, 195
Essential Tillich, The: An Anthology of the Writings of Paul Tillich, xiiin. 2
Europe, xii
European, 126
evangelist, 16–17, 21, 58, 91, 131, 133, 138, 201
evangelists, 17–18, 38, 61, 77, 97, 114–115, 129, 171, 179, 186, 201, 209
Eve, 92, 101
excommunication of the Christians, 29, 188
exile, xx, 2, 31, 41, 51–53, 58, 88, 122, 143, 171, 173–179, 181, 183, 185, 187, 189, 191, 204
Exodus, xx, 41, 88, 166, 176
Ezekiel, 145–146

F

Fall, 35, 56, 91, 100, 122, 135–136, 157, 184
Faulkner, William, 75
  Sound and the Fury, The, 75
Feeding of 5,000, 48
Felker, Pastor Paul, xvi
fertility gods, 60
fiery chariot, 175
fire, 22, 47, 122, 159, 183, 185–186, 196–200
First Amendment, xiv
forerunner, 173, 175–176, 185, 194, 199
forgiveness of sins, 89, 172, 176, 178–179, 181, 204, 206
Four Quartets (Eliot), xvi
Four Witnesses, The: The Rebel, the Rabbi, the Chronicler, and the Mystic (Griffith-Jones), 22, 28, 36, 100n. 9, 211, 220
fourth century, 39, 168
Fourth Gospel, 97, 118, 209
Fourth of July, 154n. 2
France, xiii
frankincense, 116, 124
free will, 148, 187
freedom, 9, 28, 147, 187, 201
fundamentalists, xv

G

Gabriel, archangel, 62, 65–72, 81–82, 84–85, 108, 136, 156, 180

Gandhi, Mahatma, 169
Galatians, Letter to, 4
Galilee of the Gentiles, 30
Galilee, *passim*
  northern, 23, 25
genealogy, 30, 36, 48–54, 56–58, 69n. 3, 91, 105, 172
Genesis creation story, 51
Geneva, xiii
Gentile, 4–6, 23, 25, 34, 36–37, 44, 47, 55–56, 58, 70, 83, 98–100, 125, 130–132, 134, 138, 153, 165–167, 177, 180, 187, 210
Gloria, 135n. 2
gnosis, 3, 159–160
Gnostic Gospels, The (Pagels), 159, 221
Gnosticism, 3, 159–164
  Gnostic, 3, 159–162, 221
Gobi, 174
God's anointed, 42, 100, 117
God's revelation, 36, 46, 126, 147, 209
God's saving action, 13, 42, 65, 83, 88, 96, 108, 126, 134
God's son, 23, 101, 211
gods, 41, 60, 98, 101, 122–123, 126
gold, 116, 124, 142
Golgotha, 125
Good King Henry IV, xiii
"good news," 2, 13–14, 17, 42, 62, 86, 108, 111, 113, 115, 168, 172–174, 176, 194, 198, 213, 219
good Samaritan, 36, 43
Gospel According to Saint John, The, 3n. 1, 17
Gospel According to Saint Mark, The, 2, 16, 23, 97
Gospel According to St. Matthew, The, 27, 35, 206
Gospel According to the Hebrews, The, 209
Gospel of the Ebionites, The, 209n. 13
Gospel of Thomas, 17, 27, 160, 163–164
Gospel Parallels, 13, 209–210, 209n. 13, 222
gospel stories:
  prodigal son, 36
  good Samaritan, 36
  thief on the cross, 36
Gospel Truth: The New Image of Jesus Emerging from Science and History, and Why it Matters (Shorto),120n. 11, 221

Gospels, *passim*
grace, 34, 48, 113, 126, 137, 145, 147,
    162, 167, 175, 211, 215
Great Commandment, 162
Great Commission, 30, 78, 125
great fire in Rome, 22
greater one, 204
Greco-Roman, 60, 92, 98n. 6
    culture of, 60
    world of, 92
Greece, xx
    southern, 35–37
Greek, 3, 22, 26, 34, 43, 46, 60,
    100–101, 122, 148–149, 159, 173
Greeks, 41
Greensboro, North Carolina, xvii
Griffith-Jones, Robin, 22n. 3
    *The Four Witnesses: The Rebel, the
    Rabbi, the Chronicler, and the
    Mystic,* 22, 28, 36, 211, 220
Grimball, Rev. Richard, 215
groupings of biblical text, 30

H

Halley's Comet, 124
Hannah, 65, 77, 83, 99, 137
harvest, 197
heavenly messengers, 61. *See also* angels
heavenly voice, 207, 209–212
heavenly, 61, 72, 83, 111, 114, 135, 154,
    194, 207, 209–212
Hebrew Bible, xx, 7, 31, 99–100, 122,
    132, 164, 166, 187
Hebrew, 3, 7, 22, 31, 41, 53, 96, 99–100,
    122, 132, 142, 164, 166–167, 173,
    181, 187
Hebrews, xx
Hebrews, Letter to, 34
Hell, xv, 88–89, 123
Hellenism, x
Hellenistic, 35
Henry IV, xiii
Hercules, 98
heresy, 155, 162
heretic, 3, 159
heretics, 7, 159, 162
Herod, xxi, 61, 63–64, 97, 105,
    107–109, 116–118, 124–126,
    139–142, 144–147, 149, 164, 166,
    179–180, 188, 190, 200–202
Herod Agrippa I, xxi

Herod Agrippa II, xxi
Herod Antipas, xxi, 201–202
Herod the Great, 63–64, 107, 109, 124,
    141, 144, 149, 164, 201
Herodian royal line, 97
Herodians, 109, 169, 200–202
heroes, 98
Hester, David, 44, 219
High Priest, 124, 154
hill country, 59, 61, 63, 65, 67, 69,
    71–73, 75–77, 79, 82, 85, 198
historical aspects of the Gospels, 11
historical Jesus, 11, 14, 17, 102n. 12,
    120, 220
historical Judaism, 51, 77, 88
Holy Family, xxi, 121, 130, 132, 135,
    140–141, 153, 206
Holy Innocents, 31, 64, 139, 142–143,
    145–146, 206
Holy Land, xx, 7, 143, 161, 164, 174, 191
Holy Spirit, ix, 9, 28, 45–46, 61, 68, 75,
    85, 90, 96, 133, 135, 157, 194–199,
    205, 208–210, 213
Holy Trinity Church, Greensboro,
    NC, xvii
Holy Week, 30, 55n. 14, 110, 125, 138,
    153n. 1, 187
Hosea, 143
Hughes, Rev. Tom, 215
human beings, 79, 207
human doings, 79
Hyde, Jeff, xvi
hypocrites, 30

I

Iberia, xii
idol, 143, 163, 175
Iliad, The, 149
illuminates, 196
imagery, 31, 33, 37, 121–122, 161, 194,
    197, 200
incense, 61, 64, 124
India, 126
inerrancy, 8, 18
Infancy Gospel of Thomas, 160,
    163–164
infancy gospels, 5
infidels, 7
interpretation of Scripture, 8–10, 44, 92,
    95, 149, 201–202

Iran, xx, 126
Iraq, xx, 41, 73
Irish Catholic, xv
Isaac, 40, 48–49, 65, 83, 99
Isaiah, the prophet, 118n. 8
Islam, 7, 221
Islamic Jihads, 7
Islamic tradition, 65
Israel, xxi, 7, 31, 39–43, 45, 47, 49–53,
    55, 57–58, 61, 65–66, 70, 76, 85–89,
    94, 112, 116, 118–120, 122, 124–125,
    131, 133–135, 137, 140, 142–143,
    145–146, 154, 166–167, 173–175,
    177–178, 183
    northern kingdom of (in timeline), xx
Israelite Conquests, 7
Israelites, xx, 41, 56, 86, 90–91, 112,
    142, 144, 155, 161, 164, 174, 176,
    178, 183, 190
Italy, xiii
Iturea, xx

J

Jacob, 40, 48–49, 54, 68–70, 83n. 1,
    99, 147
    house of, 68–70
James, 6, 48, 100, 114, 219, 222
January 6th, 121
Jefferson, Thomas, xi
    marketplace of ideas of, 8, 46, 148, 162
Jeffersonian wall between church and
    state, xiv
Jeremiah, 31, 139, 143, 146
Jericho, 55
Jerome, Saint, 147–148
    Vulgate, The, 148
Jerusalem:
    church leadership of, 6
    and conquest, 35, 41, 167, 167, 188
    and Herod's court, 61, 63–64,
        116–117, 124 125, 142
Jerusalem Temple, xx-xxi, 29, 41, 59,
    61, 63–65, 67, 69, 71, 73, 75, 77–79,
    130, 151–157, 159, 161, 163, 165,
    169, 190, 198, 205, 209
    destruction of the Jerusalem Temple in
        70 A.D., 22, 167, 187–188
Jesse, 49, 112, 144
Jesus, *passim*
Jesus: A Revolutionary Biography
    (Crossan), 99n. 7, 120nn. 11, 12,
    166n. 18, 195n. 1, 201n. 2, 202n. 6

Jesus, adult, 193
Jesus, infancy, 31
Jesus and his disciples feeding of the
    5,000, 48
Jesus movement, 5, 28, 32, 35, 46, 97n.
    5, 113, 136, 187–188, 190, 199
Jesus of Nazareth, 7, 43, 71
Jesus' Crucifixion, xxi
Jewish law, 4, 28, 83, 95, 130, 156, 167
Jewish leadership, 29–30, 33, 126, 142
Jewish rebellion, xxi, 29–30, 47, 78, 188
Jewish religious authorities, 29
Jewish temple, xx, 22, 64
Jewish, 4, 7, 22–23, 25, 28–30, 33–37,
    41–42, 47, 50–51, 53–55, 57–58, 60,
    63–64, 66, 69, 72, 77–78, 83, 92, 95,
    98–100, 108, 113, 119, 122, 124–126,
    130–131, 142–143, 151, 153–154,
    156, 166–168, 174–175, 177, 184,
    188, 190, 195, 200, 209–210, 220
Jewish-Roman war, 187
John the Baptist, 71, 77, 86, 165, 172,
    175–177, 179–182
    approximate date of John the Baptist's
        first appearance: 27–29 A.D., 180
    arrest of, 200–202
    as prophet, 183–191, 194–200
    baptizes Jesus, xxi, 203–212
    birth, 61, 68, 70, 78, 82, 88, 91
    crowds and, 183–184, 187, 189–190
    desert and, 174–175
    disciples of, 73, 199
    Essenes, 87, 181–182
Johnson, Luke Timothy 102, 120 n. 11,
    163, 220
    The Real Jesus: The Misguided Quest for
        the Historical Jesus and the Truth of
        the Traditional Gospels, 102, 220
Johnson, Rt. Rev. Robert, ix-x, 217
Jonah and the Great Fish, xv
Joram, 49, 53
Jordan River, 51, 54, 172, 174–177,
    179, 181, 187–188, 190–191, 193,
    195, 197, 199, 201–207, 209,
    211–213
Joseph of the Old Testament, 54
Joseph of the New Testament, 36,
    40–41, 49, 54, 67, 71, 81, 90–93,
    95–96, 102–103, 105–107, 109–112,
    120, 126, 129–132, 137, 139–149,
    151, 153–154, 156, 167, 206
Joseph's perspective, 36, 71, 90–91

Josephus, 166, 190, 195, 201–202
Joshua, 41–42, 55, 174
Journey of the Magi (Eliot), 126
journey, passim
Judah, 48–49, 54–56, 54n. 13, 99, 116,
    118, 183
Judaic law, 93, 95, 130, 132, 135, 187
Judaic practices, 31
Judaic ritual practice, 83
Judaism, 7, 29, 35–36, 51, 77, 88, 93, 95,
    123, 174, 177, 187, 210, 221
Judas Iscariot, 64n. 2
Judas Maccabeus, xx
Jude, 6
Judea, xx-xxi, 27, 41–42, 52, 61, 82, 99,
    106, 108–109, 112, 116, 118, 120,
    129, 137, 140, 144, 174–175,
    177–179, 203–204, 206
    southern kingdom of(in timeline), xx
Judean hill country, 59, 61, 63, 65, 67,
    69, 71, 73, 75, 77, 79, 85
Judeo-Christian tradition, 123
judgment, 84, 87, 95, 185, 196–197, 202
Julius Caesar, 98, 168
Jupiter, 124

K
Kelber, Werner, 139
    Mark's Story of Jesus, 138–139
King James Version, 48, 100, 114
King of the Medes, xx
King of the Jews, 116–117, 124–125
king, 41, 48–52, 54, 56, 58, 61, 63, 66,
    99–100, 108, 112, 114, 116–117,
    124–125, 140, 166, 169
King, Martin Luther, 169
kingdom: of God, 2, 14, 23, 26, 35,
    77–78, 97, 111, 136, 149, 151,
    179, 199, 216
    of heaven, 26, 78, 177, 179, 213
    of Israel, 51–52, 175, 178
    of Judea, 52, 99
Koran, 7

L
L source, 16, 43
    The Prodigal Son, 43
    The Good Samaritan, 43
    The Road to Emmaus, 43
late blessing of parenthood, 67
Latin, 6, 78, 148

latter prophets, 145, 161, 184
Leah, 54
legalists, 95
Letter to the Galatians, 4
Letter to the Hebrews, 34
Letter to the Romans, Paul's, 47n. 5, 210
Levirate law, 55n. 14
Levitical law, 132
Lewis, C.S., 102n. 12, 123, 210n. 15, 220
    Mere Christianity, 123, 210n. 15, 220
    Narnia Chronicles, The, 123
    Screwtape Letters, The, 102, 220
liberal, 77–79
Lincoln, Abraham 103, 169
literalism, 8, 11, 98, 103, 121
literalist, 30, 102
literalists, 95
literary, 11, 18, 28, 31, 35, 44, 57, 91–92,
    97, 109, 120–121, 127, 141–143,
    145–146, 149, 163, 169, 202
Little Apocalypse, 31
Little Gidding (Eliot), xvi
liturgies, 87, 161
locusts, 172, 175, 177
logos, 211
Long, Thomas G., 207nn. 10, 11, 12
    Westminter Bible Companion, Matthew,
        207nn. 10, 11, 12
Lot, 51, 56, 61, 64, 74, 215
lot, chosen by, 61, 64
Louisville Presbyterian Theological
    Seminary, 44
Love, 10, 12, 38–39, 45, 56, 60, 75,
    92–93, 95, 113, 123, 136, 158–159,
    161–162, 165, 178, 190, 205,
    215, 217
lover of God, 36, 47, 166
Luke, passim
    Lukan authorship, 34
    Lukan world, 64
    Luke's genealogy, 51, 57
    Luke's prologue, 42
    Luke's Sermon on the Plain, 27
Luke-Acts, 34–36, 47, 72–73, 124, 138,
    163, 199. See also Acts of the
    Apostles
Luther, Martin, 6, 9, 169

M
M source, 10, 16–17, 177, 219
Maccabean Revolt, xx
macro-stories, 176

Magi, 36, 105, 122, 124–126. *See also* wise men

Magnificat, the, 36, 76–78, 85, 88, 106, 135

mainline church, xv

Mannesseh's, 53

Maoists, 8

Marcion, 3, 159

Mark, *passim*

Markan priority, 15–16

Mark's Story of Jesus (Kelber), 138–139

marketplace of ideas, 8, 46, 148, 162

Mary, 36, 49, 54, 56–57, 67–73, 75–78, 83, 88, 90–93, 95–96, 101, 103, 106–108, 110–112, 115–116, 120, 129–132, 134, 136–137, 141–142, 144, 151, 153–154, 156–157, 165, 167

Mary's perspective, 36, 71

Masada, xxi, 35

matriarchs, 54

Matthean priority, 16

Matthean, 16, 26, 34, 101, 119–120, 146

Matthew, *passim*

Matthew's genealogy, 36, 49–54, 57, 105

Matthias, 64n. 2

Meaning of Jesus, The: Two Visions, by Marcus Borg and N.T. Wright, 120nn. 11, 12, 166n. 18

Medieval Church, xii, xv, 6

Mediterranean, xx, 3, 6, 34–35, 37, 92, 124, 151, 167, 220

Meier, John, 102

Memorial Day, 154n. 2

Mercer University, 107

Mere Christianity (Lewis), 123, 210n. 15, 220

Mesori Star, 124

Messenger of God, 74

Messiah, 28–31, 42, 48–53, 57–58, 87–91, 99–100, 105, 110–111, 113–121, 124, 129, 133, 135, 143–144, 162, 166, 168, 173, 179, 185, 198–199

Messianic Age, 120

Messianic expectations, 88

Messianic ideas, 88

metaphorical, 9, 31, 90

Methodist, 102

Micah, 118–121, 144, 178, 190, 208

Middle Ages, xii

Middle East, 7

midrash, 31–32, 100, 143, 149

mission, 5, 22, 30, 33, 42, 57, 65, 68, 72–73, 76, 90, 105, 114–115, 125, 129, 144, 182, 199, 207–208

missionary, 34, 36

Moabite, 54–56

Moabites, 56

Mohammed, 7, 65

monotheistic God, 2, 36, 123

monotheism, 2, 36, 123

Moore, Wilfred, xv

Mosaic law, 83

Moses, xx, 41, 50, 53, 60, 90, 130–131, 142, 146, 154, 165–167, 169, 174, 176

Mount of the Transfiguration, 176

Mount Sinai, 167

Much Ado About Nothing (Shakespeare), 92

myrrh, 116, 124

mysteries, 158, 160–161

mysterious visitors, 61

mystical, 3, 31–32, 54, 60, 105, 122, 127

mythological stories, 98n. 6

N

Nag Hammadi, 27, 159–160

Namaan of Syria, 51, 54

Naomi, 55–56

Narnia Chronicles, The (Lewis), 123

Nathan, the prophet, 56

Nathanael, 118

Nazareth, *passim*

Nazarite, 144

Nazis, 8n. 4, 47n. 5

Nazorean, 140, 143–144

Nero, Roman emperor, xxi, 22, 47n. 5, 164

New Adam, 101, 163. *See also* Adam

New Covenant, 31, 62, 78, 95, 145

new events, 7

The New Interpreter's Bible, Volume 8, New Testament Articles, Matthew (Boring), and Mark (Perkins), 10, 53, 145–146, 197, 207n.10, 219

The New Interpreter's Bible, Volume 9, New Testament Articles, Luke (Culpepper), and John, 107n. 1, 180n. 9, 190n. 16, 219

New Revised Standard Version (NRSV), 4, 13, 100, 222

New Testament Canon, 3

New World, xiii, 220

Nezer, 144

Nicene Conference, 168

Nicene Council, 157

Nicene Creed, 173

Nile River, 27

Nineveh, 164

Noah, 51, 60

North Carolina, xiv, 57, 114, 174, 215, 217

northern Ireland, 7

NRSV, 4, 13, 100, 222

numbers, and the symbolic significance of in the Bible; when the Bible uses a, 30, 51, 53, 125, 137, 153

forty years of wandering in the desert, 51

forty, 51, 90, 132

forty-day struggle with temptation, 51

fourteen generations, 49, 51–54, 57

fourteen, 49, 51–54, 57

seven, 54, 129, 131, 134, 137

sevens, 30, 51, 54

seventy times seven, 54

threes, 30

twelve books of the minor prophets, 51, 137

twelve tribes of Israel, 51, 137, 167

twelves, 51

Nunc Dimittis, 135

O

occupied Israel, 39, 41, 43, 45, 47, 49–51, 53, 55, 57–58

Odyssey, The, 149

Old Covenant, 88, 95

Old Order, 32, 57, 83, 97, 129, 137–138, 166, 171, 173, 175, 177, 179, 181, 183, 185, 187, 189, 191, 208

Old Testament Canon, 3

omens, 61

omniscience, 155

oral culture, 22, 30, 54

oral tradition, 17, 21–22, 36, 44, 109–110, 120, 154, 160

orderly account, 16, 42–43, 108, 110

Oregon State University, 41

Orthodox, 3, 5–6, 29, 159, 162–163, 165

Orthodox Canon, xxi

P

pagan polytheism, 60
pagan temple, 55, 168
pagan, 2, 55, 60, 98, 122, 124, 126, 143, 167–168, 175
Pagels, Elaine, 159n. 9, 221
    Gnostic Gospels, The, 159n. 9, 221
Palestine, xx, 26, 59, 78, 108, 190, 195
Palestinians, 7
Palm Sunday, 19
papyrus, 4, 23, 27
parables, 30, 77n. 7, 146n. 10, 197
paradox, 8, 18, 196, 213
parallels, 13, 31, 62, 87, 91, 97, 167, 171, 203, 205, 209–210, 222
Parse, Pastor Jack, xvi
parthenos, 100–101
Passover, 19, 35, 41, 152–155, 155n. 2
patriarchal society, 54
Paul, Saint, xii, xxi, 3–6, 22, 34, 37, 47, 73, 83, 97, 120n. 10, 124, 136–137, 158–159, 161–163, 165, 173, 204, 210–211, 217, 221–222
    Paul's letters, 4
Pauline mission of Acts, 73
Pauline tradition, 34
Pax Romana, 59, 109, 168
Peace of Rome, 58–59
Pentateuch, 187
Pentecost, 199
people of the Book, 7
Perea, xxi
pericope, 34, 91, 108, 138, 146, 187, 201, 203
Perkins, Pheme, 174
    The New Interpreter's Bible, Volume 8, New Testament Articles, Matthew (Boring), and Mark (Perkins), 10, 53, 145–146, 197, 207n.10, 219
persecution, xxi, 22–23, 25, 29, 78, 162, 169
Persia, xx, 41, 122, 126
Persians, xx
Peter, xxi, 22–23, 25, 47, 220
Petrine community, 34
Petty, Jim and Nancylee, xviii, 216
Pharaoh, 40, 142, 146–147, 154, 166–167
Pharisees, 19, 23, 29–30, 51, 160, 186–188, 191

Philip, 179, 201
Phillip, xxi
pilgrimage, 153, 183
Pisgah Forest of North Carolina, 174
Platonic, 60
political sovereignty, 46
polytheistic, 60
Pontius Pilate, xxi, 29, 125, 180
Pompey, xx
poor, 2, 26, 34, 36–37, 77, 106, 110, 113, 115, 132, 153–154, 190
Pope John XXIII, 148
Pope, 148
populist, 78–79
portents, 23, 61
post-Apostolic era, 31
post-exile restoration, 174
preexistence, 211
pregnancy, 55, 66, 76, 78, 92, 96
Presbyterian Church in the United States of America, xiii, 207,
priest, 61, 63–64, 85, 124, 131–132, 154
priestly order, 61, 64
Priestly story, 176
primal narrative, 41
principal texts, 165
printing press, 54, 144
prodigal son, 36, 43
prologue, 34, 42–44, 110, 172
Promised Land, 40–41, 51–52, 167, 174–175
prophecies, 31, 72, 124, 143, 158
prophecy, 31–32, 85, 91, 100, 105, 110, 119–121, 141, 143–144, 146, 166, 168, 173, 177, 179, 181, 208
prophecy/fulfillment pattern, 31, 32, 100
prophet, 31, 56, 65, 86, 88–90, 112, 116, 118, 134, 137, 139, 146–147, 172, 175, 177, 179–180, 195, 197
prophetic, 31, 50, 87, 99–100, 147, 158, 173–174, 178–180, 183, 195, 198, 202, 208, 211
proselyte, 36
prostitute, 54–55
Protestant liberty, 9
Protestant, 6, 9, 159
Protestants, xii, xiii
province of Syria, 108
Ptolemy, xxi
purification, 130–132, 153, 185, 197
purifies, 196–197
Puritan, xvi

Q

Q material, 26–27
Q source, xxi, 16–17, 26–28, 30, 35, 43, 45–46, 160, 177, 182, 187, 220–221
Q theories, 26
quelle, 16
Quiet in the Land, 135
Quirinius, xxi, 106, 108n. 3
Qumran, 86–88, 195, 204

R

Rabbi, 27–28, 100n. 9, 119, 143, 188.
    See also Luke
Rabbinic, 31, 143, 187
Rachel, 31, 54, 139, 143
Radical Christianity, Islam and Judaism, 7
Rahab, 49, 54–55
Real Jesus: The Misguided Quest for the Historical Jesus and the Truth of the Traditional Gospels, The, (Johnson), 102, 102n. 13, 120n. 11
Rebecca, 54, 65, 83, 99
Rebel, 21–22. *See also* Luke
Red Sea, 142
redeemed, 85, 92, 132
Reformation, xiii, 6
religious authorities, 23, 29
religious liberty, xiv, 9
repent, 177, 184
repentance, 90, 172, 175–176, 178–179, 181, 183–186, 194, 196–197, 202, 204, 211
resurrection, 4, 14, 23–24, 27, 163, 168, 187, 199, 210–211
return from the Babylonian exile, 52, 58, 88, 176
revelatory setting, 137
righteous, 61, 90, 92–93, 95, 103, 130, 133, 173, 207
righteousness, 86, 88, 93, 95–96, 103, 185, 205–207
risen Christ, 28, 51, 125
risen Lord, 23
Road to Emmaus, 43
Roberts, Terri, xvii, 216
Rohr, Richard, 86–87, 219
Roman authority, 63
Roman Catholic, xii, 102, 159n. 8, 162, 174
Roman Catholic Church, Medieval, xii, xv

Roman Centurion's faith, 155
Roman Church, xiv, 6
Roman Emperor Augustus, xxi, 97–98, 106, 108–109, 142, 164–169
Roman Emperor Caligula, xxi, 164
Roman Emperor Claudius, xxi
Roman Emperor Domitian, xxi
Roman Emperor Nero, xxi, 22, 47n. 5, 164
Roman Emperor Tiberius, xxi
Roman Emperor Titus, xxi
Roman Emperor Vespasian, xxi
Roman Empire, 2, 21, 28, 31, 35, 46–47, 58, 115
Roman execution, 2
Roman legionnaires, 190
Roman occupation, 42, 176, 198
Roman registration, 107
Roman Republic, 59
Roman Senate, 98, 168
Roman, 2, 6, 19, 21, 28, 31, 35, 42, 46–48, 58–60, 63, 98, 101–102, 107–110, 115, 135, 147, 155, 159, 162, 164–165, 168, 174, 176, 180, 190, 198
Romans, 29, 41, 60, 78, 98–99, 109
Romans, Paul's Letter to, 47, 210
Rome, xii, xxi, 2, 6, 22, 24–25, 30, 34–35, 37, 46–47, 58–59, 78, 88, 107–110, 144, 168, 175, 187, 190, 195
Rt. Rev. Robert H. Johnson, x, 217
Ruth, 49, 54–55

S

Sabbath, 113
Sadducees, 55n. 14, 186–188, 191
Sahara, 174
salvation, 34, 86, 88–89, 119, 133, 135–136, 180–182, 3
Samaria, xx
Samaritans, 34
Samson, 144
Samuel, 45, 66, 77, 83, 112, 137, 144
sanctuary, 61–62, 64, 66, 69, 85, 131
Sanhedrin, 142, 155
Sarah, xx, 40–41, 54, 83, 99, 185
Sarai, 39–40, 60, 65
Satan, 123
Saturn, 124
Saul, xx, 45, 66
Savoy, xiii

Sawyer, Tom, 48
sayings, 16–17, 26–27, 30, 33, 160, 182, 221
Schism, 6
scholars, 4, 15–16, 22, 26–28, 34, 36, 56, 71, 77, 87, 97, 100, 102, 107–108, 115, 120, 124, 136, 138, 142, 144, 151, 155, 157, 159–160, 165, 167, 174, 178, 180–182, 210
Screwtape Letters, The (Lewis), 102n. 12, 220
scribes, 23, 29–30, 51, 116–118, 166
Scrooge, Ebenezer, 96
Seabury-Western Theological Seminary, 180, 216
second coming of Christ, 4
Second Vatican Council of 1962–1965, 6, 148
Selucids, xx
separation of church and state, xiii, xiv
Sepphoris of Galilee, 110
Septuagint, xx, 3, 100
Sermon on the Mount, 27, 95
Sermon on the Plain, 27
serpent, 184
sexuality, 57, 96
Shakespeare, William, 92
    Much Ado About Nothing, 92
shepherds, 36, 72, 111–115, 126, 135, 156
Shorto, Russell, 120, 221
    Gospel Truth: The New Image of Jesus Emerging from Science and History, and Why it Matters, 120n. 11, 221
Simeon, 72, 133–138, 156
sin offering, 131–132
Slaughter of the Holy Innocents, 31, 64, 139, 143, 145–146, 206
slavery, 2, 40, 51, 88, 143
Socrates, 169
Sodom, 56
soldiers, 34, 190–191
Solomon, king, xx, 11, 52, 56
Son of God, 42, 68, 99, 101–102, 158, 168, 172–173, 179, 204, 207, 210–211, 213
Son of Righteousness, 88
Son of the Most High, 68–70, 72, 155, 168
Song for Simeon, A (Eliot), 135
Sonora, 174
Sound and the Fury, The (Faulkner), 75

source, 3–4, 15–17, 24, 26–27, 30, 34, 43, 55, 91, 157, 172, 182, 187, 201
South, 27, 108, 175
Southern Baptist Convention, xv, 107
speeches in character, 28
Stalinists, 8
Stanley, Charles, xiv
State of Israel, 7
Steven, Saint, 169
story of Jesus, 2, 5, 7–8, 14, 17, 21, 28, 34, 38, 42, 44, 48, 61–62, 98, 109, 137, 145, 153–154, 219
Summa Theologiae, (Aquinas), xi
symbolic, 11, 31, 70, 97–98, 101–103, 124, 126, 137, 143, 204
"synagogue across the street", 28–30, 33, 188
synagogues, 29, 35
Syria, xx, 23–25, 28, 33, 36–37, 54, 106, 108–109, 108n. 3
    southern, 23, 25
Syrian, 51
Syrian canon, 3
Syro-Phoenician woman, 30

T

Tamar, 49, 54–55
Tatian, 18
tax collectors, 189–191
tax gatherers, 190
temple authorities, 23
temple, 2, 22–23, 29, 35, 41, 55, 59, 61, 63–65, 67, 69, 71–73, 75, 77–79, 85, 87, 108, 117, 124, 130–131, 133–134, 136–139, 142, 151–157, 159–161, 163, 165, 167–169, 180, 187–188, 190, 198, 205, 209. See also Jerusalem Temple
temptation, 50–51, 201
testing of Jesus, 51, 201
theological, 4–6, 11, 44–46, 53, 92, 97, 108–109, 120, 145–146, 159, 180, 195, 202, 207, 209–210, 216
Theophilus, 35–36, 43, 46–47, 110, 165–166, 172
thief on the cross, 36
Thomas, Gospel of, 17, 27, 160, 163–164
Thomas, Infancy Gospel of, 160, 163–164
Thomas Aquinas, Saint, xi; Summa Theologiae, xi
Tiberius, Roman emperor, xxi
Tillich, Paul, xi, 221

Titus, Roman emperor, xxi
toll collectors, 190–191
tomb, 23–24
Torah, 167, 187
Tower of Babel, 199
Trachonitis, xxi
Tradition, 9, 12, 15, 17, 21–23, 27, 34,
    36, 44–45, 47, 65, 70, 83, 88, 91,
    97–99, 101, 109–110, 120, 123–127,
    131–132, 136, 144–147, 154, 158,
    160, 163, 173–174, 177, 179, 181,
    187, 202, 208, 210–211
tragedy, 92, 147, 167
trinitarian, 155
Trinity Asheville, xvii, 215–216
Trinity, 155, 157, 168, 195, 212, 215
Turkey, xx
Twelve Apostles, The, 51, 167
twentieth-century, 75, 86

U

Uncaused Cause, xi
Unitarianism, xv
United Monarchy, xx, 41, 52
United States Constitution, xiv
United States, xiv, 45, 180, 207
universal, 3, 6, 34, 48, 51, 115
universalistic, 181
University of the South, xvii
Ur in the Chaldees, xx, 1, 39–41, 43,
    45, 47, 49, 51, 53, 55, 57–58
Uriah the Hittite, 54, 56
Uzziah, 49, 53

V

Valdese, North Carolina, xiii
Vespasian, Roman emperor, xxi
vipers, 183–184, 186
Virgil, 168
Virgin birth, 68, 70, 73, 92, 96–98,
    100–103, 209–210
virgin, 67–68, 70, 73, 90–92, 94–98,
    100–103, 120, 209–210
Vulgate, The (St. Jerome), 148

W

Waldenses, iii, xii, 219
    brutal torture and slaughter of, xiii
    French, xiii
    Italian, xiii
Waldensian Presbyterian Church, xvi
Waldensian Valleys, xiii
Washington, George, 103
Wesley, John, 22n. 3
Western Church, 3, 121
Western Civilization, 7
Western North Carolina, 114, 215
Westminter Bible Companion, Matthew
    (Long), 207nn. 10, 11, 12
wheat, 196–198
Whelchel, Rev. Judith, 114n. 1, 216
Whisenhunt, Rev. Bill, xvii, 215
Whittington, Robbin Brent, publisher,
    xvii, 216
wife of Uriah, 49, 56
wilderness, 72, 86, 89, 172–177,
    179–181, 183–185, 198, 203, 213

wise men, 109, 116–117, 120–122,
    125–126, 139–140, 147–149. See also
    magi and Eastern magi
woes to the scribes and the Pharisees, 51
women, 23–24, 34, 36–37, 50, 54,
    56–58, 73, 75, 77, 83, 98, 100, 137,
    156, 197
word metaphors, 184
Word of God, 45, 179, 211
wrath, 40, 141, 181, 183–184, 186
Wright, N.T., 120nn. 11, 12,
    166n. 18, 220
    Meaning of Jesus, The: Two Visions,
    120nn. 11, 12, 166n. 18

Y

Yahweh, 2, 41–42, 64, 112, 164
Yom Kippur, 154

Z

Zealots, 7, 88
Zechariah, 61–67, 69–73, 75–76, 78,
    81–82, 84–89, 108, 130, 136,
    179–180
    dumbstruck and, 66, 69–70, 78
Zeus, xx
Zion, 52–53, 185
Zoroastrianism, 122–123, 127